The
ULTIMATE
BOOK OF
BIRTHDAY CAKES

The ULTIMATE BOOK OF BIRTHDAY CAKES

Joanna Farrow
Lindsay John Bradshaw
Lisa Tilley

MEREHURST

Published in 1999 by Merehurst
Limited
Ferry House, 51–57 Lacy Road,
Putney,
London SW15 1PR

Extracts taken with kind
permission from the authors of
the following books:
*The Merehurst Introduction to
Cake Decorating*, Joanna
Farrow
The Novelty Cake Book, Lindsay
John Bradshaw
*Sugarcraft Skills – Novelty
Cakes*,
Lisa Tilley
One Hour Party Cakes, Lindsay
John Bradshaw
*Sugarcraft Skills – Chocolate
Cakes and Decorations*, Joanna
Farrow
*Family Circle Crazy for
Chocolate*
Family Circle Cakes
*Family Circle Feeding Babies
and Toddlers*
Family Circle Kids Party Book

Designer: Anita Ruddell
Photography by James Duncan
and
Clive Streeter
CEO & Publisher: Anne Wilson
International Sales Director:
Mark Newman

Colour separation by Bright
Arts, Hong Kong
Printed in Singapore by Tien
Wah Press

Contents

Cake Making & Decorating
page 7

Skill Levels

The birthday candle
flame underneath each
cake title denotes the
degree of difficulty:

Easy

Moderate

Requires more skill

Cake Making & Decorating

Cake Decorating Equipment

Using the correct equipment not only helps to give better results, but also makes decorating easier. The following is a list of the equipment used in this book. Although most of it is basic, you will need some specialist items to decorate some of the more elaborate cakes.

CAKE BOARDS

These are available in all shapes and sizes from round and square to heart, petal, hexagonal and rectangular. Choose between thin 'cards' and thicker boards or 'drums'.

CAKE TINS (PANS)

Round and square tins (pans) are widely available in good hardware shops, kitchenware stores and even larger supermarkets. Unusual shapes can be bought or hired from specialist cake-decorating shops.

COCKTAIL STICKS (TOOTHPICKS)

Cocktail sticks (toothpicks) are useful for dotting tiny amounts of food colouring onto icing, and for precise decorative work.

CRIMPERS

These come in different shapes, such as hearts, diamonds, zigzags and scallops. They are used to emboss decorative borders and patterns in sugarpaste (rolled fondant). See page 24 for crimping technique – always practise first.

CUTTERS

A vast range of cutters can be found in kitchenware stores and specialist cake-decorating shops. Large biscuit (cookie) cutters are useful for shaping novelty cakes, while smaller cutters are better suited to more delicate work. Flower cutters come in basic petal shapes, or are specially shaped for making particular flowers, e.g., orchids and lilies. Blossom 'plunger' cutters have a wire spring which gently pushes out the flower shape once cut.

DECORATIVE SCRAPERS

These are used for creating decorative patterns around the sides of cakes.

DUSTING POWDERS (PETAL DUSTS/BLOSSOM TINTS)

Powder colours are mostly used to give colour highlights to sugarpaste (rolled fondant) flowers. They are applied with a dry paintbrush.

FLORISTRY WIRE

This is used for wiring flowers together into decorative sprays, and also for looping ribbons into sprays or attaching them to cakes. It is available from specialist cake-decorating shops as well as from florists.

FOOD COLOURINGS

Choose specialist paste and concentrated liquid colourings, which

KITCHEN PAPERS

Plastic food wrap is useful for tightly wrapping icings to prevent crusts forming. Foil, crumpled or flat, acts as a mould for drying icing decorations. Greaseproof (parchment) and non-stick papers are used for lining tins (pans) and for making paper piping bags and templates. Absorbent kitchen paper (paper towels) is sometimes used to support sugarpaste decorations while they harden.

LEAF VEINER

This provides a quick alternative to using the point of a knife for marking leaf and petal veins.

MODELLING TOOLS

These come in various shapes and sizes and are useful for making sugarpaste (rolled fondant) flowers and marzipan (almond paste) fruits. They are available from specialist cake-decorating shops. A ball modelling tool is particularly useful.

are available in a huge variety of colours from cake-decorating shops and some kitchenware stores. Liquid food colourings from supermarkets are best avoided as they do not produce the rich tones needed for dramatic effects.

FRILL CUTTER

This large cutter with a central detachable ring is used for making frilled borders and decorations.

ICING RULER

A smooth, firm ruler is used for flat icing the tops of cakes decorated with royal icing.

ICING SMOOTHER

A smooth, flat tool for giving a perfect finish to cakes covered with sugarpaste (rolled fondant).

PAINTBRUSHES

Large brushes are used for moistening cakes or boards with water before icing and for painting large areas of icing. Fine brushes are used for delicate painting and for dampening small pieces of icing before securing them to a cake.

PALETTE KNIFE (METAL SPATULA)

A palette knife (metal spatula) is useful for spreading or sandwiching cakes with cream, buttercream, chocolate or ganache.

PIPING BAGS

Bought nylon piping bags are best for piping large quantities of whipped cream, buttercream or ganache. For smaller quantities, homemade or bought paper piping bags are easier to use (for how to make a paper piping bag, see left).

To make a paper piping bag

Cut a 25cm (10in) square of greaseproof (parchment) or non-stick paper, then cut the square in half diagonally to make two triangles. Holding one triangle with its longest side away from you, fold the right-hand point over to meet the bottom point, curling the paper round to make a cone shape.

Fold the left-hand point over the cone and bring all three points together. Fold the points over twice to secure. Cut off the tip and fit with a piping tube (tip).

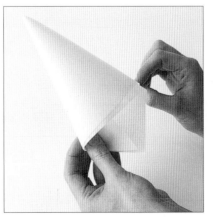

PIPING JELLY

This is useful for adding a 'wet look' effect, particularly to water on children's novelty cakes.

PIPING TUBES (TIPS)

These range from very fine writing tubes (tips) for delicately piped icing, to large tubes for piping basket-work, stars, leaves and petal shapes. Very large star or plain tubes are available in sizes 5mm–2cm (¼–¾in). They are used with large nylon piping bags to pipe large amounts of whipped cream or meringue.

RIBBON

Lengths of ribbon are frequently used to decorate cakes, either in bows on top of a cake or tied around the sides. A ribbon fixed around the cake board makes an effective finishing touch.

Wired ribbons are usually used to enhance small clusters of flowers on cakes decorated with sugar-

paste (rolled fondant) or royal icing. Use fine ribbon, no more than about 1cm (½in) wide.

Cut a 6cm (2½in) length of floristry wire and a 10cm (4in) length of ribbon. Fold the ribbon in half so the ends meet. Wrap the wire around the centre of the folded ribbon, then twist the ends of the wire tightly. (See illustration above.) Use the wire to secure the ribbon to flowers on a cake.

ROLLING PIN

An ordinary rolling pin is adequate for rolling sugarpaste (rolled fondant), although special icing rolling pins give smoother results. A small rolling pin is perfect for delicate work.

Textured rolling pins are used to texture large areas of sugar-paste, pastillage or marzipan (almond paste). There are three commercially available ones: ribbed (parallel lines) sometimes referred to as smocking; boxwood (crossed lines); and basketweave.

SPONGES (FOAM)

Special sponges, available in various sizes from cake-decorating shops, are used when shaping flowers with a ball modelling tool, or after cutting with a plunger cutter. A flat-sided bath sponge makes an adequate substitute.

Tip

☆ *When making a sponge cake, only the base of the tin (pan) needs lining.*

STAMENS

These are available from specialist cake-decorating shops in a variety of shapes and sizes. They add the finishing touch to lovely moulded flowers.

TURNTABLE

A cake turntable makes it much easier to work on a highly decorated cake.

To line a cake tin (pan)

Place the tin (pan) on a piece of greaseproof (parchment) or non-stick paper and draw around it, then cut out the shape just inside the drawn line. To line the sides, cut a strip of paper that is as long as the circumference of the tin and 2.5cm (1in) deeper. Make a 2.5cm (1in) fold along one long edge of the strip and snip the folded portion from the edge to the fold at 2.5cm (1in) intervals. Position the strip around the inside of the greased tin with the snipped edge lying flat on the base. Place the cut-out piece of paper in the base, then grease the paper.

Cake Recipes

There are all kinds of cake to make – from a Madeira (pound) or sponge (layer) mixture to a rich fruit cake or even a chocolate cake. A Madeira cake is best for novelty cakes as it can be shaped easily.

Madeira (pound) cake

For ingredients, tin (pan) sizes, baking times and flavourings, see the chart on page 16. Although this is not the traditional method for making a Madeira cake, it is very quick and easy. If you do not have an electric whisk or mixer, cream the butter or margarine and sugar together first, then gradually beat in the eggs and finally fold in the sifted flour and any flavouring.

1 Preheat the oven to 160°C (325°F/Gas 3). Grease and line the required tin (pan). Put the softened butter or margarine, sugar, eggs and sifted flour in a large bowl. Add the chosen flavouring, if desired (see chart).

2 Beat with an electric whisk for about 2 minutes or until the mixture is pale and fluffy.

3 Spoon the mixture into the pre-pared tin and level the surface. Bake in the oven for the time stated in the chart or until the cake is firm to the touch and a skewer inserted in the centre comes out clean. Leave to cool slightly in the tin, then turn out onto a wire rack and leave to cool completely. Wrap the cake tightly in foil until ready to decorate.

Rich fruit cake

For ingredients, tin (pan) sizes and baking times, see the chart on page 16. This is a very quick method for making a rich fruit cake. If you do not have an electric whisk or mixer, cream the butter or margarine and sugar together first, then gradually beat in the eggs and finally fold in the flour, spice, dried fruit, cherries and nuts.

1 Preheat the oven to 140°C (275°F/Gas 1). Grease and line the required tin (pan).

2 Put the softened butter or mar-garine, sugar, flour, spice and eggs in a large bowl and beat well with an electric whisk until creamy.

3 Stir in the mixed dried fruit, cherries and nuts until they are evenly combined.

4 Spoon the mixture into the pre-pared tin and level the surface. Bake in the oven for the time stated in the chart or until the cake is firm to the touch and a skewer inserted in the centre comes out clean. Leave to cool in the tin.

5 Remove the cake from the tin and wrap tightly in foil until ready to decorate.

Whisked sponge cake

Makes two 20cm (8in) round sandwich (layer) cakes.

4 eggs
125g (4oz/½ cup) caster (superfine) sugar
125g (4oz/1 cup) plain (all-purpose) flour

1 Preheat the oven to 180°C (350°F/Gas 4). Grease and line two 20cm (8in) round sandwich tins (layer pans).

2 Put the eggs and sugar in a heatproof bowl and set the bowl over a saucepan of gently simmering water. Beat with an electric whisk until the mixture thickens and becomes pale and fluffy and the whisk leaves a trail on the surface when it is lifted. Remove the bowl from the heat and whisk for a further 3 minutes.

3 Sift the flour onto a sheet of greaseproof (parchment) or non-stick paper, then sift again over the mixture. Using a large metal spoon, gently fold in the flour until evenly distributed.

4 Spoon the mixture into the prepared tins and bake in the

oven for 15–20 minutes or until just firm to the touch. Turn the cakes out onto a wire rack covered with greaseproof or non-stick paper and leave to cool. Wrap the cakes loosely in foil until ready to decorate.

Tips

☆ *If possible, always make cakes the day before decorating them as they cut better. This is particularly important when shaping novelty cakes. Well wrapped in foil, a whisked sponge can be kept for two days before eating; a Madeira will keep for up to a week. Both should be frozen if kept for longer.*

☆ *Rich fruit cakes store well for several months in a cool, dry place. If liked, drizzle with a little brandy from time to time to improve the flavour.*

Quick mix sponge

Makes two 20cm (8in) round sandwich (layer) cakes.

185g (6oz/¾ cup) soft margarine
185g (6oz/¾ cup) caster (superfine) sugar
3 eggs
185g (6oz/1½ cups) self-raising flour
1 tsp baking powder

1 Preheat the oven to 160°C (325°F/Gas 3). Base-line and grease two 20cm (8in) round sandwich tins (layer pans).

2 Beat all the ingredients together for 2–3 minutes with an electric mixer until light and fluffy. Spoon the mixture into the prepared tins. Bake in the oven for 25–30 minutes until golden and firm.

Genoese sponge

Made by whisking sugar and eggs to an aerated foam, Genoese sponges are particularly light. The quantities below are suitable for two 18cm (7in) round sandwich (layer) cakes. For two 20cm (8in) round sandwich cakes, increase the sugar to 125g (4oz/½ cup), the eggs to 4, the flour to 125g (4oz/1 cup) and the melted butter to 60g (2oz/ ¼ cup).

3 eggs
90g (3oz/⅓ cup) caster (superfine) sugar
90g (3oz/¾ cup) plain (all-purpose) flour
45g (1½ oz/3 tbsp) butter, melted

1 Preheat the oven to 180°C (350°F/Gas 4). Base-line and grease two round sandwich tins (layer pans).

2 Combine the eggs and sugar in a heatproof bowl. Set over a pan of hot but not boiling water. Have ready the sifted flour (with cocoa if using) and melted butter.

Using an electric mixer, whisk the egg and sugar mixture until pale and thick enough to hold the trail of the whisk, then remove the bowl from the pan.

3 Sift half of the flour over the whisked mixture. Carefully fold in, using a metal spoon. Fold in half of the melted butter, then fold in the remaining flour and butter.

4 Pour the mixture into the prepared tins, gently tilting the tins so the mixture spreads right to the side. Bake in the oven for 15–20 minutes until golden and just firm to the touch. Cool slightly in the tins, then invert onto a wire rack to cool completely.

FLAVOURINGS

Chocolate: Substitute 15g (½ oz/ 2 tablespoons) flour with cocoa (unsweetened cocoa powder).

Mocha: Make as for the chocolate, adding 1 tablespoon instant coffee powder dissolved in 2 teaspoons boiling water, with the butter.

Chocolate fudge cake

Flavoured with cocoa (unsweetened cocoa powder), Chocolate Fudge Cake has a very rich, dense texture. Top it with Chocolate Fudge Icing (see page 19) or Ganache (see page 18). The cake is particularly thick, so use a deep sturdy tin (pan). If you prefer a shallower cake, use a 23 or 25cm (9 or 10in) tin.

250g (8oz/1 cup) butter, softened, or soft margarine

375g (12oz/2 cups) soft dark brown sugar

375g (12oz/3 cups) plain (all-purpose) flour

1 tbsp baking powder

4 eggs, lightly beaten

4 tbsp golden syrup (light corn syrup)

125g (4oz/1 cup) cocoa (unsweetened cocoa powder)

185ml (6fl oz/¾ cup) warm water

155ml (¼pt/⅔ cup) plain yogurt

1 Preheat the oven to 150°C (300°F/Gas 2). Grease and line a 20cm (8in) round or 18cm (7in) square cake tin (pan).

2 Combine the butter or margarine and sugar in a large bowl and beat, using a wooden spoon or electric mixer, until pale and fluffy. Sift the flour and baking powder together in a separate bowl.

Tip

☆ *Soured cream may be used instead of the yogurt, and treacle (molasses or dark corn syrup) substituted for the golden syrup (light corn syrup) for an even darker cake.*

3 Gradually add the beaten eggs to the creamed mixture, beating well after each addition. Add 1 tablespoon of the flour to the mixture to prevent curdling.

4 Stir in the syrup. In a small bowl, blend the cocoa with the measured water to make a paste. Beat into the mixture.

5 Using a large metal spoon, fold in half of the sifted flour and baking powder mixture, using a figure-of-eight action. Fold in the yogurt, then add the remaining flour in the same way as before, until only just combined. Spoon the mixture into the prepared tin and level the surface.

6 Bake in the oven for 1¼ –1½ hours or until well risen and a skewer inserted in the centre of the cake comes out clean. Cool briefly in the tin, then invert the cake onto a wire rack and leave to cool completely.

Moist rich chocolate cake

1 For ingredients, tin (pan) sizes and baking times, see the chart on page 15. Preheat the oven to 160°C (325°F/Gas 3). Grease and line the required cake tin (pan).

2 Add the vinegar to the milk and set aside. Melt the chocolate. Combine the margarine, sugar and eggs in a bowl. Sift together the flour, bicarbonate of soda (baking powder) and cocoa (unsweetened cocoa powder). Add to the bowl with half of the milk mixture and beat until smooth.

3 Add the melted chocolate and the remaining milk mixture and beat again until the ingredients are thoroughly combined.

4 Spoon the mixture into the prepared tin. Bake in the oven for the time stated in the chart or until a skewer inserted in the centre comes out clean. Cool in the tin for 30 minutes, then transfer to a wire rack.

Tip

☆ *Where possible use an electric food mixer for cake making. It is much easier to incorporate air and is generally far quicker than a wooden spoon.*

Swiss (jelly) roll

90g (3oz/⅓ cup) caster (superfine)
sugar

3 eggs

90g (3oz/¾ cup) plain
(all-purpose) flour

½ tsp baking powder

1 Preheat the oven to 220°C (425°F/Gas 7). Grease and line a 28 x 18cm (11 x 7in) Swiss (jelly) roll tin (pan). Combine the sugar and eggs in a heatproof bowl. Whisk over hot water until the mixture is very thick, pale and creamy and the whisk leaves a trail on the surface when lifted. Remove the bowl from the heat and whisk for 3–5 minutes.

2 Sift the flour and baking powder together onto a sheet of greaseproof (parchment) or non-stick paper. Sift again over the surface of the mixture. Gently fold in, using a figure-of-eight movement to ensure that all the flour has been incorporated. Do not over-beat or the mixture will deflate.

3 Pour the mixture into the prepared tin and carefully spread level using a palette knife (metal spatula). Bake at once for 7–9 minutes, until firm to the touch. Invert the baked sponge onto greaseproof or non-stick paper dusted with caster (super-fine) sugar.

4 Trim the edges of the roll, spread with jam (conserve) and roll up tightly. If using a butter-cream filling, roll up the roll with a sheet of waxed paper inside. Leave to cool, then unroll and spread with buttercream before re-rolling. By rolling from the long side a conventional sized roll will be produced. Rolling from the short side will produce a shorter but thicker roll. For large cake shapes join two rolls together.

VARIATION

Chocolate: Substitute 15g (½oz/ 2 tablespoons) flour with cocoa (unsweetened cocoa powder).

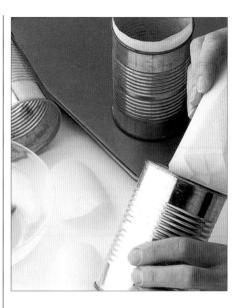

Lining empty food cans

For tubular-shaped cakes, such as the Dream Castle (see page 104) and the Messy Paints cake (see page 68), empty food cans make perfect baking tins (pans). Remove both ends from the can, then wash and dry thoroughly.

Place the can on a piece of greaseproof (parchment) or non-stick paper and draw around it. Cut out the paper circle, just inside the drawn line. Cut a strip of paper the circumference of the can and 1cm (½in) deeper. Make a 1cm (½in) fold along one long edge, then snip the paper along the folded portion, from the edge to the fold, at 1cm (½in) intervals.

Brush the inside of the can with melted margarine. Bring the two short ends of the paper strip together and push into the can. Place the can on a greased baking sheet so that the snipped portion of paper rests flat on the sheet. Fit the circle of paper in the base. Brush the paper with more melted margarine.

The can is now ready to be filled with mixture. Level the surface carefully and do not overcook.

Tip

☆ *The long shape of a Swiss (jelly) roll lends itself particularly well to many novelty cakes, in many instances forming the basic structure on which to build. Apart from being useful as a base shape, by cutting and joining pieces of Swiss roll into certain configurations you save more time in shaping and layering than you would using conventional square and round cakes. As with other types of cake, it is advisable to freeze the cake for a short period prior to shaping, making cutting and sculpting easier. Join the cakes using jam (conserve), buttercream or melted chocolate.*

Tip

☆ *To obtain a perfectly shaped roll, wrap a sheet of greaseproof (parchment) or non-stick paper tightly around the roll and leave to stand until needed.*

Moist rich chocolate cake quantities chart

Tin (pan) size	15cm (6in) round or 13cm (5in) square	20cm (8in) round or 18cm (7in) square	25cm (10in) round or 23cm (9in) square
Milk	125ml (4 fl oz/½ cup)	250ml (8fl oz/1 cup)	470ml (15fl oz/1¾ cups)
Vinegar	1 tsp	1 tbsp	2 tbsp
Chocolate, plain (semisweet)	60g (2oz/2 squares)	125g (4oz/4 squares)	250g (8oz/8 squares)
Margarine, soft	60g (2oz/¼ cup)	125g (4oz/½ cup)	250g (8oz/1 cup)
Caster (superfine) sugar	125g (4oz/½ cup)	250g (8oz/1 cup)	500g (1lb/2 cups)
Eggs	1	2	4
Self-raising flour	155g (5oz/1¼ cups)	315g (10oz/2½ cups)	685g (1lb 6oz/5½ cups)
Bicarbonate of soda (baking soda)	½ tsp	1 tsp	2 tsp
Cocoa (unsweetened cocoa powder)	1 tbsp	2 tbsp	4 tbsp
Baking time	1 hour	1½ hours	2¼ hours

Cutting and layering

Preparation of the cake is a most important part of cake decorating work. Careful handling, even cutting and neat layering all contribute to making an accurate cake base on which to build and also provide a visually pleasing appearance to the cake when cut.

To achieve even and accurate slicing, which helps good layering, use commercially available polypropylene cutting boards. Place a board each side of the cake, hold the cake steady and, using a sharp knife resting on the boards as a guide, cut through the cakes.

While working, always keep the cake covered, particularly any cut surfaces, in order to prevent loss of moisture, which will cause the cake to be dry. A good method is to slide the cake into a large polythene bag. Once cut, spread the cakes evenly with jam (conserve) and/or buttercream, according to taste.

Tip

☆ Before cutting or layering a Madeira (pound) or sponge (layer) cake, remove the thin crust or 'skin' from the top of the cake by drawing the back edge of a long knife across the cake, or use a sharp serrated knife in a conventional manner.

Rich fruit cake quantities chart

Round tin (pan)	15cm (6in)	18cm (7in)	20cm (8in)	23cm (9in)	25cm (10in)	28cm (11in)	30cm (12in)
Square tin	13cm (5in)	15cm (6in)	18cm (7in)	20cm (8in)	23cm (9in)	25cm (10in)	28cm (11in)
Butter or margarine, softened	125g (4oz/½ cup)	155g (5oz/⅔ cup)	200g (6½oz/¾ cup)	280g (9oz/1¼ cups)	410g (13oz/1⅔ cups)	470g (15oz/1¾ cups)	625g (1¼lb/2½ cups)
Dark muscovado sugar	125g (4oz/¾ cup)	155g (5oz/1 cup)	200g (6½oz/1¼ cups)	280g (9oz/1¾ cups)	410g (13oz/2⅓ cups)	470g (15oz/2¾ cups)	625g (1¼lb/3⅓ cups)
Plain (all-purpose) flour	155g (5oz/1¼ cups)	185g (6oz/1½ cups)	250g (8oz/2 cups)	275g (12oz/3 cups)	500g (1lb/4 cups)	625g (1¼lb/5 cups)	750g (1½lb/6 cups)
Ground mixed spice	1 tsp	1 tsp	1½ tsp	2 tsp	3 tsp	4 tsp	6 tsp
Eggs	2	3	3	4	6	8	9
Mixed dried fruit	440g (14oz/2½ cups)	625g (1¼lb/3¾ cups)	875g (1¾lb/5¼ cups)	1.1kg (2¼lb/6¾ cups)	1.5kg (3lb/9 cups)	1.8kg (3¾lb/11¼ cups)	2.25kg (4½lb/13½ cups)
Glacé cherries	60g (2oz/⅓ cup)	60g (2oz/⅓ cup)	90g (3oz/½ cup)	100g (3½oz/⅔ cup)	155g (5oz/1 cup)	185g (6oz/1¼ cups)	250g (8oz/1½ cups)
Chopped mixed nuts	30g (1oz/¼ cup)	30g (1oz/¼ cup)	45g (1½oz/⅓ cup)	60g (2oz/½ cup)	90g (3oz/¾ cup)	125g (4oz/1 cup)	185g (6oz/1½ cups)
Baking time	1½–2 hours	2–2¼ hours	3–3¼ hours	3½–4 hours	4 hours	4½–4¾ hours	5–5¼ hours

Madeira (pound) cake quantities chart

Round tin (pan)	15cm (6in)	18cm (7in)	20cm (8in)	23cm (9in)	25cm (10in)
Square tin	13cm (5in)	15cm (6in)	18cm (7in)	20cm (8in)	23cm (9in)
Butter or margarine, softened	125g (4oz/½ cup)	185g (6oz/¾ cup)	315g (10oz/1¼ cups)	440g (14oz/1¾ cups)	500g (1lb/2 cups)
Caster (superfine) sugar	125g (4oz/½ cup)	185g (6oz/¾ cup)	315g (10oz/1¼ cups)	440g (14oz/1¾ cups)	500g (1lb/2 cups)
Eggs	2	3	5	7	8
Self-raising flour	185g (6oz/1½ cups)	250g (8oz/2 cups)	375g (12oz/3 cups)	500g (1lb/4 cups)	625g (1¼lb/5 cups)
Flavourings: (optional choices) Ground mixed spice	1 tsp	1 tsp	1½ tsp	2 tsp	3 tsp
Citrus (grated rind of lemon/orange/lime)	1	2	3	4	5
Chopped mixed nuts	30g (1oz/¼ cup)	60g (2oz/½ cup)	90g (3oz/¾ cup)	125g (4oz/1 cup)	155g (5oz/1¼ cups)
Baking time	1–1¼ hours	1¼–1½ hours	1½–1¾ hours	1¾–2 hours	2 hours

Icing Recipes

All kinds of icings are used to cover and decorate cakes. Versatile sugarpaste provides a repertoire of decorations while royal icing is reserved for special occasions. Buttercream and chocolate icings offer more delicious choices.

Sugarpaste (rolled fondant)

You can use either bought or homemade sugarpaste (rolled fondant) for the cakes in this book. Bought sugarpaste, sold 'ready-to-roll', has a similar taste and texture to the homemade version but might work out slightly dearer if used in large quantities. The following recipe makes sufficient sugarpaste to cover a 15–18cm (6–7in) cake.

Makes 500g (1lb)
1 egg white
6 tsp liquid glucose
500g (1lb/3 cups) icing (confectioners') sugar
icing sugar for dusting

1 Put the egg white and liquid glucose in a bowl. Gradually beat in the icing (confectioners') sugar until the mixture becomes too stiff to stir. Turn it out onto a surface sprinkled with icing sugar and knead in the remaining icing sugar until the mixture forms a smooth, stiff paste.

2 Use immediately, or wrap tightly in plastic food wrap and store in a cool place for up to one week. For longer storing, wrap in a double thickness of plastic wrap, or put in a sealed polythene bag.

Pastillage

Just a few of the recipes in this book need pastillage – a hard-setting paste used for modelling. Again, it really is not worth making your own. Buy an instant dry-mix type that you simply mix with water. Alternatively, knead 1 teaspoon gum tragacanth powder into 500g (1lb) sugarpaste. To curve pastillage pieces, dry over a former.

Royal icing

Used for flat icing and piping, royal icing is mostly required for traditionally decorated celebration cakes. To prevent a crust forming once made, cover the surface of the icing with plastic food wrap, place a damp cloth over the wrap, then cover the bowl with a second piece of plastic wrap. Well sealed, royal icing will store for several days. The following recipe makes sufficient royal icing for most decorative purposes. Increase the quantities for flat icing.

Makes 250g (8oz/1 cup)
1 egg white
250g (8oz/1½ cups) icing (confectioners') sugar, sifted

Lightly whisk the egg white in a bowl, then gradually beat in the icing (confectioners') sugar, beating well after each addition until the icing forms soft peaks.

Buttercream

Buttercream is used for covering sponge (layer) cakes and gâteaux, and is particularly popular for children's novelty cakes. It can be piped or spread, flavoured and coloured, and is very easy to work with. The following recipe makes sufficient buttercream to sandwich and cover the top of a 20cm (8in) sponge (layer) cake.

Makes 375g (12oz/1½ cups)

125g (4oz/½ cup) butter or margarine, softened

250g (8oz/1½ cups) icing (confectioners') sugar

2 tsp boiling water

Put the butter or margarine in a bowl and sift over the icing (confectioners') sugar. Beat together until creamy. Add the water and beat again until soft and pale.

BUTTERCREAM FLAVOURINGS

Citrus: Add the finely grated rind of 1 orange, lemon or lime.
Coffee: Add 2 teaspoons coffee essence.
Chocolate: Add 30g (1oz) sifted cocoa (unsweetened cocoa powder).
Almond: Add 1 teaspoon almond essence.

Peaking buttercream

Buttercream is perfect for creating a quick and easy 'sea' effect. Colour some buttercream blue, then spread it thickly over the cake using a palette knife (metal spatula). Rough up the buttercream using the back of a teaspoon. For 'foaming waves', coat the back of a clean teaspoon with plain butter-

cream and use to touch the blue peaks, leaving white tips.

Glacé icing

This is used mainly as a simple topping for sponge (layer) cakes, and occasionally when making novelty cakes. The following recipe makes enough to cover the top of a 20cm (8in) cake. Add the water cautiously as too much will give a very runny icing.

Makes 250g (8oz/1 cup)

250g (8oz/1½ cups) icing (confectioners') sugar

about 1 tbsp warm water

a few drops of food colouring (optional)

Sift the icing (confectioners') sugar into a small bowl and gradually beat in enough water to make a smooth paste that thickly covers the back of a spoon. Add food colouring, if liked. Use immediately, or cover with plastic food wrap to prevent a crust forming.

Chocolate ganache

This delicious blend of melted chocolate and cream can be poured over cakes, or left to firm up, whisked and then spread or piped. The following recipe makes enough ganache to coat a 20–23cm (8–9in) cake.

155g (5oz/5 squares) plain (semisweet) chocolate

155ml (5fl oz/⅔ cup) double (heavy) cream

Break up the chocolate and put it in a heatproof bowl with the cream. Place the bowl over a saucepan of gently simmering water and leave until the chocolate has melted. Stir gently with a wooden spoon until smooth. Remove from the heat and leave until the mixture thickens enough to coat the back of the spoon very thickly. The ganache is now ready to pour over a cake.

Alternatively, leave the ganache until cool, then beat lightly until thick enough to spread or pipe.

Chocolate moulding icing

This resembles ordinary moulding icing or sugarpaste (rolled fondant) and is very versatile. It can be made using plain (semisweet), milk (German sweet) or white chocolate. The following recipe makes enough to cover a 20–23cm (8–9in) cake.

185g (6oz/6 squares) plain (semisweet) chocolate

2 tbsp liquid glucose

1 egg white

500g (1lb/3 cups) icing (confectioners') sugar, sifted

1 Break up the chocolate and put it in a small heatproof bowl over a saucepan of hot water. Add the liquid glucose and leave until melted.

2 Remove from the heat and leave for 2 minutes, then add the egg white and a little of the icing (confectioners') sugar. Beat the chocolate mixture until smooth, gradually adding the remaining icing sugar.

3 When the mixture becomes too stiff to beat, turn it onto a surface and knead in the remaining icing sugar to make a stiff paste. Wrap the paste in plastic food wrap or a polythene bag and keep in a cool place for up to three days.

Chocolate frosting

The following recipe is sufficient to cover an 18–20cm (7–8in) cake.

60g (2oz/2 squares) plain (semisweet) chocolate
185g (6oz/¾ cup) caster (superfine) sugar
1 egg white
pinch of cream of tartar

1 Melt the chocolate in a heatproof bowl over hot water. Combine the sugar, egg white and cream of tartar in a large heatproof bowl. Place the bowl over a saucepan of gently simmering water. Using electric beaters, beat the ingredients together thoroughly for 6–8 minutes, until soft peaks form.

2 Remove the bowl from the heat. Gradually whisk the melted chocolate into the egg white until evenly incorporated.

3 Immediately spread the frosting over the top and side of the cake, using a palette knife (metal spatula) to spread and swirl it.

Chocolate fudge icing

A thick covering of this rich icing can liven up a plain chocolate cake. Swirl it over the cake while still soft. The recipe below is sufficient to cover a 20–23cm (8–9in) cake.

250g (8oz/8 squares) plain (semisweet) chocolate
125g (4oz/½ cup) butter
2 eggs
250g (8oz/1½ cups) icing (confectioners') sugar, sifted

1 Break up the chocolate and melt it with the butter in a heatproof bowl over a saucepan of hot water. Stir, then leave the mixture to cool for 5 minutes.

2 Add the eggs to the cooled chocolate mixture. Beat well.

Tips

☆ For successful rolling and moulding, Chocolate Moulding Icing must be the correct consistency. If when rolled it becomes soft and sticks to the work surface, gather it up and knead in more icing (confectioners') sugar. If the icing is dry and cracks, heat it in the microwave on High for 30 seconds. If it remains dry, sprinkle it with water and knead to soften.

☆ Unlike ordinary sugarpaste (rolled fondant), Chocolate Moulding Icing does not develop a dry crust if exposed to the air for more than a minute or two. It does, however, harden slowly as the chocolate sets. If this happens, heat in the microwave on High for 30 seconds. Leave to stand for one minute, then microwave for a further 30 seconds if necessary.

☆ When rolling or moulding the icing, dust surfaces and hands with cornflour (cornstarch) to prevent sticking.

3 Add the sifted icing (confectioners') sugar, beating until smooth. Continue beating until the mixture almost holds its shape. If the icing remains too thin, chill until required.

Marzipan (Almond paste)

Marzipan (almond paste) has several uses in cake decorating. It can be used to cover cakes before adding a layer of icing, or used as an alternative to icing. Pliable in texture, it can also be moulded into novelty shapes.

Makes about 500g (1lb)

250g (8oz/2 cups) ground almonds

125g (4oz/½ cup) caster (superfine) sugar

125g (4oz/¾ cup) icing (confectioners') sugar

1 egg white

1 tsp lemon juice

1 Place the almonds and both sugars in a large bowl. Stir the ingredients together.

2 Add the egg white and lemon juice and mix until the mixture starts to bind together.

3 As soon as the mixture starts to form a paste, turn it out onto a surface dusted with icing (confectioners') sugar. Knead the paste lightly until completely smooth. Avoid overkneading as this will make the paste soft and oily.

4 When ready, wrap the marzipan in foil or a polythene bag. Store in a cool place, or refrigerate, for up to three days before using.

VARIATIONS

Chocolate marzipan: Make as before, adding 45g (1½oz/⅓ cup) sifted cocoa (unsweetened cocoa powder) and using 2 egg whites.
.

Chocolate hazelnut paste: Make as above variation, substituting ground hazelnuts for almonds.

Truffle paste

A firm paste ideal for moulding and shaping, particularly useful for difficult-to-shape pieces and sections on certain novelty cakes.

Makes about 750g (1½lb/3 cups)

500g (1lb/8 cups) cake crumbs

60g (2oz/⅓ cup) apricot jam (conserve)

60ml (2fl oz/¼ cup) evaporated milk

½ tsp vanilla essence (extract)

about 125g (4oz) melted chocolate (see Note)

1 Place the cake crumbs in a bowl, add the apricot jam (conserve), evaporated milk and vanilla. Mix the ingredients a little using a spoon, then stream in the melted chocolate and continue mixing until a firm paste is formed. (A dry mix will crumble and be difficult to mould, while a mixture that is too soft will not retain its shape when moulded.)

Tip

☆ *Truffle paste makes use of any cake trimmings left over after shaping cakes. Cake trimmings can be frozen in polythene bags and stored for subsequent use, either as they are to be used for forming shapes (see Golf Bag, page 160) or crumbed and sieved for making truffle paste (see Horse, page 86).*

2 The prepared mixture will keep for a few days sealed in an airtight container in the refrigerator.

3 To create shapes, simply mould using hands dusted with icing (confectioners') sugar. Attach to the main cake using jam, melted chocolate or buttercream.

Note

If using chocolate crumbs, use milk (German sweet) or plain (semi-sweet) chocolate. For plain crumbs, use white chocolate. The amount required will depend on whether the crumbs are dry or moist.

Covering Cakes

Before decorating a cake, it is important to obtain a good, smooth base. This is done by carefully applying marzipan (almond paste) and/or sugarpaste (rolled fondant). Apricot glaze is used to secure it to the cake; the marzipan creates a neat shape for the icing layer. Both rich fruit and Madeira (pound) cakes can be covered in the same way.

Apricot glaze

This can be made in large quantities and stored in the refrigerator for several weeks. If a recipe uses more than 3 tablespoons of apricot glaze, increase the amount of water required in proportion to the jam (conserve).

3 tbsp apricot jam (conserve)
1 tsp water

Put the jam and water in a saucepan and heat gently until the jam has melted and the mixture boiled. Press through a small sieve using a teaspoon.

Covering a cake with marzipan

The amount of apricot glaze and marzipan (almond paste) required varies from cake to cake.

Brush the top of the cake with apricot glaze. Lightly knead the required amount of marzipan to soften it slightly. Roll out two-thirds of the paste on a surface dusted with icing (confectioners') sugar to a round or square 5cm (2in) larger than the diameter of the cake. Place the marzipan on a sheet of greaseproof (parchment) or non-stick paper. Place the cake upside down on the paste and press the marzipan up against the cake to fill in any gaps around the edges. Using a sharp knife, cut off the excess paste around the top of the cake to give a neat finish. Invert the cake onto a cake board and carefully remove the lining paper.

If covering a round cake, measure the circumference of the cake with a length of string. Roll out the remaining marzipan to a strip slightly longer than the string and deeper than the cake. Using the string as a guide, cut the strip to the exact circumference, then trim it to the exact depth of the cake. Brush the side of the cake with more apricot glaze. Roll up the almond paste strip and place it against the side of the cake. Unroll around the cake, pressing it firmly into position and lightly smoothing out the join and top edge, using hands dusted with icing sugar.

Use the same method to cover a square cake, but using four strips of paste, each the exact measurement of the sides of the cake. Attach one piece at a time. Use a palette knife (metal spatula) to smooth all the joins together.

Covering a round cake with sugarpaste

The amount of sugarpaste (rolled fondant) required varies from cake to cake. The recipes in this book give the exact quantity required for each cake.

First spread the cake top and side with apricot glaze or jam (conserve). Cover with marzipan (almond paste) if using. Alternatively, buttercream (see page 18) may be used.

Lightly knead the required amount of sugarpaste to soften it slightly. Dust a work surface with icing (confectioners') sugar and roll out the sugarpaste to a round 7.5cm (3in) larger than the diameter of the cake. Lift the sugarpaste onto the rolling pin, or use your hands dusted lightly with cornflour (cornstarch), and lay it over the top of

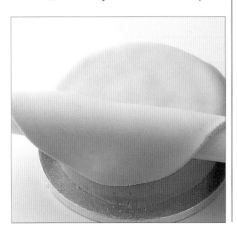

the cake. Smooth the sugarpaste over the top and down the side of the cake, easing it gently to fit around the side. If it forms folds and creases, keep smoothing the paste to eliminate them. Trim off any excess paste around the base of the cake.

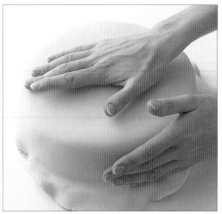

Covering a square cake with sugarpaste

Cover the cake with apricot glaze and buttercream or marzipan as for a round cake.

Roll out the sugarpaste to a square 7.5cm (3in) larger than the cake. Lift it onto the cake, draping the paste loosely. Smooth from the centre to remove any air pockets. Remove any creases and folds.

Use a small knife to trim excess paste from the base.

Tip

☆ An icing smoother (see below) gives a beautiful finish to a cake covered with sugarpaste (rolled fondant). Lightly dust the smoother with cornflour (cornstarch), then gently move it over the surface of the sugarpaste, using a circular 'ironing' action.

Sugarpaste Techniques

Sugarpaste (rolled fondant) is one of the most exciting aspects of cake decorating. Smooth and elastic, it can be moulded, rolled, cut and shaped into all kinds of decorations for party cakes.

Colouring sugarpaste

KNEADING IN COLOUR

Place the measured quantity of sugarpaste (rolled fondant) on a surface dusted with cornflour (cornstarch) and knead lightly until smooth. Using a cocktail stick (toothpick) to prevent adding too much colour at once, dot liquid or paste colouring onto the sugarpaste, then knead in until blended.

Always add colours sparingly as some are much stronger than others. For pastel shades, the icing might need only the smallest amount, while several additions of colour might be needed for deeper shades. Once the required colour is achieved, keep the sugarpaste tightly wrapped in plastic food wrap.

MARBLING

This is achieved by only partially blending the colour into the sugarpaste (rolled fondant). Dot the icing sparingly with the chosen colour, as before. Roll the icing to a long, thick sausage shape, then fold the ends to the centre and dot with a little more colour. Re-roll to a thick sausage and fold the ends in once again. Repeat the rolling and folding, without adding any more colour, until the colour starts to show in thin streaks. Add more colour and repeat the rolling and folding process if stronger marbling is required, but take care not to overwork the sugarpaste, until a uniform marbled colour has been achieved.

Once sufficiently marbled, roll out the sugarpaste and use as required.

Covering a cake board

Place the cake in the centre of the board and brush the surface of the board all around the cake with a dampened paintbrush. Colour the sugarpaste (rolled fondant) as required (see left). On a surface dusted with cornflour (cornstarch), thinly roll it out to a long, thin strip; trim one edge. Lift the strip onto the board and ease the cut edge up against the side of the cake, allowing the untrimmed edge to overhang the edge of the board. Smooth down lightly using hands dusted with cornflour, then trim off the excess sugarpaste around the edge of the board. (For large cakes you may need to cover half at a time, smoothing over the joins before trimming off the excess.)

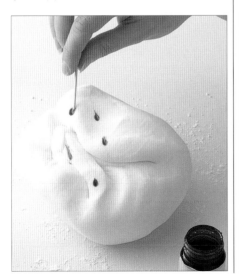

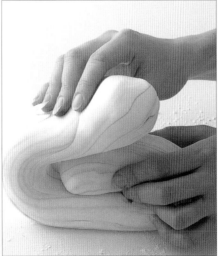

Use four separate strips of sugarpaste to cover the board around a square cake.

Alternatively, cover the board following the technique described for covering the cake (see page 22). Smooth the surface to remove any air pockets and neatly trim the edge with a sharp knife.

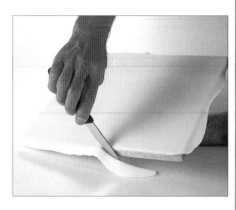

Finishing joins in sugarpaste

With a little practice, joins in sugarpaste (rolled fondant) can be smoothed out completely. Lightly dampen the edges that are to meet, then overlap them very slightly. Rub the edges together, using your fingertips. If the icing starts to feel sticky, dust your fingertips very lightly with cornflour (cornstarch) and continue to rub over the join until it disappears.

Tip

☆ *You can only hide a join successfully when the icing is freshly rolled or moulded. Once it begins to harden, it quickly forms a crust which cannot be completely concealed.*

Making frills

Frills can be applied to the sides of a cake in a scalloped pattern or as a straight border around the base. Before making frills, make sure the cake is marked with template lines (see page 28) to guide the positioning of the frills.

On a surface lightly dusted with cornflour (cornstarch), thinly roll out a little sugarpaste (rolled fondant). Cut out a scalloped circle

Tip

☆ *Some frill cutters come with adjustable centres so that the depth of the frill can be varied between 2cm (¾in) and 2.5cm (1in). Frills can also be made using a plain or fluted biscuit (cookie) cutter about 9cm (3½in) in diameter. Cut out the centre with a small cutter. For a narrower frill, put the wider centre into the frill cutter.*

using a frill cutter. Remove the centre and cut through the ring with a sharp knife.

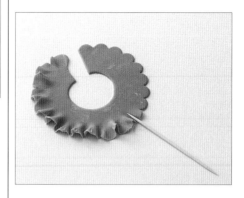

Coat the tip of a cocktail stick (toothpick) with cornflour, and roll the tip along the fluted edge of the sugarpaste until the icing begins to frill. Gradually work around the edge until the icing is completely frilled.

Lightly dampen the cake where the frill is to be applied, then attach the frill to the cake. Continue the technique, making and applying one frill at a time.

Crimping

Crimping is a quick and easy decorative technique worked on sugarpaste or almond paste while it is still soft. A variety of different-shaped crimpers is available. The most widely used is a scalloped crimper, although straight crimpers, hearts, diamonds and zigzags are also available.

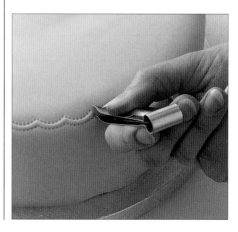

Crimping can be worked around the top edge of a cake or along a scalloped template line (see page 28) marked around the sides.

Dust the crimper with cornflour (cornstarch). Holding the ends of the crimper about 5mm (¼in) apart, carefully pinch the icing, squeezing firmly until marked. Lift the crimper away from the icing before easing the pressure or it will tear the icing above and below. Repeat the pattern all around the top or side of the cake.

Making a bow

An icing bow is easier to assemble than one made from ribbon. The pieces of bow are made separately and then assembled on the cake. The technique is always the same, regardless of size.

Colour some sugarpaste (rolled fondant) as required (see page 23) and roll it out thinly on a surface dusted with cornflour (cornstarch). Cut out one long strip and cut two long rectangles from the strip. Dampen the ends and fold the rectangles over to form loops, tucking small rolls of absorbent kitchen paper (paper towels) or tissue paper inside the loops to keep them in shape.

Cut two more rectangles and pinch one end of each. Cut the other ends of these rectangles into

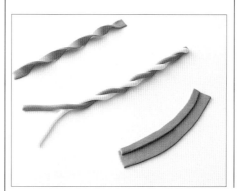

'v' shapes to resemble ribbon ends. Position the loops and bow ends on the cake so they almost meet in the centre, securing them with a dampened paintbrush.

Cut out a square of icing, dome it slightly in the centre, and position it over the centre of the bow to hide the ends. Secure with a dampened paintbrush, if necessary. Do not forget to remove the rolls of absorbent kitchen paper or tissue once the sugarpaste has hardened.

Finishing touches

A piped border of icing is the most common way of finishing the lower edge of a cake, but if you want to avoid piping, choose one of these alternative decorative finishes. Before applying, dampen the bottom edge of the cake.

TWIST

Thinly roll sugarpaste (rolled fondant) on a surface dusted with

cornflour (cornstarch). Cut out a 5mm (¼in) wide strip and lightly twist it from the ends. Lay the strip gently around the base of the cake.

ROPE

Thinly roll out two pieces of icing (in contrasting colours, if liked) under the palms of your hands. Twist the pieces together, then lay the 'rope' around the base of the cake.

STEP

Cover the edges of the cake board first. Roll out more sugarpaste and cut out a strip about 1cm (½ in) wide. Lay this strip over the iced board with one edge against the side of the cake, making a decorative 'step'.

Moulded sugarpaste flowers

ROSES

Knead colouring into the sugarpaste (rolled fondant) until it is the colour you require (see page 23). (Alternatively, roses can be shaped in white and then highlighted with dusting powder (petal dust/blossom tint) and a fine paintbrush.) Take a piece of paste about the size of a grape and shape it into a cone. Pinch the cone around the centre to form a 'waist'. Take another small ball of paste and press it between your fingers and

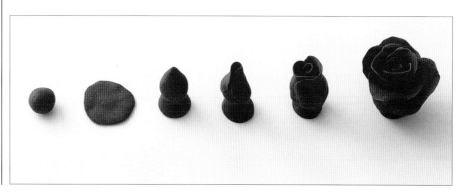

Tip

☆ *Begin with different-sized cones to vary the size of each finished rose. If possible, have a real rose, or a picture of a rose, beside you as you work to help you achieve a realistic result.*

thumb to shape it into a petal. Wrap this around the cone, overlapping the first petal. Continue building up the rose, making each petal slightly larger than the one before. Open out and roll the tips of the outer petals outwards slightly to create a realistic shape. Once completed, slice off the rose through its base and use the base to shape the next cone. Leave overnight to harden.

BLOSSOMS

To save time and effort, use a 'plunger' blossom cutter (see page 8). Colour some sugarpaste (rolled fondant) as required (see page 23). Put the sugarpaste on a surface

Tip

☆ *Moulded flowers look particularly effective using 'petal' or 'flower' paste, which can be rolled more thinly than sugarpaste (rolled fondant). It is available from specialist cake-decorating shops and requires firm kneading before use to soften. Use as for sugarpaste.*

dusted with cornflour (cornstarch) and roll it out as thinly as possible. Dip the cutter into cornflour, then press out a blossom shape. Push the shape out of the cutter onto a piece of sponge (foam) to create a curved blossom. Push a pin through the centre if attaching a stamen. Leave on the sponge overnight to harden. Thread stamens through if required. (See picture below.)

Modelling bears

When modelling the limbs for bears, always begin with equal pieces of sugarpaste (rolled fondant) for both arms and legs, to ensure a well-balanced bear. Model the limbs as shown below, tapering their ends. The legs should be turned up slightly at one end to represent feet, and the arms tapered, then shaped to form a basic hand. Brush with a little water and attach to the body.

Make round holes with the end of a paintbrush for eyes. Pipe in the whites of the eyes and a nose with a little white royal icing, using a no. 1 piping tube (tip). When dry, pipe in the blacks of the eyes and paint the nose pink.

Tip

☆ *When modelling with sugarpaste (rolled fondant) or modelling paste, always use a little cornflour (cornstarch) or icing (confectioners') sugar to prevent sticking. Do not use too much, or the paste will begin to dry out and crack.*

Modelling mice

Begin with a piece of sugarpaste (rolled fondant) the size of a golf or squash ball for each mouse. Use half for the body and the other half for the head, arms and legs. Using the shapes shown as a guide, model the body first, marking the crossed lines on the front and bending the paste slightly into a sitting position. Make indentations for the head and arms.

Roll a ball of paste for the head and gradually model the long nose, curving it up slightly. Make the ears, indenting them slightly with a ball modelling tool, and carefully attach them to the top of the head by dampening the paste. Model the arms, bending them slightly at the elbows, and shape the fingers. The arms can be modelled into different positions, as shown in the photograph of the finished cake on page 43. Roll a thin tail for each mouse and curl up the end. Make a pair of wellington boots for each mouse. Assemble the pieces, carefully sticking them in place with a little water. Use a cocktail stick (toothpick) to mark a tread pattern on the bottom of the

wellington boots, then paint lightly with grey food colouring to accentuate the pattern. Leave to dry. Paint on the eyes and mouth when the paste is dry. Dust the cheeks and inside the ears with a little pink dusting powder (petal dust/blossom tint).

Modelling figures

Colour the sugarpaste (rolled fondant) as required (see page 23) before beginning to model the figures. Roll out a piece of sugarpaste to 1cm (½in) in depth and cut out a pair of legs (trousers), about 4cm (1½in) long and 2cm (¾in) wide, as shown. Taper the legs slightly at the top and make a cut up the centre, leaving 1cm (½in) clear at the tapered end. Soften the square edges of the trousers with your fingers.

Use a smaller piece of sugarpaste to make the body. First roll the paste into a ball, then work it with your fingers until it forms an oblong with rounded edges. Taper the oblong slightly at one end. Cut a small semi-circle from the tapered end of the body to represent the

neckline and trim off the two top corners as shown. Attach the body to the legs using a little royal icing. For standing figures, place a cocktail stick (toothpick), sugar stick or piece of dry spaghetti through each leg and up into the body for extra stability. Make sure that the recipient of the cake knows that there is a cocktail stick in the model, for safety's sake!

Model the arms out of two small pieces of sugarpaste, rolled and tapered at one end. Attach to the body using a paintbrush and a little water, then make a hole in the tapered end for a hand to be inserted. The hands are small flattened circles of flesh-coloured sugarpaste, pinched at one side to fit the ends of the arms.

Make an oval-shaped head out of a piece of flesh-coloured sugarpaste, making almond-shaped indentations with a cocktail stick for the eyes. Fill the sockets with royal icing, attach a button-shaped nose and leave to dry.

Paint on facial features, including rosy cheeks, eyelashes, freckles and eyebrows. Pipe on the hair in the colour of your choice; add glasses or other details to give the figure a personality.

Special effects

More special effects for novelty cakes: grass; woodgrain; gravel.

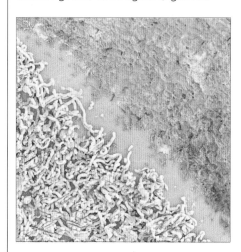

GRASS

Cover the cake or board with green-coloured sugarpaste (rolled fondant) (see page 23). Either stipple using a piece of foam sponge and browny-green royal icing or use a clay gun to force out small thin tufts of browny-green coloured sugarpaste.

WOODGRAIN

Colour sugarpaste (rolled fondant) to the required wood effect tint and use to cover the cake or board (see page 22). When dry, use a paintbrush or food colouring pen to paint or draw fine brown lines and an occasional knot.

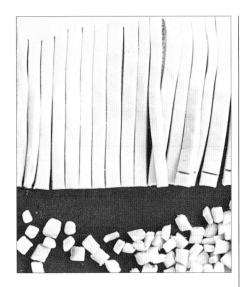

GRAVEL

Roll out some grey-coloured sugarpaste (rolled fondant) and, using a small knife, cut into very thin strips. Cut again at right angles and to the same width to make tiny cubes of paste. Accuracy isn't that important as irregularity creates a more natural effect.

Using templates

A few of the cake designs in this book use a template to create a particular shape. To use a template, first trace the outline on a piece of greaseproof (parchment) or non-stick paper, then cut it out.

On a surface dusted with cornflour (cornstarch), roll out sugarpaste (rolled fondant) or other icing in the chosen colour. Gently rest the paper template over the icing. Using a sharp knife, cut around the template, then lift it away. Use as required.

Templates are also used to mark a particular shape or area of icing on the surface of an iced cake. Cut out the template, attach it to the cake with pins, and then mark the outline on the icing, either by making a series of pin-pricks or by lightly scratching lines on the surface with a pin.

Tip

☆ Paper templates can be used to cut out any decorative shape you choose.

Securing decorations

There are two simple methods of securing decorations on a cake.

SECURING WITH WATER

For decorations that are cut out and secured to the cake while still soft, such as the scalloped border on the Garlands and Bows cake (see page 190), use a small paint-brush that has been lightly dampened with water. Dampen either the underside of the piece of icing to be secured or the area of cake to which the decoration is to be attached, whichever is the easier method.

Tip

☆ When securing decorations with water, do not 'wet' the icing or the shapes will not adhere. If using icing, only the smallest amount is required – large blobs look unsightly.

SECURING WITH ICING

Decorations that are left to harden before being applied to a cake, such as flowers and leaves, are best secured with a little icing. If the cake uses royal icing, use small dots of this to secure. Alternatively, mix a little icing (confectioners') sugar with a dash of water to make a firm paste. Dot the underside of the decoration with the icing and secure in position.

Decorative Fruits and Flowers

As well as silk, sugarpaste and piped flower decorations, frosting real flowers provides a beautiful alternative for cake decorations. White marzipan (almond paste) can be shaped into eye-catching miniature fruits for use as colourful decorating ideas.

Frosted fruits and flowers

Use egg white and sugar to 'frost' fruits, whole flowers, single petals or leaves. Frosted fruits make a stunning decoration for special occasion gâteaux, while whole frosted flowers can be used on both sugarpasted (rolled fondant) and royal-iced cakes as a quick alternative to moulded sugarpaste flowers. Ideal flowers for frosting include rose petals, primroses, pansies, petunias, violets and fruit tree blossoms. Leaves, such as rose, mint and lemon balm, also work well. Suitable fruits include grapes, currants, firm strawberries, gooseberries, cranberries and cherries.

Lightly whisk an egg white and brush over the fruit, leaf or flower. Dip in caster (superfine) sugar, coat thoroughly, then shake off the excess. Leave to dry on absorbent kitchen paper (paper towels). To avoid damaging the petals of larger flowers, wrap floristry wire or a bag tie around the stem and hang the flower upside down to dry.

Marzipan (almond paste) fruits

If liked, a little flavouring, such as finely grated orange rind or liqueur, can be kneaded in with colouring.

APPLES

Shape marzipan (almond paste) into small balls about 2cm (¾in) in diameter. Remove the round centres of cloves and press the stem end of a clove into each paste ball. Cut the wide ends off more cloves and press the stems into the opposite side of the balls for stalks. Paint the apples with diluted red and green food colourings.

STRAWBERRIES

Colour marzipan red and roll into balls about 2cm (¾in) in diameter. Mould each ball into a strawberry shape, then prick all over with a cocktail stick (toothpick). Thinly roll out a little green sugarpaste (rolled fondant) and cut out calyxes using a small calyx cutter or a five-point star. Dampen the centres and secure to the strawberries.

REDCURRANTS

Roll small pieces of soft red marzipan into balls about 5mm (¼in) in diameter. Arrange in clusters.

BLUEBERRIES

Colour marzipan deep blue, adding a touch of black. Roll into balls about 1cm (½in) in diameter and flatten slightly. Lightly mark an indentation in the centre of each with a pointed modelling tool.

BLACKBERRIES

Colour marzipan with black colouring, adding a touch of blue and red. Roll small balls of paste, about the size of a large pea, and elongate slightly. Roll tiny balls of paste and use to cover the centres.

Royal Icing Techniques

Coating and decorating a cake with royal icing is one of the cake decorating skills that requires practice but, once mastered, it provides the basis of many very attractive traditional cake designs.

Coating cakes

Three coats of royal icing (see page 17) are usually applied; the technique for each coat is the same and 24 hours should be left between each coat. Once coated and decorated, the cake can be stored in a cool, dry place for 2–3 weeks.

COATING THE TOP OF A CAKE

Spread a little of the royal icing over the top of the cake using a palette knife (metal spatula). Work the knife backwards and forwards to eliminate any air bubbles. Spread the icing right to the edges in an even layer. Draw an icing ruler, held at an angle of 45°, over the icing to create a smooth layer. (You may need to work the ruler across the icing several times before you achieve a really smooth surface.)

Using a sharp knife, trim off excess icing from the edges of the cake. Leave to dry for about 2 hours.

COATING THE SIDES OF A SQUARE CAKE

Spread some icing on one side of the cake, working the knife backwards and forwards to eliminate any air bubbles. Draw an icing scraper across it in one smooth movement to give a flat finish. Repeat this on the opposite side of the cake, then leave to harden for 2 hours before icing the remaining two sides; again, leave to harden.

After the icing has hardened slightly, use a sharp, rigid knife to trim off all the excess icing from around the top edges of the cake.

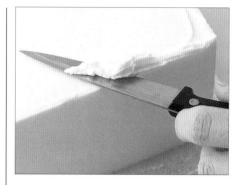

COATING THE SIDE OF A ROUND CAKE

Use the same technique as for a square cake, but spread the icing all around the cake in one go. A turntable is invaluable for icing the side of a round cake as one hand can hold the scraper in position and the other gently rotate the turntable.

Tips

☆ To save time, the icing for the three coats of flat icing can be made up in one batch and stored, tightly covered, in a cool place. This is particularly worthwhile if using a coloured icing as it is always difficult to make up a new batch of exactly the same colour.

☆ During storage, the icing will stiffen up slightly. Before using, beat well to soften, adding a few drops of water or beaten egg white if necessary.

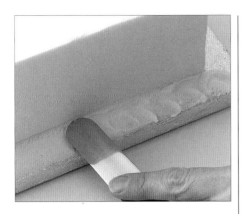

Icing the cake board

This gives a neat finishing touch to cakes decorated with royal icing. Once the sides of the cake have been coated, spread the cake board around the base of the cake with a thin layer of icing using a palette knife (metal spatula). (Cover all the board at once for a round cake, or one side at a time for a square cake.) Draw the palette knife along the icing to neaten, then trim off any excess icing from the edges. Leave to harden.

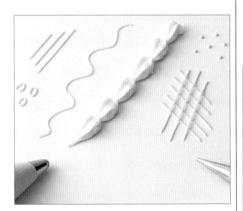

Basic piping

WRITING TUBES

Writing tubes (tips) are used to pipe words, lines, lattice work and dots. Use a fine, medium or large piping tube, depending on the thickness of the line required.

Star tubes are used to pipe decorative shell borders.

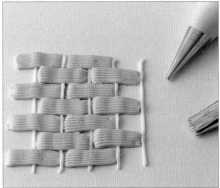

BASKETWORK

For this you will need one piping bag fitted with a medium piping tube (tip) and another fitted with a basketwork tube. If preferred, fill the bags with icing in two contrasting colours.

First pipe a straight line over the area of the cake to be covered. Using the basketwork tube, pipe 2.5cm (1in) bands of icing, a tube-width apart, over the piped line. Pipe a second line, just touching the ends of the bands of basketwork. Pipe a second row of basketwork, starting at the first line and crossing over the second line in the same way. Repeat all over the area to be covered.

Tip

☆ *The smaller the piping tube (tip) used, the thinner the icing needs to be. When using a star or basketwork tube, use royal icing that holds its shape when left to settle in the bowl. For fine lines and writing, thin the icing with a little beaten egg white or water so that it is easier to pipe.*

Runouts

Thinned royal icing can be used to 'fill in' decorative shapes, such as the bow right. Once hardened, the shapes can be used to decorate sugarpasted or royal-iced cakes.

Runout work or flooding is also a technique that can be applied directly to the surface of a cake (see the Broderie Anglaise Cake on page 183), and is particularly useful for covering flaws in flat icing.

Trace the outline of a decorative shape, e.g., a heart, star, butterfly or bow, onto greaseproof (parchment) or non-stick paper. Place another piece of paper over the tracing. Using a piping bag fitted with a fine piping tube (tip), pipe royal icing in a fine line around the outline of the shape.

Thin more royal icing with a little beaten egg white or water until it becomes completely level when left to settle in the bowl for several seconds. Place in a paper piping bag. Snip off 2.5mm (⅛ in) from the end. Gradually fill the outline with the thinned icing, easing the icing into the corners using the tip of a cocktail stick (toothpick). For best results, fill the shape with as much icing as it will hold without flooding over the piped outline. Leave to harden for 24 hours, then carefully peel away the paper.

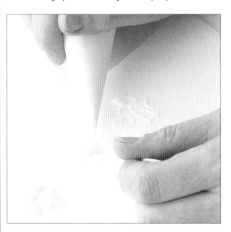

Tip

☆ *Bows made in this way would look very pretty as an alternative decoration to the silk roses and bows of the Broderie Anglaise Cake (see page 183).*

Chocolate Techniques

To achieve good results with chocolate it is important to melt it correctly. This is crucial if it is to be used for decorating purposes such as runout work, or for swirling over a cake.

Melting chocolate

Break chocolate into small pieces and place in a heatproof bowl. Bring a saucepan of water to the boil, then remove from the heat. Place the bowl of chocolate over the pan, above the water level. Leave the chocolate until completely melted. Stir lightly before use.

Chocolate which has been overheated may develop discoloured streaking or a mottled appearance once set.

Small pieces of chocolate can be melted in a non-stick pan, keeping the heat very low. Stir until melted.

MELTING CHOCOLATE IN THE MICROWAVE

While the microwave is perfect for melting chocolate for mousses, puddings, cake mixtures and icings, care must be taken when melting chocolate for decorative work, as the temperature is much more difficult to control. Chocolate heated in the microwave retains its shape and should be tested with a fork.

Break the chocolate into pieces and place in a suitable bowl. Heat on Medium power, allowing 3 minutes for 185–250g (6–8oz/6–8 squares) chocolate. Leave to stand in the microwave for 5 minutes; reheat briefly if necessary.

COVERING A CAKE WITH MELTED CHOCOLATE

Melted chocolate makes an easy cake covering.

For a 20cm (8in) sponge (layer) cake you will need 250g (8oz/8 squares) chocolate. Place the cake on a serving plate or on a wire rack over a plate. Lightly stir the melted chocolate, then pour it over the cake. Using a palette knife (metal spatula), swiftly spread the choco-

late evenly over the top and down the sides of the cake to cover it completely.

As the chocolate cools, lightly swirl the surface with a clean palette knife. Alternatively, run the serrated edge of a plastic cake decorating scraper over the surface. Leave the cake in a cool place to set.

Tempering couverture

Couverture must be tempered before being used: break up to 500g (1lb) couverture into small pieces. Melt it in a heatproof bowl over a pan of simmering water. When the chocolate reaches 46°C (115°F) on a sugar or chocolate thermometer, remove from the heat and place in a larger bowl of cold water. Stir the chocolate until the temperature falls to 27–28°C (80–82°F). Return the bowl to the heat and heat to 31°C (88°F). The chocolate is now tempered and ready to use.

Caraque

Melt 250g (8oz/8 squares) plain (semisweet) or white chocolate. Pour onto a marble slab or other clean, smooth surface. Spread it quite thinly and leave to set. Draw

the blade of a large knife, held at an angle of 45°, across the surface of the chocolate to remove or shave off a thin layer that will roll into curls. Transfer the curls to a large plate as you make them. Chill the caraque or keep it in a cool

Tip

☆ *If the caraque breaks off in brittle pieces, it is probably too cold to curl. Leave in a warm place for several minutes, then try again. If the caraque is too warm to curl, refrigerate briefly.*

place until you are ready to use it.

For Double Chocolate Caraque, use 125g (4oz/4 squares) each plain and white chocolate. Melt in separate heatproof bowls as before. Spread the dark chocolate over the slab, then swirl with the white. Leave to set, then make the caraque as above.

Chocolate cut-outs

Melted chocolate can be thinly spread on greaseproof (parchment) or non-stick paper and left to set, ready for cutting out numerous novelty shapes or dainty boxes. A simple cake for a child's birthday

could be made by cutting out milk (German sweet) chocolate shapes and securing them to a cake covered in white chocolate. Squares or panels of chocolate can also be made for covering the tops or sides of cakes, a technique which has been used to good effect on the Chequered Parcel illustrated on page 213, and the White Chocolate Box illustrated on page 209.

Chocolate boxes

These can be made in miniature *petit four* sizes or slightly larger for individual cakes.

To create each box cut out five equal squares of chocolate, each 2.5cm (1in) in diameter. Place one square on a work surface and cover with 1cm (½in) square of chocolate sponge. Spread a little whipped cream or ganache (see page 18) over the sponge, then secure the four remaining squares around the filling to make a box. Finish the cake boxes with strawberries or other fresh fruit and sprigs of mint or chocolate leaves.

To make larger chocolate boxes increase the size of the squares to 4cm (1½in) and use 2.5cm (1in) squares of sponge.

Chocolate modelling paste (clay)

Chocolate modelling paste (clay) is made from chocolate and liquid glucose. Easy to manage, it can be shaped into stunning flowers, figures, ribbon and novelty shapes – with a little practice the possibilities are endless, particularly if a mixture of plain (semisweet), milk (German sweet) and white chocolate is used.

To make 155g (5oz) chocolate modelling paste you will need 125g (4oz/4 squares) chocolate and 2 tablespoons liquid glucose.

Melt the chocolate in a heatproof bowl over hot water. Remove from the heat and beat in the glucose until a paste is formed which comes away from the side of the bowl. Place the paste in a polythene bag and chill for 1 hour until firm but pliable.

Chocolate roses

To make a chocolate rose, take a piece of modelling chocolate about the size of a grape and shape it into a cone. Press down on the surface and squeeze a 'waist' into the cone near the base.

Take another piece of paste about half the size of the cone and press it as flat as possible to create a petal shape. Secure this around the cone. Shape another slightly larger petal and wrap this around the first, overlapping it slightly. Continue building up the flower, making each petal slightly larger than the previous one, until you have a complete flower comprising 7–8 rose petals, as illustrated above.

Bend and tuck the outer petals to create a realistic shape. Once completed, slice just below the petals; use the base to shape the next cone.

To create a posy, vary the sizes of the roses. For buds use just 3–4 petals, tucking them tightly around the cone.

Tip

☆ *For variety, cover different types of leaves with chocolate, such as rose, lemon balm, mint, bay and holly.*

Drizzling chocolate

This makes a simple and attractive decoration for cakes covered with melted chocolate or ganache (see page 18).

Put some melted chocolate (in a contrasting colour to that used on the cake, see photograph) in a paper piping bag and snip off the smallest tip so the chocolate flows out in a fine stream. Holding the piping bag about 5cm (2in) above the cake, pipe some lines by gently squeezing the bag and moving your hand quickly over the cake. Tilt the cake slightly so that the sides can be covered with piped lines as well as the top.

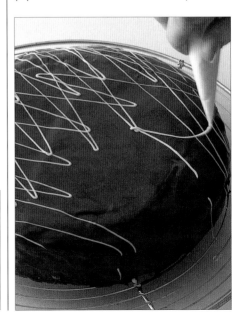

Chocolate cases

Small *petit four* or paper sweet cases (candy cups) make perfect moulds for shaping chocolate cases. These can be filled with piped ganache (see page 18), used as a container for whipped cream or lemon mousse, or scattered over a chocolate cake for decoration, as on the White Chocolate Box illustrated on page 209. They also make tasty containers for truffles.

To coat about 20 paper sweet cases, melt 125g (4oz/4 squares) plain (semisweet), milk (German sweet) or white chocolate (see page 32). Using the back of a small teaspoon, thickly coat the base and side of the paper cases. Scoop out the excess chocolate, then invert the cases to set. When set, check the sides for any thinly coated areas; re-coat if necessary. Peel away the paper case.

Chocolate runouts

Chocolate runouts can be made in almost any shape. You can trace designs from greetings cards or books or even make up your own. If experimenting for the first time, it is best to stick to simple shapes.

Trace the chosen design. Secure each tracing to a flat surface with waxed paper on top.

Place a little melted chocolate in a paper piping bag fitted with a piping tube (tip); pipe over outlines, making sure joins are neat. Set.

Place more melted chocolate in a bag fitted with a clean tube. Working fairly quickly, fill in the outline with melted chocolate, easing the chocolate into corners with the tip of a cocktail stick (toothpick) if necessary. Cornelli work can be used if a lacy effect is preferred. When set, carefully pull the paper away from the runouts.

(Cornelli work is done by piping long, continuous curvy lines, see page 205.)

Chocolate for dipping

Fresh and crystallized fruits, truffles and nuts make delectable cake decorations when dipped in chocolate. Nuts and truffles are best completely coated in chocolate, while fruits such as seedless grapes, strawberries and cherries look more attractive if half dipped. Nuts, truffles and crystallized fruits can be dipped several days in advance, but fresh fruits should be dipped on the day they are to be eaten.

Before you start, wash and dry all fruit thoroughly. Line a baking sheet with greaseproof (parchment), non-stick or waxed paper. Melt plain (semisweet), milk (German sweet) or white chocolate (see page 32). Leave the bowl over the pan of hot water while dipping the fruits.

Holding the fruit by its stalk end, half dip into the chocolate and twist slightly. Allow excess to drip back into the bowl, then transfer the fruit to the paper to dry. Dip nuts one at a time; remove using a dipping fork.

Further Decorating Ideas

With a little creativity, you can make great use of bought plastic and fabric decorations, from plastic lettering, numbers, beads and bells to fabric butterflies, ribbons, flowers and leaves. The secret is not to use them straight from the pack – tweak the flowers, curve the leaves, trim the lettering to suit and then attach them to your cake. You will be surprised at the difference!

Bought plastic and fabric decorations

Fabric, wafer and piped flowers, all available commercially, will benefit from a quick tint with dusting powder (petal dust/blossom tint), just to make them more individual.

Writing on cakes is usually the most difficult part, so take advantage of the many cut-out letters, numbers and popular inscriptions that are available, and don't forget ribbons, bows and cake candles – birthday cakes are not the same without colourful ribbon trimmings and candles to blow out. If you think sticking candles in your cake will spoil the look of it, insert them just before the party, or see right.

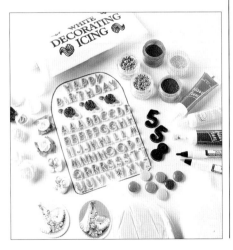

Tip

☆ *Do not attempt to decorate a cake that is beyond your level of skill. It is far better to give a neat finish to a simple cake with bought decorations than struggle to perfect a more intricate hand-made design.*

READY-MADE EDIBLE DECORATIONS

Edible decorations are becoming increasingly popular and you can now obtain everything from lettering to ready-made icing in tubes.

ADDING CANDLES

If there is no room on the cake for candles and holders, or you feel they will interfere with the design, use the cake board instead.

Candle holders can be made out of sugarpaste (rolled fondant). Roll small balls in your chosen colour

and flatten them slightly. Secure to the board with a dampened paintbrush. Dampen the base of the candles and press them into the balls of sugarpaste.

Alternatively, cut out small flower or star shapes using a cutter and secure in the same way.

ICING CUT-OUTS

One of the simplest ways to decorate a child's cake is to cover the cake with simple cut-outs made using biscuit, numeral, alphabet or novelty shape cutters.

Thinly roll out some sugarpaste (rolled fondant) in your chosen colour on a surface dusted with cornflour (cornstarch). Dip the cutters in cornflour to prevent sticking, then cut out the shapes. Dampen the underside of each shape and secure to the cake. By using a selection of cutters, or cutting shapes by hand, you can build up complete sugarpaste pictures, such as a clown's face, a simple house etc.

Fun Party Cakes

Clown Cake

A colourful clown makes an appealing cake for any child – and some adults too!

CAKE AND DECORATION

20cm (8in) round Madeira (pound) cake (see page 16)

125g (4oz/½ cup) buttercream (see page 18)

3 tbsp apricot glaze (see page 21)

1.5kg (3lb) sugarpaste (rolled fondant)

cornflour (cornstarch) for dusting

blue, red, yellow and green paste food colourings

250g (8oz/1 cup) royal icing (see page 17)

2 stamens

candles and holders (optional)

1m (1yd) decorative ribbon for board edge

EQUIPMENT

25cm (10in) round silver cake board

7.5cm (3in) piece of wooden dowelling

paintbrush

frill cutter

paper piping bag

no. 1 piping tube (tip)

plunger flower cutter

1 Level the surface of the cake by cutting off any peak that formed during baking. Cut the cake horizontally in half and sandwich the layers together again with the buttercream (see page 15). Place the cake on the board.

2 Brush the cake with apricot glaze. Reserve 500g (1lb) sugarpaste (rolled fondant); use the remainder to cover the cake (see page 22).

3 Cut a long, thin strip of greaseproof (parchment) or non-stick paper measuring 71 x 5cm (28 x 2in). Fold the strip in half, then in half twice more to give a rectangle of eight layers. Unfold. Trace the template on page 40 onto one of the end rectangles on the strip. Refold the paper, then cut out the shape.

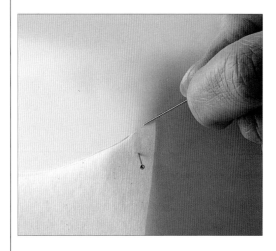

4 Open out the template and wrap it around the cake, securing the ends with pins. Using another pin, mark the curved outline of the template on the cake. Remove the template.

5 Colour 250g (8oz) of the remaining sugarpaste blue. Reserve a small piece and use a little of the rest to cover the cake board around the base of the cake (see page 23). Use more blue sugarpaste to make frills (see page 24) and position around the side of the cake with the unfrilled edge just covering the template line.

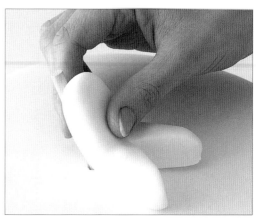

6 Press the dowelling into the top of the cake, just off centre, so that it sticks out at an angle. Shape 60g (2oz) white sugarpaste into a sausage shape 7.5cm (3in) long and flatten it slightly. Cut the sausage lengthways in half from one end to the centre. Position the uncut end against the dowelling on top of the cake. Open out the cut pieces for the clown's legs. Lightly dampen with a paintbrush.

7 Thinly roll out a little more white sugarpaste on a surface dusted with cornflour (cornstarch) to a 7.5cm (3in) square. Make a cut from one side into the centre. Wrap the square around the

'clown' on top of the cake, fitting it around the legs and tucking the excess around the back of the dowelling. Mark 'creases' with a knife at the bottom of each leg of the clown's trousers.

8 Colour a little sugarpaste pale pink with a dot of red food colouring. Shape some into a small ball and position for the clown's head. Shape two small hands from the remaining pink paste. Shape two puffed sleeves from white paste and secure to the sides of the clown. Secure the hands to the ends of the sleeves.

9 Roll out the small piece of reserved blue sugarpaste and cut out a small frill. Attach it around the neck of the clown.

Tip

☆ *Lengths of fine dowelling are available from cake decorating shops. Alternatively, buy some from a hardware shop, or use a wooden toffee apple or lollipop stick.*

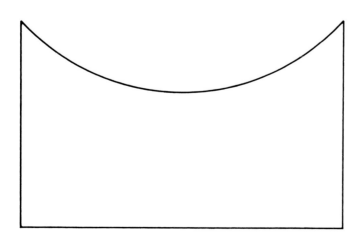

10 Reserve a small dot of white paste for the eyes, then divide the remainder into three and colour red, yellow and green.

11 Using a paper piping bag fitted with a no. 1 piping tube (tip) and white royal icing, pipe small dots over the blue frills. Pipe decorative lines of small shells around the base of the cake and around the top of the frill on the side of the cake.

12 To make the clown's hair, thinly roll out some yellow paste and cut into strips about 5cm (2in) long and 1cm (½ in) wide. Make cuts from one long side of each strip, almost through to the other side. Dampen the clown's head, then secure the strips of hair in position, in overlapping pieces. Press two small white eyes onto the clown's face. Add a red nose and mouth.

13 Shape two large red boots and secure to the legs. Roll small balls of icing in different colours. Flatten and press onto the clown's clothes.

14 Shape small juggling balls, scarves and a hat from the trimmings of coloured paste. For the hat, wrap a strip of red around a flattened ball of green paste. Make two small flowers with a plunger cutter. Push a stamen through each and press into the hat. Paint crosses on the clown's eyes. Position candles if using and trim the board with ribbon.

Sofa Mice

Create your own living-room family of lovable, edible mice.

1 Cut the cake into three pieces: 15cm (6in), 6cm (2½in) and 3cm (1¼in). Stand the largest piece on end, longest side to the board, and shape the top to whichever style you prefer for the back of the sofa (see page 42). Round off the edges as illustrated above.

2 Cut the 25 x 3cm (10 x 1¼in) strip of cake in half to make the arms of the sofa. Trim off any rough sides or edges and shape the ends as shown.

3 Sandwich the cake with the filling of your choice. Stick the individual pieces to each other and to the board with a little royal icing. The arms should be slightly higher than the seat; if necessary, build them up by placing a small piece of sponge or sugarpaste underneath. Coat with apricot glaze.

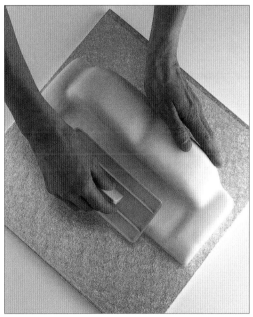

4 Colour the sugarpaste (rolled fondant) with a little cream and a little raspberry red food colourings. Roll out to approximately 5mm (¼in) thick and cover the cake, using a smoother for a better finish. Leave to dry for 24 hours.

5 Colour a small piece of modelling paste a darker pink, roll out and make a frill (see page 24). Attach the frill to the bottom edge of the sofa with a little water.

CAKE AND DECORATION

25cm (10in) square Madeira (pound) cake (see page 16)

strawberry jam (conserve), lemon curd or buttercream (see page 18) for filling

125g (4oz/½ cup) royal icing (see page 17)

250ml (8fl oz/1 cup) apricot glaze (see page 21)

1kg (2lb) sugarpaste (rolled fondant)

turquoise, cream and raspberry red liquid food colourings

500g (1lb) bought modelling paste

dark brown, liquorice black, mint green, blueberry, melon yellow, orange and Christmas red paste food colourings

peach and pink dusting powders (petal dusts/blossom tints)

1.5m (1⅔yd) pink or peach ribbon for board edge

EQUIPMENT

36cm (14in) square cake board

plastic smoother

cocktail stick (toothpick)

paper piping bag

no. 3 piping tube (tip)

nos. 0 or 1 and 3 paintbrushes

ball modelling tool

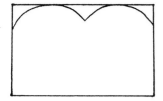

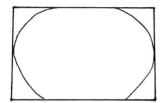

Sofa back variations

6 Using the no. 3 piping tube (tip) and a little pink royal icing, pipe single lines of shells along the outside edge of each arm, along the top two edges of the back of the sofa and around the bottom of the cake, just above the frill.

7 Paint on a design of your choice randomly, using a fine paintbrush, no. 0 or 1, and a little food colouring, as shown below.

8 Colour the remaining modelling paste light brown with a hint of peach and model the mice following the instructions on page 26 and as illustrated. Take five small pieces of sugarpaste and colour each of them differently – red, blue, green, yellow and orange – and model the wellington boots.

9 Colour a piece of sugarpaste dark brown and make noses for the mice. Paint on eyes and mouth when dry.

10 Arrange the mice on the sofa. Make a rug to decorate the board and leave to dry before painting a pattern on it and adding a piped or painted greeting. Trim the board edge with ribbon.

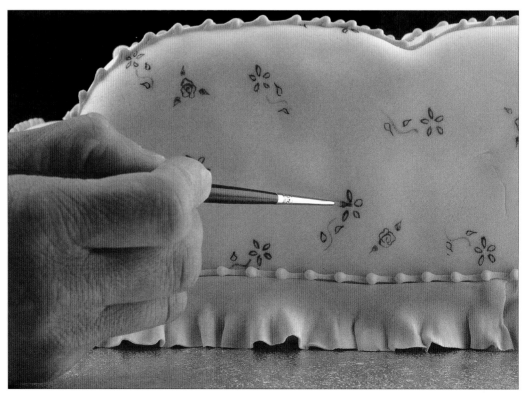

Yellow Kite

CAKE AND DECORATION

25cm (10in) square
Madeira (pound) cake
(see page 16)

250g (8oz/¾ cup) jam
(conserve) for filling

375g (12oz/1½ cups)
buttercream (see
page 18)

1kg 185g (2lb 6oz)
sugarpaste (rolled
fondant)

yellow, blue, red,
chestnut and black paste
food colourings

60g (2oz/¼ cup) royal
icing (see page 17)

30cm (12in) blue ribbon,
about 2.5cm (1in) wide

EQUIPMENT

40 x 30cm (16 x 12in)
oblong cake board

crimper

small oval cutter

paper piping bag

no. 3 piping tube (tip)

*Eye-catching and easy to make, this kite can't fly
– but does look and taste good.*

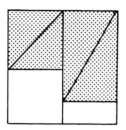

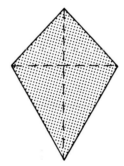

Tip

☆ *To make cutting and layering
simpler, the diamond shape required
to make the kite can be cut in one
complete piece from a large cake.
However, this would create consider-
ably more cake trimmings to be
re-utilized (see page 20).*

1 Prepare and layer the cake (see page 15), then cut and join as shown above. Cover the cake completely with a thin spreading of buttercream.

2 Colour 500g (1lb) sugarpaste (rolled fondant) yellow and use to cover the cake (see page 22).

3 Colour 500g (1lb) sugarpaste blue and cover the board (see page 24). Make a template of the cloud design on page 251 and make three clouds from white sugarpaste. Inlay on the board. Crimp the board edge (see page 24).

4 Roll out some white sugarpaste and cut out two oval shapes for the eyes. Colour a piece of sugarpaste red and model the nose and tongue. Cut out and make the bows using the template on page 251 and picture below. Colour sufficient sugarpaste chestnut to make the cross pieces. Use the rest, coloured black, for the beads, mouth and eyes. Attach the pieces by lightly moistening with water. Finally pipe the mouth and eyebrows using the no. 3 tube (tip) and black icing. Position and attach the ribbon and bows with dabs of royal icing.

Piece of Cake!

CAKE AND DECORATION

two 20cm (8in) round
Madeira (pound) cakes
(see page 16)

1.5kg (3lb) sugarpaste
(rolled fondant)

blue, red, pink, yellow
and brown paste food
colourings

red piping jelly
(optional)

cornflour (cornstarch)
for dusting

4 tbsp raspberry or
strawberry jam
(conserve)

250g (8oz/1 cup)
buttercream made using
white vegetable fat
(shortening) (see
page 18)

EQUIPMENT

cocktail sticks
(toothpicks)

fine paintbrush

33cm (13in) round silver
cake card

large paintbrush

paper piping bag

large star piping
tube (tip)

Tip

☆ *A lot of sponge
must be trimmed off
this cake to shape an
impressive 'wedge'.
The trimmings can
be kept and used to
make a trifle or simi-
lar dessert, or frozen
for a later date.*

---

*The colours on this giant slice of cake can easily be varied,
as long as they remain garish and over the top!*

1 First make the candles. Colour 125g (4oz) sugarpaste (rolled fondant) pale blue. Reserve 15g (½oz) blue, then roll the remainder to a 2cm (¾in) thick sausage. Cut across into two 7cm (2¾in) lengths and shape one end of each to resemble the top of a melted candle. Halve a cocktail stick (toothpick) and singe the ends. Press one into each 'candle' top. Make small 'teardrop' shapes from the trimmed icing and secure down the side of each candle with a dampened paint-brush, to resemble drips.

2 Colour 60g (2oz) sugarpaste dark red and roll into two balls. Using the end of a paintbrush, make a dent in the top of each ball so they resemble cherries. Paint with piping jelly if wished. Shape several tiny 'crumbs' of white sugarpaste. Leave the candles, crumbs and cherries on greaseproof (parchment) or non-stick paper to harden for at least 24 hours.

3 Trace the template on page 254 onto greaseproof or non-stick paper. Level the surface of the cakes by trimming off any peaks and place one on top of the other. Lay the template over the top. Cut through both cakes to shape a wedge.

4 Thinly roll out 315g (10oz) white sugarpaste and use to cover the cake card (see page 24). Roll out a long thin strip of sugarpaste, 4cm (1¾in) in diame-ter. Dampen the edge of the board icing, then lay the strip around the edge to make the rim of the 'plate'. Trim.

5 Sandwich the wedges together with the jam and 3 tablespoons butter-cream. Reserve 4 tablespoons butter-cream; spread the rest over the cake.

6 Roll out half of the remaining sugar-paste and cover the flat sides of the cake. Colour remainder dark pink. Use half to cover the outside of the wedge and the remainder to cover the top and hang over the edge. Using a cocktail stick, mark two bands of wavy lines along the sides to indicate areas of 'filling'.

7 Mix yellow and brown food colour-ings and dilute with water. Paint the 'sponge' areas on the cake sides and the shaped sugarpaste crumbs. Make more 'teardrop' shapes from dark pink trim-mings and secure along the top edges.

8 Thinly roll lengths of blue sugarpaste and secure in loops around the outside of the cake. Fill a piping bag fitted with a large star tube (tip) with the reserved buttercream and pipe swirls along the top edge. Paint lines of jam 'filling' on the cake sides, and paint thin bands of pink and blue around the 'plate'. Position candles, cherries and crumbs.

Jungle Cake

Animals of any description appeal to most children. This simple creation, in buttercream and sugarpaste, is perfect for younger boys and girls.

CAKE AND DECORATION

two 15cm (6in) round Madeira (pound) cakes (see page 16)

1kg (2lb) sugarpaste (rolled fondant)

yellow, red, black, brown, pale green and dark green paste food colourings

cornflour (cornstarch) for dusting

500g (1lb/2 cups) chocolate buttercream (see page 18)

0.5m (½yd) green ribbon for board edge

EQUIPMENT

fine paintbrush

cocktail sticks (toothpicks)

23cm (9in) round silver cake board

Tips

☆ *Small, round, bought cakes are perfect for this. Stack three together as they tend to be shallower than homemade sponges.*

☆ *If liked, cut out extra giraffe shapes and press together to make double-sided giraffes with the cocktail sticks in the middle. Paint markings on both sides.*

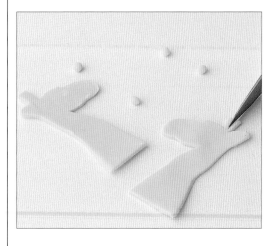

1 To make the giraffes, colour 60g (2oz) sugarpaste (rolled fondant) yellow. Trace the giraffe template (below) onto greaseproof (parchment) or non-stick paper and cut it out. Thinly roll out the yellow sugarpaste on a surface dusted with cornflour (cornstarch). Lay the template on the sugarpaste and

cut around it. Make another giraffe, then turn the template over and cut out another two facing the other way. (One set acts as a spare.)

2 Using a knife, cut down between the horns to separate them. Roll small balls of yellow sugarpaste and secure to the ends of the horns with a dampened paintbrush. Dampen the ends of wooden cocktail sticks (toothpicks) and lay them under the base of each giraffe. Press down lightly to secure. Transfer to a sheet of greaseproof or non-stick paper and leave for at least 24 hours to harden. Wrap the remaining sugarpaste in plastic food wrap.

3 Using a fine paintbrush and slightly diluted colourings, paint red markings and black facial features on the giraffes.

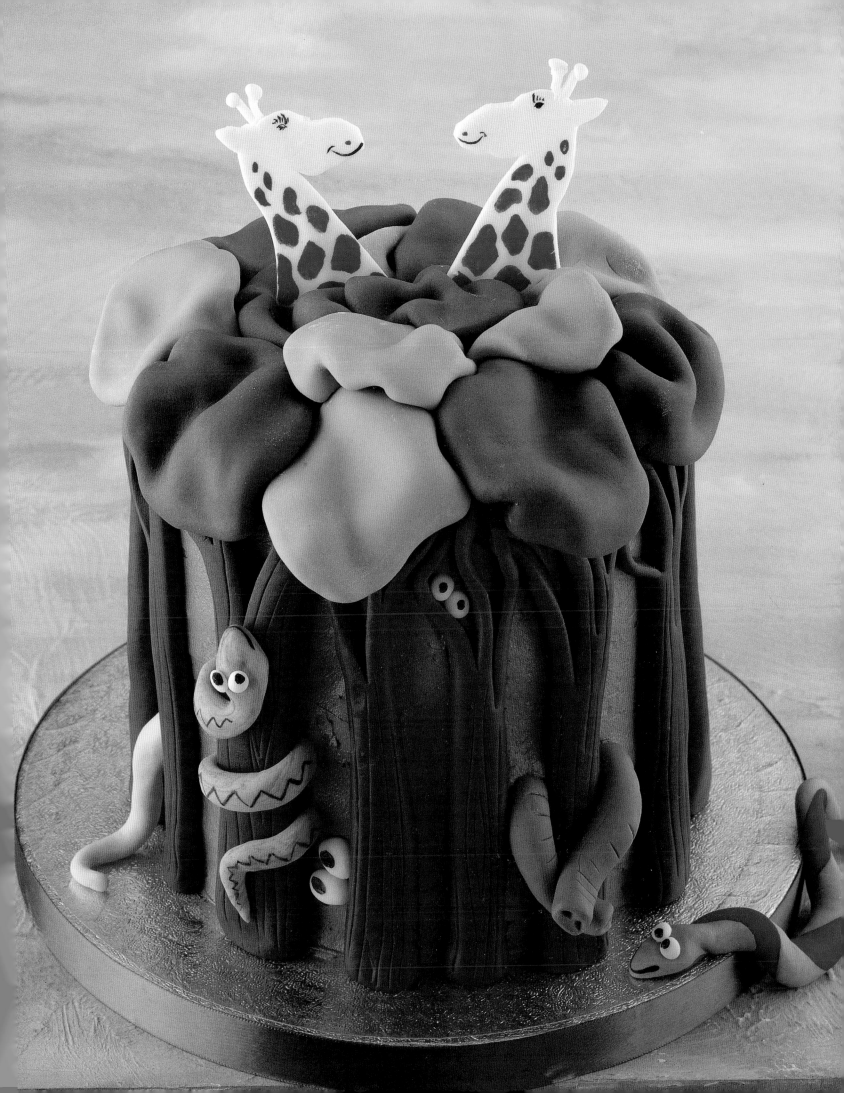

Tip

☆ *If you only have one green food colouring, make half the treetops, then darken the remaining green sugarpaste by adding extra green and a little black food colouring.*

4 Level the surface of one cake by cutting off any peak that formed during baking. Place the cake on the board. Spread with a little buttercream, then cover with the second cake. Completely spread the top and side with the remaining buttercream, smoothing it with a palette knife (metal spatula). Trim the board with green ribbon.

5 Colour 500g (1lb) of the remaining sugarpaste brown. Roll out a little to a long sausage, roughly the depth of the

cake. Flatten slightly, then cut slits down one end and open out slightly for branches. Make long, shallow lines with the tip of a knife for bark markings and secure to the side of the cake. Make more trees in the same way, varying the size of each.

6 Colour 155g (5oz) of the remaining sugarpaste pale green and another 155g (5oz) dark green (see TIP). Roll out a small ball of one colour to a 12cm (4½ in) round. Pull up the edge and pinch together. Turn the piece of sugarpaste over and press into position on the top of the cake to resemble a tree. Make more treetops in the same way. Arrange them on the cake so the colours alternate and overlap slightly.

7 Roll small balls of white sugarpaste and position around the cake in pairs to resemble peering eyes.

8 Colour more trimmings grey and shape elephants' trunks. Press into the buttercream and secure to the trees with a dampened paintbrush.

9 Make brightly coloured snakes from the remaining trimmings. Secure to the tree trunks. Make snakes' eyes as above. Paint the centres of the eyes and snake markings with a fine paintbrush and black food colouring.

Aqua Zoom

Water shoots or flumes are now a highlight of many leisure pools. This cake should appeal to most children, even if they've never had a go on one.

1 Level the surface of the cake by cutting off any peak formed during baking. Using a large, sharp knife, cut the cake in half from one top edge to the opposite lower edge. Turn the upper piece round so that the thin sides are together, creating a slope.

2 Using a knife, cut out an inverted 's' shape from the cake. Reserve one of the large trimmed sections.

3 Use a third of the buttercream and 4 tablespoons of the jam (conserve) to sandwich the split cakes together. Press the remaining jam through a sieve to remove any pieces, then brush it over both pieces of cake.

4 Place the large cake towards the back of the cake board. Roll out 1kg (2lb) sugarpaste (rolled fondant) to a 36cm (14in) circle. Lay this over the large cake and smooth down the sides, easing it to fit. Trim off excess icing around the base. Use the trimmings and another

375g (12oz) sugarpaste to cover the small piece of cake. Place on the cake board.

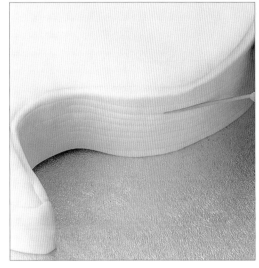

5 Before painting stripes on the side of the cake, mark guidelines with a cocktail stick (toothpick). Using a fine paintbrush and diluted blue food colouring, paint the sides of the cake with stripes for a tile effect.

6 Colour another 375g (12oz) sugarpaste blue. Roll a little under the palms of your hands to a long sausage. Secure this down the centre of the large cake, then press all along to a point. Roll out the remaining blue paste and cut out two strips, each 30 x 7.5cm (12 x 3in).

7 Dampen the flat surface of the cake. Fit one blue strip down one side of the shoot, so that one side rests on the blue ridge in the centre. Curve the other

CAKE AND DECORATION

23cm (9in) square Madeira (pound) cake (see page 16)

500g (1lb/2 cups) buttercream (see page 18)

7 tbsp strawberry or raspberry jam (conserve)

2kg (4lb) sugarpaste (rolled fondant)

cornflour (cornstarch) for dusting

blue, flesh, red, green and yellow paste food colourings

1.5m (1½yd) yellow ribbon for board edge

plastic greenery, such as palm trees, foliage, etc.

EQUIPMENT

33cm (13in) square silver cake board

cocktail stick (toothpick)

fine paintbrush

Tips

☆ *If you cannot get any plastic foliage, mould some out of green sugarpaste.*

☆ *A dot of red food colouring can be used to create a 'flesh' colour for the figures.*

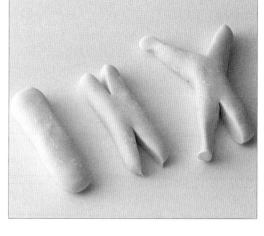

11 Make more figures in the same way. For the boy leaving the shoot, support the back with a cocktail stick, then lean it up against the shoot with the feet touching the water. Shape two or three 'head and shoulder' figures in the water. Add hair using coloured sugarpaste.

12 Use the remaining sugarpaste to shape extra decorations, such as a beach ball. Add plastic palm trees or other foliage as wished.

side of the strip up, supporting it with crumpled absorbent kitchen paper (paper towels). Position the second strip on the other side of the shoot.

8 Set aside 2 tablespoons of the remaining buttercream; colour the rest blue. Spread this over the board with a palette knife (metal spatula), peaking it in some areas (see page 18). Spread a thin covering of blue buttercream down the shoot. Peak the blue buttercream around and down the shoots with the reserved white buttercream. Trim the board with ribbon.

9 Colour half of the remaining sugarpaste with flesh colouring. Roll a little to a thin sausage about 6cm (2½in) long. Flatten slightly, then make a 2cm (¾in) cut from each end towards the centre. Mould the cut sections into outstretched arms and legs.

10 Place the figure halfway down one of the shoots. Add a small head and paint a swimsuit on the body using a fine paintbrush.

Baby Dinosaur

A baby dinosaur, just hatched from its egg, provides an interesting and fun variation on the current craze for anything prehistoric.

CAKE AND DECORATION

Madeira (pound) cake mixture for 20cm (8in) round tin (pan) (see page 16)

1.5kg (3lb) sugarpaste (rolled fondant)

cornflour (cornstarch) for dusting

blue, black, orange, green and red paste food colourings

6 tbsp strawberry or raspberry jam (conserve)

125g (4oz/½ cup) buttercream (see page 18)

0.5m (½yd) green ribbon for board edge

EQUIPMENT

2.3 litre (4pt) ovenproof mixing bowl

several Easter egg moulds in various sizes

fine paintbrush

33cm (13in) round silver cake board

large paintbrush

1 Preheat the oven to 160°C (325°F/Gas 3). Grease and line the base of the mixing bowl. Spoon the Madeira (pound) cake mixture into the bowl and level the surface. Bake in the oven for 1¼ hours or until firm. Turn out onto a wire rack and leave to cool. Wrap tightly in foil and store until ready to be decorated.

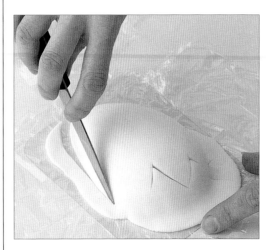

2 To make the 'egg shells', lightly knead 500g (1lb) sugarpaste (rolled fondant). Cover the outside of four or five Easter egg moulds with plastic food wrap. Roll out a little of the sugarpaste on a surface dusted with cornflour (cornstarch), then lay it over one of the moulds. Using the tip of a sharp knife, cut a zigzag line across the sugarpaste towards one end of the mould, then trim off the excess around the base.

3 Reroll the trimmings and shape several more shells. For small pieces of shell, mark the zigzag line across the centre of the mould so that both halves can be used. From the remainder of the 500g (1lb) sugarpaste, shape small whole eggs. Leave the shells to harden for 24 hours. Wrap the remaining sugarpaste in plastic food wrap.

4 Carefully pull away the Easter egg moulds and peel the food wrap away from the sugarpaste. Leave the shells to harden for a further 24–48 hours.

5 Using a fine paintbrush and diluted blue and black food colourings, paint dots of colour on the outside of the shells.

6 Level the surface of the cake by cutting off any peak formed during baking so that it sits flat when inverted. Halve the cake horizontally. Reassemble the cake on the board, sandwiching the layers together with 4 tablespoons of the jam (conserve) and the buttercream. (See page 15.)

7 Sieve the remaining jam and brush over the cake.

8 Colour another 750g (1½lb) sugarpaste orange and roll out to a 36cm (14in) round. Lightly dampen the edge of the cake board with water. Lay the sugarpaste over the cake and board, and smooth out using hands dusted with cornflour. Trim off the excess.

9 Colour 125g (4oz) of the remaining sugarpaste dark green. Reserve another small piece of white sugarpaste, about the size of a grape. Reserve 30g (1oz) of the green paste. Knead together the remaining green and white paste until mottled with colour. Shape a small 2.5cm (1in) ball of sugarpaste into the baby dinosaur's head. Cut a slit, almost through to the centre, for the mouth, and mark two nostrils with the tip of a knife.

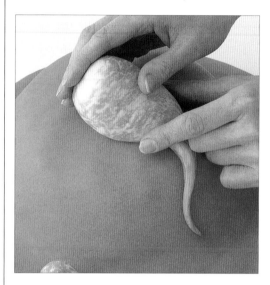

10 Form the remaining green paste into a ball, then gradually roll and pull out one end into a long thin tail. Lightly dampen the centre of the top of the cake, then position the dinosaur's body, pressing down lightly to secure in place. Place the dinosaur's head in position and secure with a little water.

11 While the dinosaur is still soft, tuck two egg shells around it, lifting the dinosaur gently and repositioning it on the edges of the shells to secure in place. Position the remaining shells and eggs around the cake.

12 Shape and position two small white balls for the dinosaur's eyes. Shape and position a small red tongue.

13 From the reserved green paste, shape a small 'quiff' of hair and several triangular spikes. Position on the dinosaur's head and along the body and tail. Paint the centres of the eyes with black food colouring. Trim the cake board with green ribbon.

Tip

☆ *To make the cake easy to assemble, the 'egg shells' should be made several days in advance. If possible, use Easter egg moulds in various sizes, available from cake-decorating shops. Do not worry if an egg shell cracks during assembly – it all adds to the effect!*

Two's Company

This slightly different idea for a novelty cake is ideal for animals lovers and any child who is interested in nature.

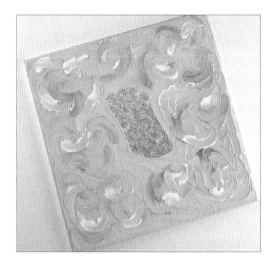

1 Colour half of the royal icing medium blue and coat the cake board up to 7.5cm (3in) in from the edge. Spread the icing roughly, applying with a swirling motion to produce a water image. Add swirls of a darker blue and white royal icing for a better effect.

2 On a separate board, turn the cake upside down and, using the template on page 253, cut out the shape of the iceberg. Build up a rough but structured shape using the sponge cake trimmings.

3 Cut and sandwich the cake with the filling of your choice, then coat with apricot glaze. Roll out 750g (1½lb) sugarpaste (rolled fondant) a little thicker than usual, approximately 5mm (¼in) thick – this will allow ample thickness for moulding the paste into iceberg peaks. Cover the iceberg, but do not attach it to the coated board yet.

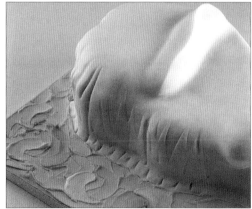

4 To give the iceberg texture, make grooves and dents in the sugarpaste using the tail-end of a paintbrush and a tapered knife blade. Use your fingers to draw up the icing to form ice walls and ice slides as illustrated. Model some mini icebergs to scatter on the top of the large iceberg and in the sea. The more uneven the appearance the better.

5 Carefully transfer the iceberg to the iced board, attaching it with a little royal icing.

6 Pipe the wave pattern around the sides of the iceberg using a grease-proof (parchment) paper piping bag and

CAKE AND DECORATION

25cm (10in) square
Madeira (pound) cake
(see page 16)

375g (12oz/1½ cups)
royal icing (see page 17)

turquoise and blue
liquid food colourings

strawberry jam
(conserve), lemon curd
or buttercream (see
page 18) for filling

125g (4oz/½ cup) apricot
glaze (see page 21)

1kg (2lb) sugarpaste
(rolled fondant)

liquorice black and berry
blue paste food
colourings

250g (8oz) bought
modelling paste

1.25m (4ft) blue ribbon
for board edge

EQUIPMENT

30cm (12in) square
cake board

nos. 1, 2 and 3
paintbrushes

paper piping bag

nos. 0 and 1 piping
tubes (tips)

Tip

☆ *When modelling animals of any kind, have a book or photograph to refer to, because it is amazing how many tiny details you miss working from memory.*

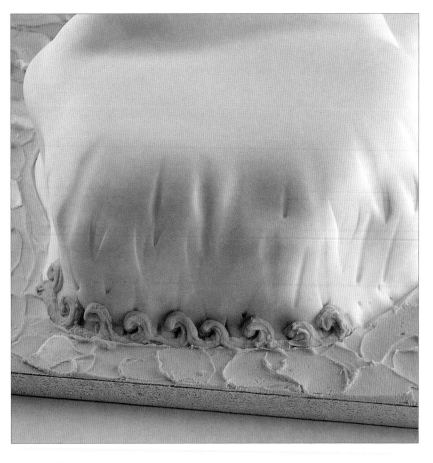

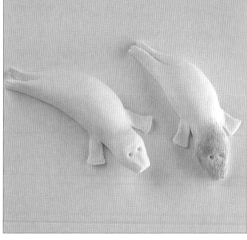

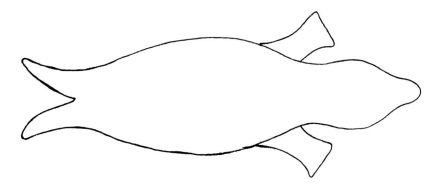

Tip

☆ *Modelling paste dries out much quicker than sugarpaste, so work as quickly as you can, but do not panic! Keep it stored in cling film when not using.*

---

blue royal icing. Snip the end off the piping bag to leave a hole the size of a no. 3 piping tube (tip).

7 Finally, to give the iceberg more depth, paint a little grey food colouring into some of the crevices and grooves, and brush the crests with white royal icing.

8 Knead 125g (4oz) each of modelling paste and sugarpaste together and use to model the seals. Begin by moulding the basic shape, as shown below. Mark lines on the flippers with a knife and quickly make holes for the eyes and nose before the paste dries.

9 Make up a brushing solution of royal icing by adding water to a teaspoon of royal icing, mixing it until it resembles a thin paste. Colour half of the icing grey and, using a no. 2 paintbrush, brush the icing over the seals to create a textured appearance. Mark eyes, nose and flippers. When the seals are dry, brush on some patches of darker grey and cream to give them a little more depth and variance.

10 Pipe in the eyes with a little black royal icing and the no. 1 piping tube (tip). Paint fine dark lines around the eyes, paint in the eyebrows and any other remaining details to give better definition to the features. Pipe on the whiskers with the no. 1 piping tube and a little grey royal icing.

11 Place the seals on the iceberg cake and trim the edge of the board with ribbon.

Bunny Cake

A perfect idea for the tinies! Finished with simply moulded rabbits and cut-out grass, this cake is assembled in no time at all.

CAKE AND DECORATION

20cm (8in) hexagonal Madeira (pound) cake made using mixture for 20cm (8in) round tin (pan) (see page 16)

7 tbsp raspberry or strawberry jam (conserve)

250g (8oz/1 cup) buttercream (see page 18)

1.5kg (3lb) sugarpaste (rolled fondant)

yellow, green, pink and black paste food colourings

cornflour (cornstarch) for dusting

12 bought flower cake decorations

0.5m (½yd) pink ribbon for board edge

EQUIPMENT

23cm (9in) round silver cake board

fine paintbrush

Tips

☆ As an even quicker alternative to the moulded bunnies, use other plastic animals bought from a cake-decorating or toy shop.

☆ A 20cm (8in) round cake can easily be substituted for the hexagonal.

1 Level the surface of the cake by cutting off any peak that formed during baking, then cut the cake horizontally in half. Place one layer on the cake board and spread with 4 tablespoons of the jam (conserve). Cover with the buttercream, then position the second layer on top.

2 Press the remaining jam through a sieve to remove any pieces. Brush the cake with the jam.

3 Colour 1.1kg (2¼lb) sugarpaste (rolled fondant) yellow. Roll out on a surface dusted with cornflour (cornstarch) and use to cover the cake (see page 22).

4 Colour another 125g (4oz) sugarpaste green. Thinly roll out a

little and cut out a 13 x 2.5cm (5 x 1in) strip. Make cuts down one long side of the strip, through to the centre. Dampen the uncut edge of the strip with water, then lay it against the base of the cake so that the cut edge falls away from the cake to resemble grass. Make more strips and attach all around the base of the cake.

5 Colour another 60g (2oz) sugarpaste pale pink and roll it out thinly. Cut into 13 x 5mm (5 x ¼in) strips, reserving the trimmings. Lightly dampen the points around the top edge of the cake. Gently twist a pink strip and secure it between two points on top of the cake. Repeat all around the cake. Secure small balls of white sugarpaste at the points where the strips meet.

6 To shape a simple bunny, start by rolling a piece of white sugarpaste into a ball, about 2.5cm (1in) in diameter, for the body. Add a head, ears and tail. Secure on the centre of the cake. Shape and secure three smaller bunnies. Add small noses and centres of ears using pink icing trimmings. Paint facial features on the bunnies, using a fine paintbrush and diluted black food colouring.

7 Make more grass as described in step 4, but cut into 2.5cm (1in) lengths and roll into 'tufts'. Secure the grass and bought flower decorations to the top of the cake. Trim the board with ribbon.

NUMBER ONE – CLOWN

20cm (8in) square buttercake, made with 1 quantity basic mix (see right) ☆ 1½ quantities buttercream (see page 18) ☆ yellow, pink, red, blue, green and black food colourings ☆ hundreds and thousands (non pareil) ☆ liquorice ☆ 46 x 30cm (18 x 6in) cake board

1 Trim the edges of the cake to neaten. Cut the cake in half and place vertically on the cake board to form a 'one' shape.

2 Cut the corners of the base cake to a rounded shape. Cut diagonally across the top corners of the upper cake for the hat. Cut the cake away from each side to shape the head.

3 Colour the buttercream as follows: yellow for the body; pale pink for the hands, face, frill and hat; red for the shoes and tie; and blue for the hat band.

4 Mark lines on the cake as a guide for different coloured areas and spread on the appropriate buttercream. Outline the shapes and pipe on details with black leftover buttercream.

5 Decorate the cake with piped coloured dots. Attach liquorice to represent hair. Sprinkle the hat with hundreds and thousands (non pareil).

NUMBER TWO – ALLIGATOR

26 x 8 x 5cm (10½ x 3¼ x 2in) long bar and 20cm (8in) ring buttercakes made with 2 quantities basic mix (see above right) ☆ 1½ quantities buttercream (see page 18) ☆ green, black, brown, yellow and red food colourings ☆ 25 x 36cm (10 x 14in) cake board

1 Cut off a quarter from the bar cake and one-fifth off the ring cake. Cut a triangular piece from the small rectangle. Assemble the pieces on the cake board to make an alligator shape.

BASIC BUTTERCAKE

155g (5oz/⅔ cup) butter ☆ 185g (6oz/¾ cup) caster (superfine) sugar ☆ 3 eggs, lightly beaten ☆ 1 tsp vanilla essence (extract) ☆ 220g (6½oz/1⅓ cups) self-raising flour, sifted ☆ 75ml (2½fl oz/⅓ cup) milk

1 Preheat the oven to 180°C (350°F/Gas 4). Brush the specified cake tin (pan) with oil. Line the base and sides with greaseproof (parchment) paper, then grease the paper.

2 Beat the butter and sugar in a small mixing bowl until light and creamy. Gradually add the eggs, beating thoroughly after each addition. Add the essence (extract) and beat until combined.

3 Fold in the flour alternately with the milk. Stir until just combined and almost smooth.

4 Spoon the mixture into the prepared tin and smooth the surface. Bake in the oven for 35 minutes or until a skewer inserted in the centre of the cake comes out clean.

5 Leave in the tin for 5 minutes, then turn out onto a wire rack to cool.

2 Trim the edges of the long base cake to shape for the alligator's mouth.

3 Colour half of the buttercream dark green and a quarter a paler green and spread over the cake following the picture.

4 Decorate by piping with various coloured buttercream – brown for feet, plain for eyes and teeth, black to outline.

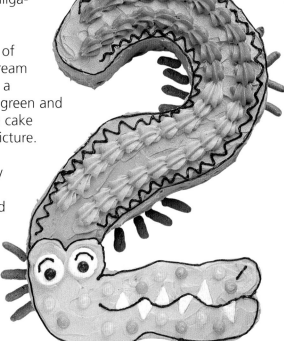

NUMBER THREE – CATS

two 20cm (8in) ring buttercakes, made with 2 quantities basic mix (see above left) ☆ 1½ quantities buttercream (see page 18) ☆ orange, brown, black and caramel food colourings ☆ 2 large wheatmeal biscuits (cookies) ☆ liquorice 'lace' ☆ 25 x 40.5cm (10 x 16in) cake board

1 Remove a quarter of one ring cake and set aside. Place the remainder on the cake board as the base of the number three. Cut out one-third of the second cake and set aside. Position the remainder against the buttercake as shown to form the number three. Cut the edges to round the corners.

2 Colour two-thirds of the buttercream orange-brown. Leave a little plain. Colour the remainder brown.

3 Cover the cake and biscuits (cookies) with orange-brown buttercream. Position the biscuits as shown. Use brown icing for the cat's markings, following the illustration, and the plain buttercream to make a face on the biscuits.

4 Outline the whole cake with a fine piped black line (colour leftover icing) and pipe on features. Use the liquorice to make whiskers.

NUMBER FOUR – BEARS

three 26 x 8 x 5cm (10½ x 3¼ x 2in) long bar buttercakes, made with 1 quantity basic mix (see far left) ☆ 1½ quantities buttercream (see page 18) ☆ 3 chocolate wheatmeal biscuits (cookies) ☆ pink, brown, blue, black and caramel food colourings ☆ rainbow chocolate buttons (freckles) ☆ 38cm (15in) square cake board

1 Place one cake bar on the cake board. Cut a quarter off the second cake and set aside, then cut diagonally across each end of the remaining cake.

2 Assemble the cakes into the number four shape, using the picture as a guide.

3 Position the biscuits (cookies) for the teddy bears' bodies. Mark the head, arm and leg shapes on the cake around them.

4 Colour two-thirds of the buttercream pink. Colour three-quarters of the remainder brown, a little blue and leave the remainder plain. Spread pink icing all over the cake, around the marked shapes. Spread brown icing inside the marked shapes, and blue for the hats.

5 Use plain buttercream to pipe on face details and hats. Colour leftover buttercream black and pipe a fine line around the bears. Position the buttons (freckles) as shown.

NUMBER FIVE – TRAIN

20cm (8in) ring and 26 x 8 x 5cm (10½ x 3¼ x 2in) long buttercakes, made with 1½ quantities basic mix (see page 62) ☆ 1 quantity buttercream (see page 18) ☆ 60g (2oz/2 squares) plain (semisweet) chocolate ☆ red and yellow food colourings ☆ 1 jam (conserve) mini-roll ☆ liquorice pieces ☆ sugar-coated chocolate buttons ☆ liquorice sweets (candies) ☆ candy bananas ☆ coloured popcorn ☆ jelly sweets (jube jels) ☆ barley sugar ☆ liquorice ☆ marshmallows ☆ liquorice 'lace' ☆ white mint with hole ☆ cotton wool ☆ cake board or serving plate

1 Cut the cakes into shapes as illustrated. Reserve 125g (4oz/½ cup) buttercream. Colour the rest with melted chocolate, beating until smooth.

2 Colour half of the reserved buttercream red, the other half yellow. Cover the cut pieces of cake with chocolate buttercream and position on the cake board as shown, using the ring cake to form the curve. Trim the mini-roll to sit flat on the cabin; cover with chocolate buttercream. Join the cake pieces with liquorice as shown and attach chocolate buttons for wheels.

3 Decorate with sweets (candies) as shown. Fix cotton wool into the mint for steam.

NUMBER SIX – SKATEBOARDER

26 x 8 x 5cm (10½ x 3¼ x 2in) long bar and 20cm (8in) ring buttercakes, made with 1½ quantities basic mix (see page 62) ☆ 1 quantity buttercream (see page 18) ☆ blue, caramel and yellow food colourings ☆ 2 orange snakes for arms and legs ☆ green and yellow roll-ups ☆ 3 marshmallows for socks and shirt collar ☆ sugar-coated chocolate buttons ☆ oval chocolates for shoes ☆ small black jelly beans (jube jels) for wheels and eyes ☆ liquorice 'lace' for hair ☆ red 'snake' for mouth ☆ pink candy for shorts ☆ hundreds and thousands (non pareil) ☆ 25 x 46cm (10 x 18in) cake board

1 Taper one end of the bar cake. Position the cakes on the cake board to form a number six.

2 Reserve one-third of the buttercream; colour the remainder blue. Colour one-third of the reserved buttercream brown and the remainder yellow.

3 Mark the shape of the skateboarder's head and shirt on the cake. Spread blue buttercream all over the cake, around the marked shapes. Fill the shirt shape with yellow.

4 Using scissors, cut and position the orange snakes for arms and legs. Cut the roll-ups for the hat and skateboard. Complete the skateboarder with sweets (candies) as listed above and shown. Sprinkle the cake with hundreds and thousands (non pareil).

NUMBER SEVEN – PALM TREE

two 26 x 8 x 5cm (10½ x 3¼ x 2in) long bar buttercakes, made with ⅔ quantity basic mix (see page 62) ☆ 1 quantity buttercream (see page 18) ☆ blue, green and yellow food colourings ☆ green mint leaves ☆ dark green roll-ups ☆ large and small candy bananas ☆ toy bird ☆ cake board or serving plate

1 Trim the cake and position on the cake board or plate to form a number seven.

2 Colour 60g (2oz/¼ cup) buttercream blue. Divide the remaining buttercream in half. Colour one half yellow and the other green. Spread yellow buttercream over the lower part of the seven and blue over the top part.

3 Cut the mint leaves in half lengthways. Cut the roll-ups into large palm-leaf shapes. Decorate the tree with leaves and bananas as illustrated. Place the toy bird in the tree.

4 Colour a small portion of yellow leftover icing darker. Spread randomly over the tree trunk to create a bark effect.

NUMBER EIGHT – FAIRY

20cm (8in) round and 20cm (8in) ring buttercakes, made with 2 quantities basic mix (see page 62) ☆ purple and pink (or peach) food colourings ☆ green, yellow, pink and white thin marshmallows ☆ coloured sugar balls (dragees) ☆ 1 purple jelly bean (jube jel), halved, for eyes ☆ 3 orange jelly beans for eyebrows and nose ☆ 2 pink heart-shaped sweets (candies) for cheeks ☆ banana sweet for mouth ☆ fried noodles for hair ☆ cardboard wand ☆ 25 x 40cm (10 x 16in) cake board

Fluffy Icing:
300g (10oz/1¼ cups) caster (superfine) sugar ☆ 125ml (4fl oz/½ cup) water ☆ 3 egg whites, whisked stiffly

1 First make the fluffy icing. Place the sugar and water in a small pan and heat gently, stirring constantly, until the mixture boils and the sugar has dissolved. Simmer, uncovered, without stirring, for 5 minutes. Pour the hot syrup in a thin stream over the whisked egg whites, beating constantly until the icing is thick, glossy and increased in volume.

2 Trim the cakes and position on the cake board to form a number eight, using the ring cake for the lower half.

3 Divide the icing in half. Colour one portion purple. Set aside 90g (3oz/⅓ cup) of the remaining icing. Colour the remainder pale pink or peach.

4 Mark the shape of the clown's face and shoulders on the upper cake and the hands on the lower cake. Spread purple icing all over the upper cake around the marked shape. Spread pink or peach icing all over the ring cake and inside the shoulder shape.

5 Colour a small portion of the pink icing darker and use to pipe the outline of the face, body and hands, and to pipe on neck and sleeve frills. Use the reserved plain icing for the face and hands. Decorate with the sweets (candies) as shown. Lay the wand in position. If liked, decorate the edge of the clown's hat with silver paper stars.

Patch

This endearing little pup will appeal to most young children, particularly if it bears a resemblance to a family pet.

CAKE AND DECORATION

Madeira (pound) cake mixture for 15cm (6in) round tin (pan) (see page 16)

1 tbsp cocoa (unsweetened cocoa powder), sifted

500g (1lb/2 cups) buttercream (see page 18)

60g (2oz) sugarpaste (rolled fondant) (see TIP)

black paste food colouring

3 liquorice 'laces'

15cm (6in) tartan ribbon, about 1cm (½in) wide

1 chocolate coin

EQUIPMENT

3.5 litre (6–7 pint) ovenproof mixing bowl

30cm (12in) round gold or silver cake board

cocktail stick (toothpick)

fine paintbrush

Tip

☆ *As only a little sugarpaste (rolled fondant) is required for this cake, buy a small packet rather than make your own. Tightly wrapped, the remainder will keep for several weeks.*

---

1 Preheat the oven to 160°C (325°F/Gas 3). Grease and line the base of the mixing bowl. Spoon the Madeira (pound) cake mixture into the bowl and level the surface. Bake in the oven for about 40 minutes or until firm. Turn the cake out of the bowl onto a wire rack and leave to cool.

2 Level the surface of the cake by cutting off any peak that formed during baking, so that the cake sits flat when inverted onto the cake board. Beat the cocoa into a third of the buttercream.

3 Reserve 3 tablespoons of the plain buttercream, then spread the remainder over the cake, covering it as smoothly as possible. Spread a little buttercream on the board at the bottom of the cake and build it up to form a 'neck'. Gently fluff up the surface of the buttercream with the tip of a cocktail stick (toothpick).

4 Spoon the reserved plain buttercream onto the cake in a mound just below the centre and spread it into a snout shape. Dampen a palette knife (metal spatula), then smooth down the snout area to contrast with the fluffed-up surface of the rest of the buttercream.

5 Spread a little of the chocolate buttercream over one eye area of the cake. Shape two white eyes from the sugarpaste (rolled fondant) and position

on the cake, placing one over the area of chocolate buttercream.

6 Colour a small piece of sugarpaste black and shape it into a nose. Press gently into position.

7 Arrange pieces of liquorice 'lace' around the eyes, pressing them gently into the buttercream. Form a smiling mouth from a little more liquorice.

8 Spread small spoonsful of the chocolate buttercream down each side of the dog's face. Flatten with a palette knife, widening at the base to shape ears. Fluff up lightly with a cocktail stick. Secure more liquorice around the ears.

9 Paint the centres of the eyes black with food colouring and a fine paintbrush. Arrange the ribbon around the base of the cake, securing the gold coin on it with a dot of buttercream.

Messy Paints

When lack of time prevents you from creating 'fiddly' cakes, a set of messy paint pots provides a welcome alternative.

CAKE AND DECORATION

Madeira (pound) cake mixture for 18cm (7in) round tin (pan) (see page 16)

3 tbsp apricot glaze (see page 21)

1kg (2lb) sugarpaste (rolled fondant)

cornflour (cornstarch) for dusting

black, red, blue, green and silver paste food colourings

500g (1lb/3 cups) icing (confectioners') sugar

EQUIPMENT

3 empty 400g (14oz) food cans, thoroughly washed and dried

large paintbrush

41 x 25cm (16 x 10in) silver cake card

Tip

☆ *If you cannot get a large enough cake card, use a plain coloured tray. For a personal touch, add the child's name and age in the coloured icings.*

1 Preheat the oven to 160°C (325°F/Gas 3). Grease and line the food cans (see page 14). Divide the Madeira (pound) cake mixture between the cans and level the surfaces. Bake in the oven for about 30 minutes or until firm. Turn the cakes out of the cans on to a wire rack and leave to cool.

2 Level the tops of the cakes by cutting off any peaks formed during baking. Brush the cakes with apricot glaze. Dampen the cake card.

3 Thinly roll out 185g (6oz) sugarpaste (rolled fondant) on a surface dusted with cornflour (cornstarch). Place over one side of the cake card then trim, at an angle, to a square. Thinly roll out another 185g (6oz) sugarpaste and place over the other side of the card, overlapping the first piece. Trim to a square, cutting around the first piece to resemble sheets of paper. Use trimmings to shape more pieces of paper showing beneath the large sheets.

4 Colour a small piece of sugarpaste, about the size of a grape, with black food colouring. Roll into a ball, then pull to a point for the tip of the brush.

5 Colour the remaining sugarpaste pale grey using black colouring. Reserve 60g (2oz), then divide the remainder into three. Roll out one piece and trim to a 23 x 11cm (9 x 4½in) rectangle. Wrap one cake in the sugar-

paste so that its base is in line with one long edge, if liked.

6 Stand the cake vertically on one square of sugarpaste on the card. Cover the remaining cakes in the same way and position on the card.

7 Roll the reserved grey icing into a paintbrush handle and lay it beside the cakes. Secure the black 'brush' tip in position.

8 Divide the icing (confectioners') sugar between three bowls. Add enough cold water to each to make a paste that becomes level when left to stand for several seconds. Colour one red, one blue and one green.

9 Spoon the red icing onto one pot, 'spilling' plenty down the sides and over the 'paper'. Repeat with the remaining colours. Using a large paintbrush dipped in the coloured icings, paint simple shapes on the white 'paper'. Paint the end of the paintbrush with a little silver food colouring.

Mice in a basket

These two mice snug in a basket would make a lovely birthday cake for twins.

CAKE AND DECORATION

18cm (7in) round Madeira (pound) cake (see page 16)

buttercream (see page 18) or jam (conserve) for filling and covering

950g (1lb 14½oz) sugarpaste (rolled fondant)

brown, coffee, black and pink food colourings

30g (1oz/2tbsp) royal icing (see page 17)

1m (1yd) spotted pink ribbon 5cm (2in) wide

1m (1yd) pink ribbon for board edge

EQUIPMENT

25cm (10in) round cake board, covered with decorative paper, if wished (see TIP page 188)

basketweave rolling pin

string

ball modelling tool

no. 2 piping tube (tip)

cocktail stick (toothpick)

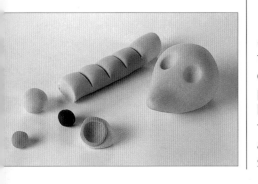

1 Cut the cake in half and sandwich with filling. Cover with a thin layer of jam (conserve) or buttercream. Colour 250g (8oz) sugarpaste (rolled fondant) chocolate, roll out and cover the cake (see page 22). Place the cake on the cake board, positioning it slightly off-centre.

2 Colour 375g (12oz) sugarpaste coffee coloured. Roll out quite thickly and texture the surface with the basketweave rolling pin. Ensure that the paste is long enough to fit around the cake – measure the cake with string to give you an idea of the length required. Use a scalloped template to cut out the shape, moving the template along the paste to complete. Attach the piece to the cake side with water, neatening the join at the back of the cake.

3 Colour 185g (6oz) sugarpaste grey, using black food colouring. Model the mice heads by making a large, pointed pear shape for each and, while the paste is still soft, indent the eyes using a ball modelling tool. Roll two ball shapes for the ears. Colour 125g (4oz) sugarpaste pink and use a little to make two small balls. Press one into each grey paste ball, for inner ear. Using the modelling tool, indent both together to create the finished ear. Attach the ears to the head with water. With a no. 2 tube (tip), pipe the eyes using white and black royal icing. Colour 15g (½oz) sugarpaste black, roll out two balls for the noses and attach in position with water. Use a cocktail stick (toothpick) to make whisker marks, if liked.

4 Attach the ribbon and a bow around the cake, ensuring that the bow is positioned at the front. Gather up any sugarpaste trimmings, knead together and model two pear shapes similar to those made for the heads but slightly smaller. Attach the pieces to the cake top and press gently to flatten slightly – these will represent the bodies of the mice.

5 Roll out the remaining pink sugarpaste quite thinly and cut out an 18cm (7in) circle, using a template, dinner plate or other suitable guide. Moisten the top area of the cake and the mice bodies and lay the circle on top, allowing it to find its own level. Fix the edge around the mouse heads to make them appear to be peeping from beneath. Trim the board with ribbon.

Sunny Valley Farm

A charming cake for a small child. The decorations can be as simple or as detailed as you like, depending on time and patience.

CAKE AND DECORATION

18cm (7in) square
Madeira (pound) cake
(see page 16)

750g (1½lb/3 cups)
buttercream (see
page 18)

500g (1lb) sugarpaste
(rolled fondant)

brown, blue and green
food colourings

cornflour (cornstarch)
for dusting

bought sugar flowers

2 shredded wheat

plastic fencing and
farm animals

green ribbon for board
edge

EQUIPMENT

33cm (13in) round silver
cake board

paper piping bags

no. 2 piping tube (tip)

Tip

☆ *A bag of cheap
plastic farm animals
is ideal for this cake.
Try to find one that
includes sections of
plastic fencing.*

1 Level the surface of the cake by cutting off any peak that formed during baking. Cut the cake vertically in half, then sandwich the two pieces together again, side by side, with a little buttercream.

2 Cut the two top edges off each side of the cake. Arrange the pieces with cut sides facing out to form the top of the roof. Secure to the top of the cake with buttercream.

3 Position the cake to one side of the cake board. Using a palette knife (metal spatula), cover all sides of the cake with a little buttercream, spreading it as smoothly as possible. Using a knife, make brick markings around the sides.

4 Colour half of the sugarpaste (rolled fondant) brown and roll it out on a surface dusted with cornflour (cornstarch). Cut out small squares and use to 'tile' the roof. Reserve the trimmings. Colour more sugarpaste blue, roll it out and cut out small windows, reserving the trimmings. Press the windows into position. Use the brown trimmings to make shutters and a door.

5 Reserve 4 tablespoons buttercream. Colour the remainder green and place 2 tablespoons in a paper piping bag fitted with a no. 2 piping tube (tip). Spread the remainder over the cake board, mounding up the buttercream in places to create small 'hills'. Lightly roll out the blue sugarpaste trimmings and press onto the buttercream for a pond.

6 Colour 2 tablespoons of the reserved buttercream brown and spread across the board for a mud track.

7 Use the reserved green buttercream to pipe trailing greenery up the sides of the house and on the roof. Secure the sugar flowers.

8 Clean the piping tube and fill a new paper piping bag with plain buttercream. Pipe ripples on the pond, windows and blossom.

9 Lightly break up the shredded wheat and tie in bundles with a little thinly rolled brown sugarpaste. Arrange in a stack.

10 Arrange the plastic fencing and farm animals around the cake. Trim the board with ribbon.

Spotty snake

CAKE AND DECORATION

90g (3oz/⅜ cup) royal icing (see page 17)

tan, pink, lemon, green, black and red food colourings

75g (2½ oz/½ cup) light brown sugar

1kg (2lb) truffle paste (see page 20)

611g (1lb 3¾oz) sugarpaste (rolled fondant)

1m (1yd) pink ribbon for board edge

EQUIPMENT

28cm (11in) round cake board

2 small graduated round cutters

A colourful fun cake with a delicious cake mixture inside that children will love.

1 Colour the royal icing tan and spread on the cake board. Sprinkle with brown sugar.

2 Roll the truffle paste into a sausage shape about 60cm (24in) long. Colour 500g (1lb) sugarpaste (rolled fondant) pink, then roll out 375g (12oz) of it into a long narrow strip and brush with water. Wrap around the truffle paste as shown below, taking care to seal the join. Arrange the body shape in a coil on the prepared board. Shape the head from remaining pink paste and attach to the body. Shape the end of the tail to a point.

water, and position a green circle on top of alternate lemon circles.

4 Colour 7g (¼ oz) sugarpaste black and 7g (¼ oz) red. Shape eyes, nose and tongue from black, red and white paste and attach to the snake. Trim the board with ribbon.

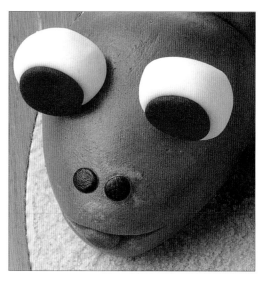

3 Colour 60g (2oz) sugarpaste lemon and 30g (1oz) green. Very thinly roll out yellow and green sugarpaste and cut out two sizes of circles. Attach the lemon circles to the snake with a little

Tip

☆ *Give your finished cake added interest and appeal by painting the surface with confectioner's varnish (glaze) to add an attractive sheen.*

Toy Box

A child's dream – this cake will enthral children of all ages. Model the child's favourite toys to surround the box.

CAKE AND DECORATION

three 15cm (6in) square
Madeira (pound) cakes
(see page 16)

1.5kg (3lb) sugarpaste
(rolled fondant)

blue, red, yellow and
black paste food
colourings

about 125g (4oz/½ cup)
royal icing (see page 17)

75g (2½oz/¼ cup) jam
(conserve) for filling

280g (9oz/generous
1 cup) buttercream (see
page 18)

about 1kg (2lb)
sugarpaste in assorted
colours, for toys

1.75m (1¾yd) red ribbon
for board edge

EQUIPMENT

flower cutter

petal or leaf cutter

craft knife

paper piping bag

nos. 1 and 2 piping
tubes (tips)

36cm (14in) square cake
board

Tip

☆ *It is useful when making the edible toys to have to hand a child's nursery or colouring book from which to glean inspiration and also to provide you with proportions of size and colour ideas.*

1 Colour 60g (2oz) sugarpaste (rolled fondant) blue and 60g (2oz) red; set aside. Colour 625g (1lb 4oz) sugarpaste bright yellow. Make a template the size of one cake top, about 15cm (6in) square. Roll out the yellow sugarpaste and cut out five squares. Lay the squares carefully on a waxed paper-lined flat tray or board. While the sugarpaste is still soft, use the flower and petal cutters to remove a pattern from the centre of four of the squares. Roll out the red and blue sugarpaste. Using the same cutters, inlay shapes in the yellow sugarpaste squares, smoothing gently with the fingers to conceal the joins.

2 Make a tracing of the word 'TOYS' (see page 78) for the lid and transfer onto parchment. Using a sharp craft knife, cut out the letters to make a stencil. Colour 30g (1oz) royal icing red and, using a palette knife (metal spatula), stencil the wording onto the undecorated yellow paste square.

3 Roll out the yellow sugarpaste trimmings and cut them into long narrow strips. Moisten the edges of the lid and attach the strips, using a small knife to cut neat mitred corners. Leave the lid to dry.

4 Prepare and layer the cakes with jam (conserve) (see page 15), one on top of the other to make a cube shape, ensuring that all the sides are equal. Trim if necessary. Cover the cake completely with a thin spreading of buttercream.

5 Colour 750g (1½lb) sugarpaste black and roll out 125g (4oz). Cut out a square the size of the cake top and attach – the buttercream will secure it in place. Roll out the remaining black sugarpaste and cover the board (see page 24).

6 Carefully attach the prepared toy box sides to the cake, securing them to the buttercream. Conceal the joins with strips of yellow sugarpaste. Attach the prepared toy box lid with a dab of royal icing. Place the cake on the board and trim the board with ribbon.

7 Each individual child for whom you make this attractive novelty will no doubt have their own favourite toys to be copied and featured on the cake. Edible toys are quite simple to make from various colours of sugarpaste – rolled, textured, modelled and joined. Eyes and features can be piped on using royal icing. Rather than make the toys and letting them dry, make each one and position on the cake, securing with royal icing; in this way they look as if they have been casually dropped around the box and on top of each other.

TOYS

Cute Teddy

Always popular, this friendly teddy bear cake could be used for children's birthdays and christening celebrations.

1 Split and sandwich the cakes with the chosen filling, then join to make two complete ball shapes. The smaller cake may be left round, or you may prefer to sculpt it to more of an oval shape for the head. (Use a sharp knife dipped in warm water to make clean cuts. Chilling or part-freezing the cake prior to shaping makes the task easier.) Cover each cake separately with buttercream or jam.

2 Colour 1kg 375g (2¾lb) sugarpaste (rolled fondant) light brown. Roll out separate circles and cover the cakes (see page 22). Attach the head to the body with reconstituted egg white or, to ensure that the cake is firmly attached, you may prefer to insert a plastic cake pillar dowel into the body and then push the head onto the dowel. Place the teddy very carefully on the cake card.

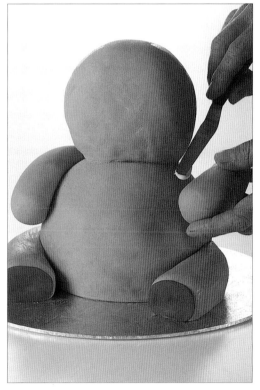

3 Shape two arms and two legs from the remaining paste and stick to the body with royal icing. Colour 30g (1oz) sugarpaste dark brown, roll out and cut out two circles; attach to the legs as shown with royal icing or softened sugarpaste.

4 Thickly roll out some more light brown paste and cut out a circle. Cut the circle in half and indent each with your thumb to form two ears. Stick them onto the head.

CAKE AND DECORATION

two 15cm (6in) diameter bowl-shaped Madeira (pound) cakes*

two 13cm (5in) diameter bowl-shaped Madeira (pound) cakes**

buttercream (see page 18) or jam (conserve) for filling and covering

about 1.5kg (3lb) sugarpaste (rolled fondant)

brown and black paste food colourings

egg white

little royal icing (see page 17)

peach dusting powder (petal dust/blossom tint)

1 large ribbon bow

EQUIPMENT

1 plastic cake pillar dowel (optional)

30 x 25cm (12 x 10in) oval cake card

dusting brush

paper piping bag

no. 2 piping tube (tip)

* use the 15cm (6in) or 18cm (7in) square Madeira mixture (see page 16), depending on size required; cut to shape if necessary

** use the 13cm (5in) or 15cm (6in) square Madeira mixture (see page 16), depending on size required; cut to shape if necessary

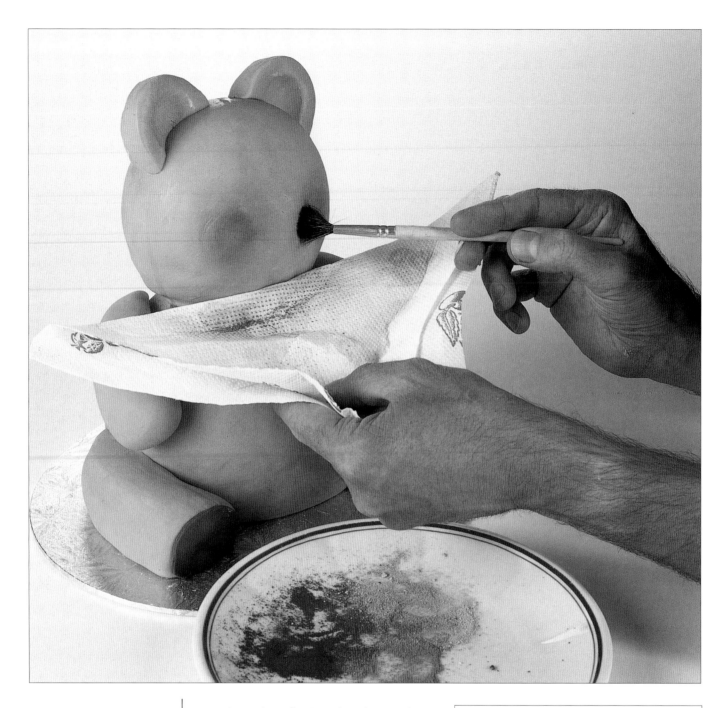

5 Using the dusting brush, apply a light blush of dusting powder (petal dust/blossom tint) to the cheeks as shown. It is a good idea to make a temporary 'bib' of absorbent kitchen paper (paper towels) for the teddy to catch any falling powder that may otherwise stain the body.

6 Make two small flat circles of black sugarpaste for the eyes and a small oval for the nose; attach to the face. Pipe the mouth and stitching using a no.

2 piping tube (tip) and black royal icing. Attach the bow to the teddy's neck.

DINO THE DINOSAUR

23cm (9in) square and 20 x 30cm (8 x 12in) rectangular buttercakes made with 2½ quantities basic mix (see page 62) ☆ 2 quantities buttercream (see page 18) ☆ blue and black food colourings ☆ purple candy-covered chocolate sweets, for the body ☆ white jelly beans (jube jels), for the eyes ☆ large cake board

1 Place the square cake beside the short side of the rectangular cake and secure with a little buttercream. Cut out the dinosaur shape with a small, sharp flat-bladed knife and place on the cake board.

2 Colour three-quarters of the buttercream blue. Leave half of the remainder plain and colour the remainder black.

3 Cover the whole cake with blue buttercream, then add yellow as shown. Outline with fine lines of black icing and decorate with sweets.

Note: Enlarge the photographs of these cakes on a photocopier for an outline guide.

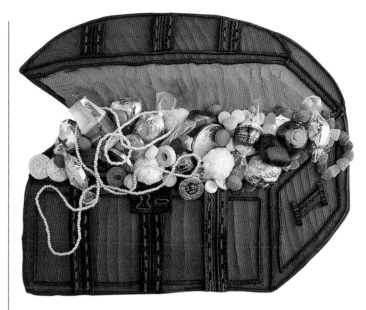

TREASURE CHEST

two 20 x 30cm (8 x 12in) rectangular buttercakes, made with 1½ quantities basic mix (see page 62) ☆ 1½ quantities buttercream (see page 18) ☆ red, pink and black food colourings ☆ liquorice 'lace' ☆ assorted sweets (candies) ☆ string of thin pearls ☆ large cake board

1 Join the cakes together at the long sides and secure with a little buttercream. Cut out the treasure chest shape with a small, sharp flat-bladed knife and place on the cake board.

2 Colour three-quarters of the buttercream red. Divide the remainder in half and colour one portion pink and the remainder black. Cover the cake with buttercream, using pale pink for the inside of the lid. Pipe with a black outline.

3 Cut the liquorice 'lace' and position on the cake to represent a trunk. Pipe fine lines of red buttercream on the liquorice for stitching. Pipe on a red lock. Decorate with assorted sweets (candies) and pearls for treasure.

PETE THE PENGUIN

23cm (9in) square and 20 x 30cm (8 x 12in) rectangular buttercakes, made with 2½ quantities basic mix (see page 62) ☆ 1½ quantities buttercream (see page 18) ☆ black, yellow and blue food colourings ☆ white chocolate button (disc), for eye ☆ small marshmallow, for inner eye ☆ small black jelly bean (jube jel), halved, for pupil ☆ orange 'snake', for mouth ☆ large cake board

1 Place the square cake beside the short side of the rectangular cake and secure with a little buttercream. Cut out the penguin shape with a small, sharp flat-bladed knife and place on the cake board.

2 Divide the buttercream into quarters. Colour one portion black, one yellow, one blue and the remainder a pale blue-green. Use to cover the cake as illustrated.

3 Position the sweets (candies) for the eye and mouth.

SUNSHINE CAKE

two 20 x 30cm (8 x 12in) rectangular buttercakes, made with 1½ quantities basic mix (see page 62) ☆ 2 quantities buttercream (see page 18) ☆ yellow and orange food colourings ☆ 2 marshmallows, for eyes ☆ 3 red jelly beans (jube jels), for inner eye and nose ☆ black jelly bean, halved, for pupils ☆ 1 red and 2 orange 'snakes', for mouth and eyebrows ☆ 2 flying saucers, for cheeks ☆ large cake board

1 Join the cakes together at the long sides and secure with a little buttercream. Cut out the sunshine face, shaping it with a small, sharp flat-bladed knife, and place on the cake board.

2 Colour the buttercream yellow, then colour a small portion of yellow icing orange. Cover the cake with yellow buttercream, then wipe strokes of orange icing randomly around the cake to give highlights. Use the sweets (candies) to create a face as shown.

LOOPY LION

two 20 x 30cm (8 x 12in) rectangular buttercakes, made with 3 quantities basic mix (see page 62) ☆ 1½ quantities buttercream (see page 18) ☆ 100g (3½ oz/3½ squares) plain (semisweet) chocolate, melted (see page 32) ☆ caramel food colouring ☆ 2 large white marshmallows, for eyes ☆ 2 white chocolate buttons, for ears ☆ 1 large milk chocolate button (disc), for nose ☆ 2 black chocolate sweets, for eyes ☆ liquorice 'lace', for tail, mouth and whiskers ☆ red sweet, for mouth ☆ large cake board

1 Join the cakes together at the long sides and secure with a little buttercream. Cut out the lion shape with a small, sharp flat-bladed knife and place on the cake board.

2 Divide the buttercream in half. Beat melted chocolate into one portion. Divide the remaining buttercream in half again and colour one portion caramel and the other pale beige. Use to cover the cake as illustrated.

3 Position the sweets (candies) to create a face and tail.

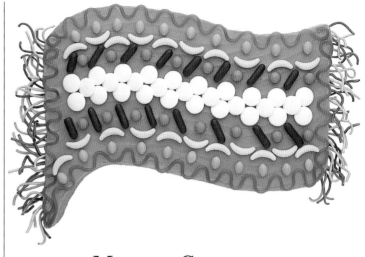

MAGIC CARPET

23cm (9in) square and 28 x 18cm (11 x 7in) rectangular buttercakes, made with 2½ quantities basic mix (see page 62) ☆ 1 quantity buttercream (see page 18) ☆ green and yellow food colourings ☆ dried fried noodles ☆ assorted sweets (candies) for decoration, e.g., candy bananas, jelly beans (jube jels), candy-coated chocolate round sweets (candies) ☆ mint imperials ☆ large cake board

1 Place the square cake beside a short side of the rectangular cake and secure with a little buttercream. Cut out the carpet shape with a small, sharp flat-bladed knife and place on the cake board.

2 Colour the buttercream green and use to cover the cake. Decorate with assorted sweets (candies), using the picture as a guide.

3 Colour half of the fried noodles green and half yellow. Leave to dry, then attach to the cake at the shorter ends.

SNAKE CAKE

500g (1lb/16 squares) plain (semisweet) chocolate ☆
250g (8oz/8 squares) milk (German sweet) chocolate ☆
250g (8oz/8 squares) white chocolate ☆ two 20 x 30cm
(8 x 12in) rectangular buttercakes, made with
3 quantities basic mix (see page 62) ☆ 2 quantities
buttercream (see page 18) ☆ caramel food colouring ☆
liquorice 'lace' ☆ small black jelly bean (jube jel),
halved, for pupils ☆ orange jelly sweet (jube), cut, for
mouth ☆ large cake board

1 Line several baking sheets with greaseproof (parchment) paper. Melt half of the plain (semisweet) chocolate (see page 32) then, using a paper piping bag, pipe small, medium and large buttons (discs) on the sheets. Leave to set, then peel off the paper. Repeat with the milk (German sweet) and white chocolate.

2 Join the cakes together at the long sides and secure with a little buttercream. Cut out the snake shape with a small, sharp flat-bladed knife and place on the cake board.

3 Melt the remaining chocolate and beat into two-thirds of the buttercream. Use to cover the head and body of the snake.

4 Colour the remaining icing caramel and use to cover the neck of the snake.

5 Attach the chocolate buttons (discs) to the body of the snake, starting with large ones at the neck end and graduating to a small one at the tip. Reserve 2 white buttons.

6 Cut the liquorice 'lace' into thin strips and use to outline the head and neck, and for eyelashes and nostrils (see illustration). Attach the reserved white buttons for eyes and place the black jelly bean (jube jel) in position. Attach the orange mouth.

Tip
☆ *Use bought chocolate buttons in white, milk (German sweet) and dark chocolate.*

TOM TEDDY

23cm (9in) square and 20 x 30cm (8 x 12in) rectangular
buttercakes, made with 2½ quantities basic mix (see
page 62) ☆ 1½ quantities buttercream (see page 18) ☆
250g (8oz/8 squares) plain (semisweet) chocolate ☆
brown and caramel food colourings ☆ ½ quantity fluffy
icing (see page 65) ☆ 2 white chocolate buttons (discs),
for eyes ☆ 3 candy-covered chocolate sweets (candies),
for eyes and nose ☆ liquorice 'lace' ☆ red sweet
(candy), for mouth ☆ large cake board

1 Place the square cake beside the short side of the rectangular cake and secure with a little buttercream.

2 Cut out the teddy bear shape with a small, sharp flat-bladed knife and place on the cake board.

3 Melt the chocolate (see page 32) and beat into the buttercream. Colour 60g (2oz/¼ cup) chocolate buttercream dark brown and set aside. Colour the fluffy icing caramel brown. Ice the cake as shown.

4 Use a skewer or fork to fluff edge of darker icing to emphasise the fur. Pipe on details as shown with the reserved dark brown icing.

5 Use the sweets (candies) to create a face as shown.

Horse

*Eating this horse is a lot less strenuous
than riding one and it is a perfect choice of cake for a
pony-mad child!*

CAKE AND DECORATION

25cm (10in) square
Madeira (pound) cake
(see page 16)

100g (3½oz/⅓cup) jam
(conserve) for filling

90g (3oz/⅓cup) truffle
paste (see page 20)

375g (12oz/1½cups)
buttercream (see
page 18)

about 1.6kg (3¼lb)
sugarpaste (rolled
fondant)

egg yellow, brown,
chestnut, black, pink
and red paste food
colourings

90g (3oz/⅓cup) royal
icing (see page 17)

gold food colouring

EQUIPMENT

38 x 33cm (15 x 13in)
oval cake board

crimper

small piece of foam
sponge for stippling

small round cutter

no. 3 sable paintbrush

Tip

☆ *Using the basic
method and
techniques described,
you can create a host
of different animal
heads. Simply pre-
pare a template of
the head shape
required and adapt
the facial features
and colourings.*

1 Make the templates on page 254. Cut the cake to shape, see below right, and layer as described on page 15. Mould the truffle paste to form a shallow dome for the cheek and attach to the face with buttercream. Cover the cake completely with a thin spreading of buttercream.

2 Colour 625g (1¼lb) sugarpaste (rolled fondant) egg yellow and use to cover the board (see page 24). Crimp the board edge (see page 24).

3 Reserve 220g (7oz) sugarpaste and colour the remainder using brown and chestnut colourings. Roll out and use to cover the cake (see page 23). Stipple the face with brown royal icing. Place the cake on the board.

4 Colour 125g (4oz) sugarpaste black and, using the templates, cut out the mane, tuft, ear and nostril. From white paste, cut out two small circles and the eye. Colour some paste pink and make the inner ear. Dry all parts. Cut narrow strips of red paste for the reins. Attach all pieces with icing. Paint the circles with gold colouring and the eye with black.

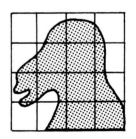

Pussy Cat

A purrrfect cake for a feline lover's party. Adapt the cat's colouring to match a favourite pet.

CAKE AND DECORATION

15cm (6in) round Madeira (pound) cake (see page 16)

20 x 15cm (8 x 6in) oval Madeira cake*

315g (10oz/1 cup) jam (conserve) for filling

470g (15oz/2 cups) buttercream (see page 18)

2.5kg (5lb) sugarpaste (rolled fondant)

green, cream, pink, red and black paste food colourings

90g (3oz/⅓ cup) royal icing (see page 17)

liquorice 'laces'

EQUIPMENT

38 x 33cm (15 x 13in) oval cake board

no. 3 sable paintbrush

* use the 18cm (7in) square Madeira mixture (see page 16)

1 Prepare and layer both cakes (see page 15), then cut and join as shown left. Cover the cake with a thin spreading of buttercream.

2 Colour 560g (1lb 2oz) sugarpaste (rolled fondant) green and use to cover the board (see page 24).

3 Reserve 125g (4oz) sugarpaste and colour the remainder off-white using cream food colouring. Roll out the sugarpaste and cover the cake (see page 22). Place the cake on the prepared board.

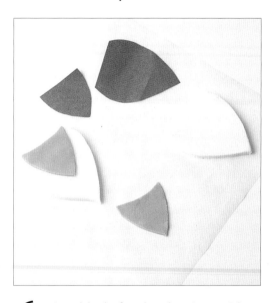

6 Using black food colouring with a small amount of royal icing added to thicken, paint on the body markings. Attach all the prepared pieces and six liquorice whiskers with royal icing.

4 Colour 22g (¾oz) sugarpaste pink, a tiny piece red and the remainder black. Using the off-white coloured trimmings and prepared colours, model the eyes, nose, mouth, tail and paws.

5 Make templates from the drawings opposite for the inner and outer ears. Roll out the pink sugarpaste and white trimmings, then cut out the ears. Leave all these pieces to dry.

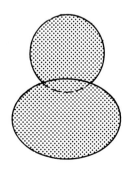

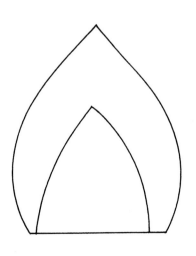

Goldfish Bowl

CAKE AND DECORATION

two 20cm (8in) diameter bowl-shaped Madeira (pound) cakes (see page 16), made using the 5-egg mixture

1.6kg (3¼lb) sugarpaste (rolled fondant)

orange, blue, yellow and green paste food colourings

100g (3½oz/⅓ cup) jam (conserve) for filling

280g (9oz/generous 1 cup) buttercream (see page 18)

blue, yellow and orange dusting powders (petal dusts/blossom tints)

155g (5oz) pastillage (see page 17)

90g (3oz/⅓ cup) royal icing (see page 17)

gold food colouring

EQUIPMENT

25cm (10in) round cake board

piece of soft material

curved former

paper piping bag

nos. 1 and 2 piping tubes (tips)

no. 66 leaf tube (tip)

Using the same techniques and decoration, this novelty could be made from stacking rectangular or square cakes to create an aquarium shape.

1 Colour 375g (12oz) sugarpaste (rolled fondant) orange and use to cover the cake board (see page 24). Leave to dry.

2 Prepare and layer both cakes (see page 15), then join to make a complete ball shape. Cover the cake completely with a thin spreading of buttercream.

3 Colour 875g (1¾lb) sugarpaste blue and cover the cake (see page 23). Due to the awkward shape you will need to cut a few tucks around the base and smooth the paste back together to create a neat finish. Use blue dusting powder (petal dust/blossom tint) or an airbrush with blue colouring to create a deeper blue shaded colour.

4 On a saucer, mix a small amount of orange colouring with a little alcohol. Scrunch up a small piece of material and use to dab the colour randomly onto the board to create a ragging effect. Leave to dry.

5 Make templates for the fish design. Colour the pastillage yellow, roll out and neatly cut out three fish shapes. Place the shapes over a curved former to dry completely. Pipe on the detail using a no. 1 piping tube (tip) and yellow royal icing. When dry, colour the fish using yellow and orange dusting powders and gold food colouring.

6 Turn the cake upside down and, using a no. 66 leaf tube (tip) and green royal icing, pipe the foliage. Turn the cake right way up and secure to the cake board with icing. Trim the board with ribbon, if liked.

7 Use the remaining white sugarpaste to make the bowl rim. Roll out into two long sausage shapes, one slightly narrower than the other. Moisten the top of the wide roll with a little water and attach the narrow roll on top. Shape into a circle and attach to the cake top with icing.

8 Carefully position the fish on the side of the bowl and attach with royal icing. Using a no. 2 piping tube and white royal icing, pipe a few bubbles onto the side and top of the cake.

Rock Pool

A simple buttercream cake, finished with sugarpaste 'sea life' that young explorers will love searching for.

CAKE AND DECORATION

Madeira (pound) cake mixture for 18cm (7in) round tin (pan) (see page 16)

750g (1½ lb/3 cups) buttercream (see page 18)

black, blue, orange, green, brown, red and yellow food colourings

60g (2oz/⅓ cup) light brown sugar

500g (1lb) sugarpaste (rolled fondant)

candles (optional)

0.5m (½yd) gold ribbon for board edge

EQUIPMENT

1.7 litre (3½ pt) ring tin (pan)

36cm (14in) round silver cake board

fine paintbrush

Tips

☆ A 23cm (9in) round Madeira (pound) cake can be substituted for the ring cake. Make a deep hollow in the centre and round off the edges before shaping.

☆ For a colourful finishing touch, mould the sugarpaste trimmings into decorations such as sandals, towels, buckets and spades.

1 Grease and line the base of the tin (pan). Spoon the cake mixture into the tin and level the surface. Bake in the oven for about 1 hour or until firm. Turn the cake out onto a wire rack to cool.

2 Level the surface of the cake by cutting off any peaks that formed during baking. Invert the cake onto a work surface and make angular cuts in the sponge, all around the cake, to create rocks. Place the cake on the board and pack the trimmings into the centre.

3 Colour half of the buttercream with black food colouring until pale grey. Using a palette knife (metal spatula), spread the buttercream over the cake, covering the trimmings in the centre. Spread the remaining grey buttercream around a quarter of the cake board. Sprinkle with the sugar.

4 Partially knead black food colouring into half of the sugarpaste (rolled fondant) until the icing is marbled in colour (see page 23). Mould into rocks of various sizes and press into the buttercream. Mould some of the paste into small pebbles and scatter them over the cake.

5 Reserve 2 tablespoons of the remaining buttercream. Colour the rest blue. Spoon a little into the centre of the cake, over the trimmings. Use the back of a teaspoon to level.

6 Spread the remaining blue buttercream on the board around the cake. Use the back of a teaspoon to pull the icing up into peaks. Use the reserved buttercream to add white tips to the peaks (see page 18).

7 Colour 60g (2oz) of the remaining sugarpaste dark orange. Roll it out thickly on a surface dusted with cornflour (cornstarch) and cut out several starfish in various sizes. Position them on the cake. Mould the trimmings into one or two small crabs and position them on the cake.

8 Colour another 60g (2oz) sugarpaste green and shape into seaweed. Scatter around the rocks.

9 From the remaining sugarpaste, shape small shellfish, such as winkles, mussels, limpets and whelks. Use a fine paintbrush and brown food colouring to add details to the shells. Press candles into the buttercream, if liked. Trim the board with gold ribbon.

Grey Rabbit

Both girls and boys would welcome the friendly smile of this cheerful rabbit at their party.

CAKE AND DECORATION

20 x 15cm (8 x 6in) oval* or 20cm (8in) round Madeira (pound) cake (see page 16)

13cm (5in) round Madeira cake

buttercream (see page 18) or jam (conserve) for filling and covering

1.1kg (2¼lb) sugarpaste (rolled fondant)

grey, pink, brown, black, red and peachy pink paste food colourings

60g (2oz/¼ cup) royal icing (see page 17)

EQUIPMENT

45.5 x 30cm (18 x 12in) oblong cake board

paper piping bag

no. 3 piping tube (tip)

* use the 18cm (7in) square Madeira mixture; cut to shape if necessary

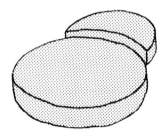

1 Split the oval cake in half and sandwich with filling. Cut the small round cake into two semi-circles and sandwich with filling to make one deep semi-circle. Trim the cake to the same height as the oval cake and join together with buttercream or jam (conserve) as shown.

2 Colour 470g (15oz) sugarpaste (rolled fondant) grey and use 220g (7oz) to cover the top part of the cake. Cover the lower part with 345g (11oz) white sugarpaste, shaping the join where the two colours meet (see picture). Place the cake on the board.

3 Roll out the remaining grey sugarpaste and use the templates on page 96 to cut out two ear shapes. Attach the ears to the head with water. Colour 100g (3½oz) sugarpaste pink, roll out quite thinly and use the smaller template to cut out the inner ears. Attach to the grey ears with water. Bend over the top of one grey ear.

Tip

☆ *If this cake looks too big for your requirements or too expensive to make, keep the costs down a little by using a smaller cake board and either reduce the size of the ears or bend them over.*

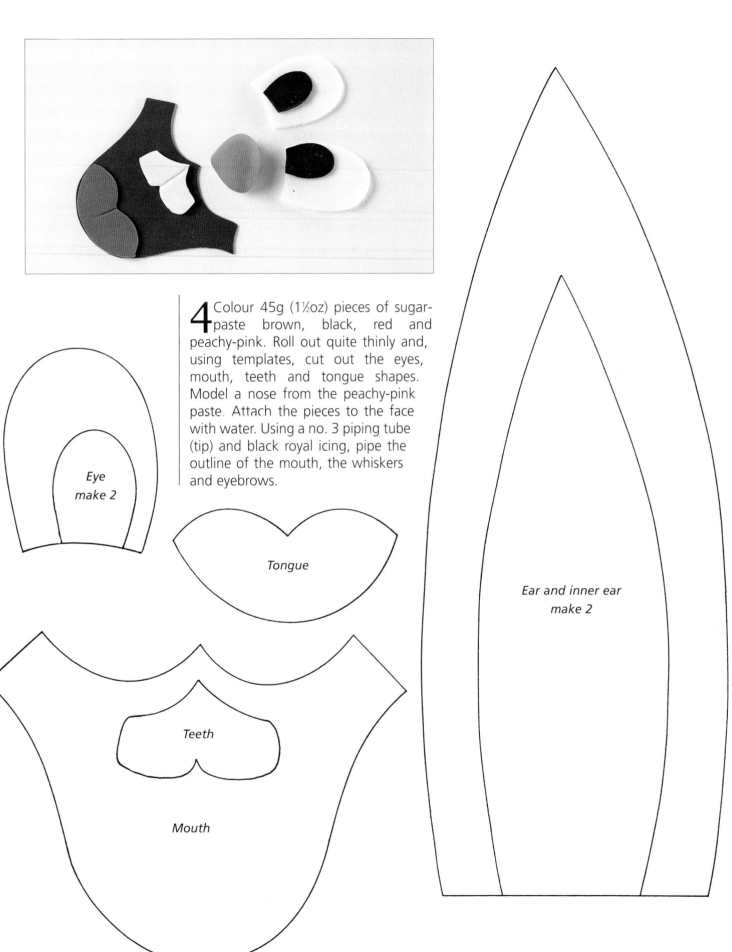

4 Colour 45g (1½oz) pieces of sugar-paste brown, black, red and peachy-pink. Roll out quite thinly and, using templates, cut out the eyes, mouth, teeth and tongue shapes. Model a nose from the peachy-pink paste. Attach the pieces to the face with water. Using a no. 3 piping tube (tip) and black royal icing, pipe the outline of the mouth, the whiskers and eyebrows.

*Eye
make 2*

Tongue

*Ear and inner ear
make 2*

Teeth

Mouth

Party Cakes

FOR GIRLS

Lady in Red

CAKE AND DECORATION

Madeira (pound) cake
mixture for 25cm (10in)
round tin (pan) (see
page 16)

125g (4oz/½ cup)
buttercream (see
page 18)

1kg (2lb) sugarpaste
(rolled fondant)

red, purple and gold
paste food colourings

cornflour (cornstarch)
for dusting

3 tbsp apricot glaze (see
page 21)

gold dragees

gold food dusting
powder (petal
dust/blossom tint)
(optional)

EQUIPMENT

1.4 litre (2½ pint)
ovenproof mixing bowl

15cm (6in) round
cake tin

standard 29cm (11½in)
doll

25cm (10in) round gold
cake board

cocktail stick (toothpick)

fine paintbrush

medium blossom
plunger cutter

*Little girls will adore this glamorous cake. And when the
cake is gone, there is the added bonus of a new doll!*

1 Preheat the oven to 160°C (325°F/Gas 3). Grease and line the base of the mixing bowl and side of the cake tin (pan). Divide the Madeira (pound) cake mixture between the bowl and the tin. Level the surfaces and bake in the oven for about 1¼ hours or until firm. Turn both cakes out onto a wire rack and leave to cool.

2 Level the surfaces of the cakes by cutting off any peaks that formed during baking. Place the bowl cake upside down on top of the round cake. Using a long, thin knife, cut the centre out of each cake and remove completely. Cut the curved edges off the bowl cake, then position the doll inside the cakes, checking that it fits comfortably.

3 Separate the cakes, then sandwich them back together with the buttercream. Place on the cake board and re-position the doll.

4 Reserve 250g (8oz) sugarpaste (rolled fondant) and colour the remainder red. Roll out a little on a surface dusted with cornflour (cornstarch) and cut out a 13 x 4cm (5 x 1¾in) strip. Dampen the underside, then wrap it around the doll for a bodice, trimming off excess at the back. Cut two more strips, each 7.5 x 2.5cm (3 x 1in). Dampen the underside of one and make a fold in the strip. Place over one of the doll's shoulders, securing to the bodice at the back and front. Repeat with the other strip. Wrap a little red icing around the doll's waist to secure to the cake.

5 Thinly roll out a little of the reserved white sugarpaste and cut out a 25 x 7.5cm (10 x 3in) strip. Dampen the underside, then secure around the base of the cake, pinching the icing as you work around the cake to create folds.

6 Thinly roll out more icing and cut out a 25cm (10in) semi-circle. Coat a cocktail stick (toothpick) with cornflour. Roll one half of the cocktail stick along the straight edge of the icing until it begins to frill. Dampen the underside of the semi-circle with water, then secure to the front of the cake so that the lower frilled edge sits about 2cm (¾in) above the board.

7 Brush the cake with apricot glaze. Thinly roll out more red sugarpaste and use to cover the skirt area of the cake in sections. Start at the front with a rectangle measuring about 15 x 13cm

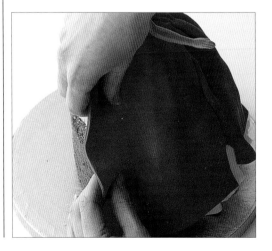

(6 x 5in). Taper the end that will fit around the waist and position on the cake, pinching around the waist to form gathers. Repeat with more rectangles around the remaining skirt area, making the strips longer at the back so they trail on the board behind the doll.

8 Press the gold dragees into the skirt, securing with a dampened paint-brush. Press a 'belt' of gold dragees around the doll's waist.

9 Roll a thin band of white sugarpaste and wrap around the doll's head, securing at the back with water or glaze. Thinly roll out a little red and white paste. Cut out a white flower using a medium blossom plunger cutter. Dampen the underside of the flower while it is still in the cutter, then press it out of the cutter onto the front of the doll's bodice. Press a gold dragee into the centre. Use the same technique to make the doll's headband out of several red and white blossoms.

10 Twist two thin ropes of icing together and secure around the doll's neck.

11 Colour the remaining sugarpaste purple. Roll it out and cut out a 25 x 5cm (10 x 2in) rectangle. Loosely drape over the doll's arms and around her back for a shawl. Leave for 1–2 hours to harden.

12 Using a fine paintbrush, paint the necklace and edges of the shawl and frill with gold food colouring. If liked, use a dry brush and gold dusting powder (petal dust/blossom tint) to dust the white frills.

Tip

☆ *If, once arranged on the cake, the icing 'dress' sections are too big, simply cut with scissors to fit.*

Sleeping Beauty

*This delightful fairytale cake will amuse
and delight young girls.*

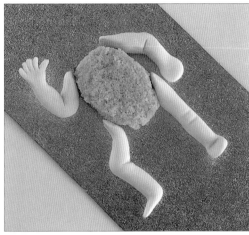

1 Cut the cake into three pieces across the width: two pieces should be 11 x 18cm (4½ x 7in) and one piece 5 x 18cm (2 x 7in); the latter will be the pillow. Carve a small hollow in the centre to support the head. Sandwich the pieces of cake together with the filling of your choice, then attach to the board with a little royal icing. Coat with apricot glaze.

2 Roll out half of the sugarpaste (rolled fondant) thinly and cover the base of the bed. Cover the pillow separately. Pipe a frill around the edge of the pillow using a no. 57 petal piping tube (tip) and a little pink royal icing. Shake the tube gently from side to side as you pipe to produce a gathered effect.

3 Shape a piece of cake to represent a body under the sheets. Model the arms and legs using a plum-sized piece of flesh-coloured sugarpaste. Model the head as shown in the illustration, using equal quantities of sugarpaste and modelling paste. When dry, paint on the eyes and eyebrows and blush the cheeks

with pink dusting powder (petal dust/ blossom tint).

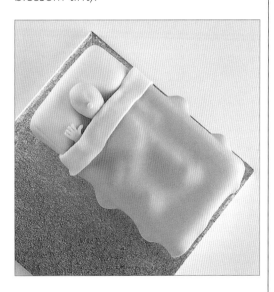

4 Colour 250g (8oz) sugarpaste pink. Roll out to make the bed cover, slightly overlapping and shaping as illustrated. Paint the darker pink and yellow design on the bed covering using a fine paintbrush and food colourings. Add a 3cm (1¼ in) border of white sugarpaste,

CAKE AND DECORATION

28 x 18cm (11 x 7in) oblong Madeira (pound) cake*

strawberry jam (conserve), lemon curd or buttercream (see page 18) for filling

250g (8oz/1 cup) royal icing (see page 17)

125ml (4fl oz/½ cup) apricot glaze (see page 21)

1kg (2lb) sugarpaste (rolled fondant)

raspberry red food colouring

berry blue, mint green, dark brown and melon yellow paste food colourings

mango and pink dusting powders (petal dusts/blossom tints)

250g (8oz) bought modelling paste

4 x 15cm (6in) long pink and white striped candy sticks or dowels

16 x 23cm (6½ x 9in) piece of lace or netting

1.25m (4ft) pink ribbon for board edge

EQUIPMENT

30cm (12in) square cake board

paper piping bag

nos. 2, 3 and 57 piping tubes (tips)

nos. 1 and 2 paintbrushes

small pieces of foam sponge

round cutter

* use 18cm (7in) square Madeira cake mixture (see page 16)

101

folding over the top edge and underneath the bottom cover. Alternatively, leave the cover plain pink.

5 Pipe a frill edge around the cover as for the pillow once it is in position on the bed. Use a no. 3 piping tube to pipe the edging around the bottom of the cake.

6 Model the prince's body out of blue modelling paste as shown below. Warn guests he includes cocktail sticks (toothpicks). Using a no. 3 piping tube

and a little royal icing, pipe a sword onto waxed paper. Use the diagram left as a guide or trace it to make a template if you are nervous about piping the shape freehand. Pipe hair with a no. 2 piping tube. Also create a crown. Use small pieces of foam to support the prince's body while it dries.

7 To create the four-poster bed effect, use either four pink and white striped candy sticks or four pieces of dowel. Sink the four candy stick posts or dowels carefully into the cake corners,

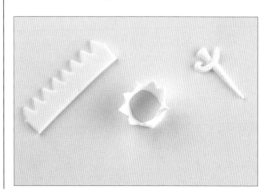

Tip

☆ *If a cake uses cocktail sticks or dowelling to support figures, always warn guests about this.*

not too close to the edge or the sugarpaste will crack. Put a little dab of icing on the top of each post and drape a piece of lace or net curtain over the top to represent the canopy.

8 Decorate dowels with trailing roses, stems and leaves. Stick small balls of leftover paste on the top of the dowels and paint with silver food colouring, if wished.

9 Trim the board with pink ribbon. Complete the decoration by colouring a small piece of sugarpaste yellow and using it to make a small circular rug. Mark the rug with a round cutter which is slightly smaller than the paste to make a fringe effect around the edge. Add piped flowers and a greeting to the rug.

Roses

☆ *Use a no. 57 petal piping tube (tip). Grease the tip of a cocktail stick (toothpick) with white vegetable fat (shortening). With the narrow end of the tube upwards, pipe a cone of icing on the stick for a bud. Pipe 3 overlapping petals to complete the rose. Leave to dry on the stick.*

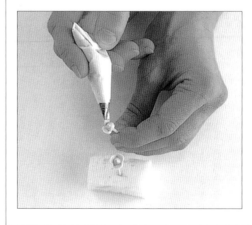

Dream Castle

CAKE AND DECORATION

Madeira (pound) cake
mixture for 23cm (9in)
round tin (pan) (see
page 16)

1.5kg (3lb) sugarpaste
(rolled fondant)

cornflour (cornstarch)
for dusting

6 tbsp apricot glaze (see
page 21)

2 packets of round
sherbet sweets (candies)

selection of pastel-
coloured sweets
(candies)

250g (8oz/1 cup) royal
icing (see page 17)

gold dragees

yellow and pink food
colourings

gold dusting powder
(petal dust/blossom tint)

0.5m (½yd) pink ribbon
for board edge

EQUIPMENT

20cm (8in) round
cake tin

3 empty 400g (14oz)
food cans, thoroughly
washed and dried

25cm (10in) round silver
cake board

2.5cm (1in) plain round
cutter

paper piping bag

no. 2 piping tube (tip)

fine paintbrush

*Fairy-tale castles are always popular with little girls.
This dreamy creation hides plenty of sweet treasures.*

1 Preheat the oven to 160°C (325°F/Gas 3). Grease and line the base and side of the round cake tin (pan) and the three food cans (see page 14). Spoon the Madeira (pound) cake mixture into the prepared food cans, filling each one two-thirds full. Spoon the remaining mixture into the cake tin. Bake the cakes in the oven until firm, allowing about 30 minutes for the cakes in cans and 1¼ hours for the large cake. Turn out onto a wire rack and leave the cakes to cool.

2 Roll out a little sugarpaste (rolled fondant) on a surface dusted with cornflour (cornstarch) and cut out a 7.5cm (3in) square. Transfer to a sheet of greaseproof (parchment) or non-stick paper. Using the tip of a sharp knife, cut out a small archway from one side and notches from the opposite side. Leave to harden for at least 24 hours. Wrap the remaining sugarpaste in plastic food wrap until required.

3 Place the large cake on the cake board and brush it all over with half of the apricot glaze. Roll out 750g (1½lb) sugarpaste to a 36cm (14in) circle. Lay it over the cake and smooth it around the side, letting the excess icing overhang the edge of the board. Trim off the excess sugarpaste around the side of the board so the board around the base of the cake is covered.

4 Level the tops of the small cakes by cutting off any peaks formed during baking. Cut a 2.5cm (1in) slice off one

cake and secure it with a little apricot glaze to another to make three towers of different sizes. Use a 2.5cm (1in) plain round cutter to take a 5cm (2in) deep notch out of one side of each of the two tallest towers.

5 Cover the towers with sugarpaste (see page 22). Place the towers on the cake. Roll out a little sugarpaste, cut

out circles and use to cover the tops of the towers. To make windows, cut crosses in the sugarpaste around the towers with a knife, then press the end of a piping tube (tip) into the ends of the arms of each of the crosses.

6 Roll out two 5cm (2in) squares of sugarpaste. Arrange a line of sweets (candies) down the centre of each. Wrap the icing around the sweets to cover them. Dampen one edge and secure the ends. Dampen the notched corners on the two towers, then press the mini-towers into position, with the joins facing inwards. Make windows in the mini-towers.

7 Peel the paper away from the hardened sugarpaste archway and secure it against the front towers. Make two more mini-towers and place one at each end of the archway. Leave to harden for several hours or overnight.

Tip

☆ *Assemble this cake several days in advance so that it has plenty of time to harden. Once it is covered, it will keep well for up to 10 days.*

8 Cut an 18cm (7in) round of rice, greaseproof (parchment) or non-stick paper into two semi-circles and shape into cones. Make a third cone from another round of paper. Pile sweets on top of each tower, then dampen the top edges of the towers. Gently rest the cones in position. Make smaller cones from 2.5cm (1in) rounds of paper for the mini-towers.

9 Place the royal icing in a paper piping bag fitted with a no. 2 piping tube and pipe a dot on top of each cone. Top with a gold dragee.

10 Roll out 2cm (¾in) strips of sugarpaste. Cut out notches and secure a strip around each tower with the notched end uppermost. Place thinner notched strips around the mini-towers.

11 Dilute some yellow food colouring with water, then use a fine paintbrush to paint the lower third of each tower and each notched strip. Paint the lower area of the large cake. Dilute some pink food colouring and use to paint the remaining areas of the towers.

12 Using a dry paintbrush, dust the cones and white areas of the lower cake with gold dusting powder (petal dust/blossom tint). Colour the remaining sugarpaste pale pink and shape into small boulders. Position around the base of the cake. Trim the cake board with pink ribbon.

Café

This is a lovely cake to make if you enjoy small-scale modelling. The idea also lends itself to several other themes, such as a sweetshop (candy store) or market stall.

1 Level the surface of the cake by cutting off any peak that formed during baking, then split the cake horizontally into three. Sandwich the cake layers back together with 6 table-spoons of the strawberry or raspberry jam (conserve). Halve the cake vertically and stand each piece on its side.

2 Brush the cake board with a little water. Thinly roll out 315g (10oz) sugarpaste (rolled fondant) on a surface dusted with cornflour (cornstarch) and lay it over the cake board. Smooth the icing with cornflour-dusted hands, and trim off the excess around the side.

3 Using a large knife, mark lines across the sugarpaste 2.5cm (1in) apart, then mark lines in the opposite direction to make squares. Using a fine paintbrush and diluted red food colouring, paint alternate squares to give the board a chequered appearance.

4 Press the remaining jam through a sieve to remove any pieces. Brush over the top and sides of the cakes, then position the cakes 2.5cm (1in) apart on the chequered board. Trim the board with ribbon.

5 Partially knead a dot of black food colouring into 125g (4oz) sugarpaste so that the icing is marbled with colour (see page 23). Thinly roll it out and cut out two 20 x 5cm (8 x 2in) rectangles. Lay one on top of each cake.

6 Colour another 500g (1lb) sugarpaste pale yellow. Roll it out and cut it into 9.5cm (3¾in) wide strips. Trim the ends, then position around the sides of the cakes, pinching up the edges to gather. Use more strips until all the sides are covered with paste. While the paste is still soft, lift up part of one side and support it so that it will dry in that position, enabling the cat to be positioned later.

CAKE AND DECORATION

20cm (8in) square Madeira (pound) cake (see page 16)

8 tbsp strawberry or raspberry jam (conserve)

1.5kg (3lb) sugarpaste (rolled fondant)

cornflour (cornstarch) for dusting

liquid red and green food colourings

0.5m (½yd) blue ribbon for board edge

black, yellow, brown and silver paste food colourings

1 sheet of leaf gelatine

125g (4oz/¾ cup) icing (confectioners') sugar

chocolate vermicelli (sprinkles)

EQUIPMENT

30cm (12in) round silver cake board

fine paintbrush

paper piping bag

no. 2 piping tube (tip)

2cm (¾in) and 1cm (½in) plain round cutters

Top (1)

Sides (2)

Front (1)

7 Mould a little white sugarpaste into a cylindrical shape and position it at one end of one counter for the urn. Roll and shape several small white trays, each measuring 4 x 2.5cm (1¾ x 1in).

8 To make the display cabinet, trace the templates (left) onto greaseproof (parchment) or non-stick paper and cut out. Lay the pieces, one at a time, on the leaf gelatine and cut out. Blend the icing (confectioners') sugar with water to make a fairly stiff glacé icing. Put in a paper piping bag fitted with a no. 2 piping tube (tip) and pipe a line along the two sloping sides of the gelatine. Position the narrow rectangle of gelatine against the iced ends to secure. Pipe more icing around the top edges of the gelatine, then rest the large rectangle over the top. Pipe a small dot of icing near the base of the front rectangle.

9 To make crockery, roll out some white sugarpaste and cut out 1cm (½in) and 2cm (¾in) circles, using cutters. Curve the edges up slightly. For cups, roll small balls of sugarpaste and press the end of a wooden spoon into the centre of each. Add tiny rolls of icing for handles. Shape the teapot and milk jug in the same way. Place all the sugarpaste shapes on a sheet of foil or greaseproof paper and leave to harden.

10 Colour a little sugarpaste pale brown. Shape a little into sliced bread and the remainder into whole loaves, French bread sticks and individual rolls. Halve the rolls and tuck in a little crumpled white sugarpaste. Using a fine paintbrush, paint the filling green. Paint green rings on the crockery.

11 Shape and colour more food in the same way, e.g., sausage rolls, sandwiches, iced buns and tray bakes. Make a large gâteau by shaping a drum of icing. Dampen the side, then roll in chocolate vermicelli (sprinkles). Pipe dots of glacé icing around the edge and top each with a tiny red ball.

12 Use the remaining sugarpaste to shape other suitable items, such as a bread board, basket or milk cartons, a tea-towel and napkin dispenser. Leave all the shaped pieces to harden for around 24 hours.

13 From the paste trimmings, shape a tiny mouse and position on the cake board, slightly under the icing drape. Colour a little paste black and shape it into the back half of a cat. Press gently into position. Roll a thin tail and secure with a dampened paintbrush.

14 Position all of the shaped sugarpaste pieces on the cakes, using a little glacé icing to secure. Using a fine paintbrush, paint the knife blade, urn and napkin dispenser silver, and the teapot and knife handle red.

Pretty Heart

Decorated with a simple tulle 'flounce' and pink hearts, this cake will appeal to girls who love 'pretty' cakes.

CAKE AND DECORATION

Madeira (pound) cake mixture for 18cm (7in) round tin (pan) (see page 16)

250g (8oz/1 cup) buttercream (see page 18)

1.5kg (3lb) sugarpaste (rolled fondant)

cornflour (cornstarch) for dusting

2m (2¼yd) pink or white tulle, about 15cm (6in) wide

pink paste food colouring

silver dragees

66cm (26in) silver ribbon, about 2.5cm (1in) wide

1 tbsp icing (confectioners') sugar

candles (optional)

EQUIPMENT

18cm (7in) heart-shaped cake tin

23cm (9in) heart-shaped or round silver cake board or cake card

cocktail stick (toothpick)

small heart-shaped cutters, preferably in two sizes

fine paintbrush

1 Preheat the oven to 160°C (325°F/ Gas 3). Grease and line the base and sides of the cake tin (pan). Spoon the Madeira (pound) cake mixture into the tin and level the surface. Bake in the oven for about 1½ hours or until firm. Turn out on to a wire rack and leave to cool.

2 Level the surface of the cake by cutting off any peak formed during baking. Cut the cake horizontally in half, then sandwich back together with half of the buttercream. Place on the board. Use a palette knife (metal spatula) to spread the remaining buttercream on top.

3 Thinly roll out 375g (12oz) sugarpaste (rolled fondant) on a surface dusted with cornflour (cornstarch). Cut out a 30cm (12in) strip and secure it to one side of the cake. Cut out another 30cm (12in) strip and secure it to the other side of the cake. Dampen the sugarpaste around the base of the cake.

4 Fold the tulle almost in half. Lay it against the base of the cake with the narrow half uppermost and the fold

against the base of the cake. Using the tip of a cocktail stick (toothpick), tuck the fold of the tulle just under the base of the cake, gathering the tulle slightly as you work. Complete all around the base of the cake.

5 Colour 125g (4oz) sugarpaste pink and reserve. Roll out the remainder to a 30cm (12in) circle. Lift this over the cake and let the sugarpaste fall around the sides. Lightly arrange the icing around the sides so that it falls in soft folds but does not crush the tulle. Trim.

6 Thinly roll out the pink sugarpaste and cut out heart shapes. Secure to the top of the cake and to the tulle using a dampened paintbrush. Lightly press silver dragees onto the cake, if necessary using a dampened paintbrush to secure them. Scatter more around the tulle.

7 To secure the ribbon around the cake, make a paste by mixing the icing (confectioners') sugar and a dash of water. Wrap the ribbon around the cake and secure the ends to the cake with a dot of the paste. Place candles on top of the cake, if required.

Tip

☆ *If you cannot get a heart-shaped tin, use a 20cm (8in) round cake and cut out the top and point of the heart. Or, use a round cake – the effect will be just as pretty.*

Jewellery Box

This pretty little jewellery box will make the perfect party cake as the contents of the box can be shared out at the end of the party.

CAKE AND DECORATION

Madeira (pound) cake mixture for 15cm (6in) square tin (pan) (see page 16)

1kg (2lb) sugarpaste (rolled fondant)

250g (8oz/1 cup) buttercream (see page 18)

pink and violet paste food colourings

1m (1yd) pink ribbon for board edge

1 tbsp icing (confectioners') sugar

2m (2¼yd) fine pink ribbon

1m (1yd) strip of spotted or plain tulle, about 7.5cm (3in) wide

selection of pastel-coloured jewellery, dolls' hairbrushes, etc.

EQUIPMENT

20cm (8in) square cake tin

20 x 10cm (8 x 4in) rectangular cake card

large paintbrush

23cm (9in) square cake board

medium blossom plunger cutter

Tip

☆ *Make the sugarpaste box pieces at least 24 hours in advance so they have plenty of time to harden before assembling.*

1 Preheat the oven to 160°C (325°F/ Gas 3). Grease and line the base and sides of the cake tin (pan). Spoon the cake mixture into the tin and level the surface. Bake in the oven for 1¼-1½ hours or until firm. Turn it out onto a wire rack and leave to cool.

2 Wrap 250g (8oz) sugarpaste (rolled fondant) in plastic food wrap and set aside. Roll out the remaining sugarpaste on a surface dusted with cornflour (cornstarch). Using the rectangular cake card as a guide, cut out four 20 x 10cm (8 x 4in) rectangles. Cut one into two equal squares. Brush the card with water and cover with one of the rectangles to make a lid. Reserve the trimmings and wrap in plastic food wrap. Leave all the shapes on pieces of greaseproof (parchment) or non-stick paper for at least 24 hours or until hardened.

3 Level the surface of the cake by cutting off any peak that may have formed during baking. Halve the cake vertically, then sandwich the two pieces together, one on top of the other, with half of the buttercream.

4 Colour 60g (2oz) of the reserved sugarpaste pale pink. Colour the remainder violet. Lightly dampen the surface of the cake board. Roll out the violet sugarpaste on a surface dusted with cornflour to a 25cm (10in) square and use to cover the cake board (see page 24).

5 Position the cake on the board. Spread the remaining buttercream over the sides of the cake. Carefully peel the paper away from the box sides and press them into position. Trim the board with pink ribbon.

6 Thinly roll out the white paste trimmings and use to cover the sponge inside the box. Make a paste with the icing (confectioners') sugar and a dash of water. Wrap ribbon around the top and bottom edges of the box, and the lid edges, and secure with dots of paste.

7 Thinly roll out the pale pink paste and cut out blossoms (see page 26). Press the blossoms out of the cutter directly onto the box to decorate. (If the blossoms do not stay in position, dampen the undersides first.) Crumple the tulle into the top of the box and fill with the jewellery. Rest the lid on top.

Rag Dolly

CAKE AND DECORATION

23 x 18cm (9 x 7in) oval Madeira (pound) cake*

buttercream (see page 18) or jam (conserve) for filling and covering

1kg 60g (2lb 2oz) sugarpaste

lemon, pink, peach, brown, black and red paste food colourings

2 white ribbon bows

EQUIPMENT

33 x 28cm (13 x 11in) oval cake board

crimping tool

paintbrush

* use the 20cm (8in) square Madeira mixture (see page 16)

This attractive cake will be popular with little girls as they will love the hair and ribbon bows.

1 Split and sandwich the cake with chosen filling (see page 15) and cover with buttercream or jam (conserve).

2 Colour 345g (11oz) sugarpaste (rolled fondant) lemon. Roll out and use to cover the cake board, then crimp the edge while the paste is still soft (see page 24).

3 Colour 440g (14oz) sugarpaste peachy-pink. Roll out and use to cover the cake (see page 22). Place on the prepared board.

4 Colour 220g (7oz) sugarpaste brown. Roll out and use the template on page 116 to cut out two hair shapes. Texture with the point of a

Tip

☆ *To cut down on time and enable you to make a better job of the face and hair detail, use a cake board covered with decorative paper rather than covering with sugarpaste and crimping, making sure the cake sits on another, smaller board first.*

paintbrush handle. Make two plaits from the remaining brown paste as shown. Attach the hair and plaits to the cake.

5 Prepare the doll's eyes, nose, mouth and cheeks using the templates below and coloured sugarpaste. Attach to the face. Pipe in some eyelashes if liked. Attach a ribbon bow to each plait with a dab of icing.

features

hair

Teddy Bears' Picnic

Let your imagination run wild creating the party spread of your dreams, including goodies ranging from sausage rolls to chocolate fudge cake.

1 Trim the top of the cake level. Slice the cake into two layers and sandwich them together with the filling of your choice. Attach to the board, off-centre towards the back of the board, with a little royal icing and coat with apricot glaze.

2 Colour 250g (8oz) sugarpaste (rolled fondant) pale blue. Roll it out to 5mm (¼in) thick and cut a strip deep enough and long enough to cover the side of the cake.

3 Colour 250g (8oz) sugarpaste pink. Roll it out and cut a wavy-edged circle, at least 2.5cm (1in) larger than the top of the cake. Lay the sugarpaste over the cake as illustrated. Pinch and lift the edge of the sugarpaste with your

CAKE AND DECORATION

20cm (8in) round Madeira (pound) cake (see page 16)

strawberry jam (conserve), lemon curd or buttercream (see page 18) for filling

375g (12oz/1⅓ cups) royal icing (see page 17)

125ml (4fl oz/½ cup) apricot glaze (see page 21)

1kg (2lb) sugarpaste (rolled fondant)

blueberry, pink, dark brown, melon yellow, liquorice black, Christmas red, mint green and tangerine paste food colourings

1 tsp red piping gel

caster (superfine) sugar for sprinkling

1 glacé cherry

icing (confectioners') sugar for dusting

5 chocolate-covered mini rolls

raspberry red and cream liquid food colourings

1.25m (4ft) pink ribbon for board edge

EQUIPMENT

30cm (12in) round cake board

plastic smoother

1.5cm (¾in), 2cm (⅞in) and 3cm (1¼in) diameter round cutters

no. 2 paintbrush

paper piping bag

nos. 0, 1, 2, 3 and 41 piping tubes (tips)

ballpoint pen top

ball modelling tool

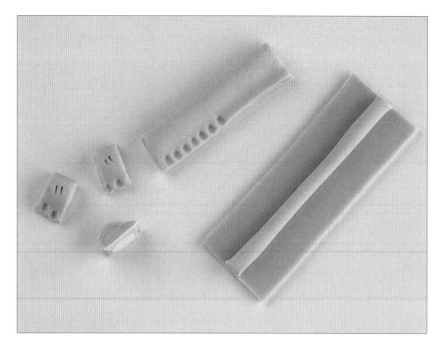

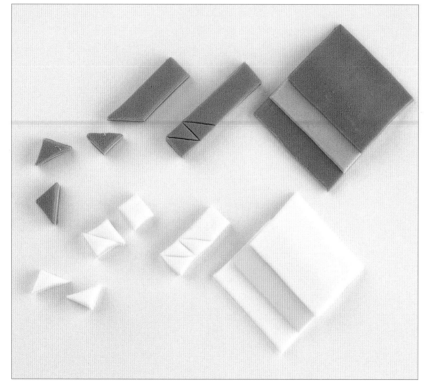

out 5 small plates and the 2cm (⅞in) cutter to cut out 5 saucers. Colour remaining sugarpaste various colours and model the food as illustrated and outlined below.

6 Make sandwiches by rolling out two colours of sugarpaste thinly. Sandwich the coloured paste between white or brown paste, brushing with a little water to stick them together. Cut into 1cm (½in) strips, then into 1cm (½in) squares. Cut in half diagonally. Stick to plates with water.

7 For sausage rolls, colour sugarpaste pale golden brown and roll out thinly. Cut it into 10 x 1cm (4 x ½in) strips. Make long sausages of pink sugarpaste and attach one to the centre of each strip with a little water. Fold one side of the strip over the sausage and stick to the other side. Seal using the tail-end of a paintbrush. Cut into small rolls. Make slits in the rolls with a knife point.

8 Shape a small wedge of yellow sugarpaste to represent cheese, making holes with the tail-end of a paintbrush. Pipe the mice with a no. 2 piping tube (tip) and a little white royal icing. Pipe a small shell for the body, adding black eyes, brown ears and tail, and a pink nose when dry, using a no. 0 piping tube.

9 Use a sterilized ballpoint pen lid to cut bases for the tiny iced gems from rolled-out brown sugarpaste. Pipe on the top of each one with a no. 41 rosette piping tube and top with a spot of pink icing.

10 Make the jam tarts and Swiss (jelly) roll with pale golden sugarpaste; the tarts are the same size as the iced gems, but indented with a ball modelling tool. For the Swiss roll, roll out a thin strip of sugarpaste to about 4 x 1.5cm (1½ x ¾in). Spread with red piping gel and roll up. Moisten the top and sprinkle with caster (superfine) sugar. Cut a slice to lay beside the roll.

Tip

☆ *Vary the colour of the tablecloth and ribbon board trimming for boys and girls, if you like.*

fingers to give a draped-cloth effect as shown opposite.

4 Colour 250g (8oz) sugarpaste brown and model the bears (see page 26).

5 Colour 60g (2oz) paste pale green. Use the 3cm (1¼in) cutter to cut out 17 large plates, the 1.5cm (¾in) cutter to cut

rosette tube. Cut a cake candle short and place in the centre of the cake.

13 To make the fruit bowl, model the fruit with coloured sugarpaste. Roll the oranges and strawberries on a nutmeg grater to give them texture.

14 Sandwich two rounds of brown sugarpaste together with brown royal icing and dust with icing (confectioners') sugar to make the chocolate cake. Plait three thin sausages of white sugarpaste to make the plaited loaf, then brush with brown food colouring. Model the teapot, milk jug, sugar bowl and cups out of reserved green sugarpaste. Paint on a pattern when dry.

11 Model a fish out of orange sugarpaste, marking it by using the piping end of a no. 2 piping tube. Pipe éclairs with a no. 3 piping tube. Pipe a short straight line of white royal icing, leave to dry, then pipe a line of chocolate brown icing on the top of each one with a no. 2 piping tube.

15 Colour some royal icing green and coat the board surrounding the cake. Stipple the icing to represent grass by dabbing it with a paintbrush held vertical to the surface. Attach the chocolate roll seats with a little royal icing. Fill a greaseproof (parchment) piping bag with any leftover green icing and pipe some grass around the bottom edge of the table and seats.

12 To make the jelly, cut a glacé cherry in half and pipe a dot of royal icing on top. Make a mini cake from a small round of sugarpaste and pipe around the edge with a no. 41

16 Trim the edge of the board with pink ribbon, or a colour to match the cloth.

Cutter templates

Party Cakes

FOR BOYS

Travelling Trucks

Simple shapes in bright colours appeal to very young boys. This theme works equally well with cars or trains.

CAKE AND DECORATION

20cm (8in) round
Madeira (pound) cake
(see page 16)

7 tbsp strawberry or
raspberry jam (conserve)

125g (4oz/½ cup)
buttercream (see
page 18)

1.5kg (3lb) sugarpaste
(rolled fondant)

cornflour (cornstarch)
for dusting

green, red, brown, blue,
black and yellow paste
food colourings

candles

0.5m (½yd) decorative
ribbon for board edge

EQUIPMENT

25cm (10in) round silver
cake board

fine paintbrush

Tip

☆ *The simple design
of this cake is very
effective. However,
you could add
more detail – for
instance, windows
and number plates
on the trucks.*

1 Cut the cake horizontally in half. Place the lower half on the cake board and spread with 4 tablespoons of the jam (conserve). Spread the jam with the buttercream, then cover with the second layer.

2 Sieve the remaining jam to remove any pieces, then brush over the top and side of the cake.

3 Roll out 1kg (2lb) sugarpaste (rolled fondant) on a surface dusted with cornflour (cornstarch) and use to cover the cake (see page 22).

4 Colour another 125g (4oz) sugarpaste green. Reserve a little, then roll out the remainder to a strip as long as the circumference of the cake. Cut one edge straight and the other in a wavy line. Dampen the bottom edge of the cake with water, then wrap the strip around the cake and secure.

5 Trace the template (page 251) onto greaseproof (parchment) or non-stick paper and cut out. Colour another 185g (6oz) sugarpaste red. Thinly roll out half. Lay the template on the sugarpaste and cut around it to shape a truck. Dampen the underside, then secure the truck to the side of the cake above the green strip. Make and secure more trucks.

6 Shape the remaining red sugarpaste into a solid rectangle and cut out a wedge to form a truck shape (see right).

7 Colour another 125g (4oz) sugarpaste brown. Shape into a thick semi-circle, then cut out the centre with a knife or round cutter to shape a bridge.

8 Colour a little more sugarpaste pale blue. Roll out and position on top of the cake. Carefully arrange the bridge over the blue 'water'. Shape a small path from brown trimmings and secure to the top of the cake. Secure the truck on top of the cake, raising it off the cake slightly on a piece of red sugarpaste trimmings.

9 Colour a little more sugarpaste black and shape into wheels. Secure to all the trucks.

10 Shape tiny balls of green sugarpaste from trimmings and arrange in rings on the top of the cake. Press candles into the centres, or fill the centres with a dot of red icing. Shape small yellow 'headlights' and secure to the front of the truck. Trim the board with decorative ribbon.

Control Pad

A simple but effective cake for games console fans. The design could be adapted to resemble the child's own control pad as closely as possible.

CAKE AND DECORATION

18cm (7in) round Madeira (pound) cake (see page 16)

3 liquorice 'laces'

4 tbsp apricot glaze (see page 21)

1kg (2lb) sugarpaste (rolled fondant)

cornflour (cornstarch) for dusting

black food colouring

black, red, blue and green paste food colourings

candles (optional)

2m (2yd) purple ribbon for board edge

EQUIPMENT

36cm (14in) square silver cake board

9cm (3½in) plain round cutter

2.5cm (1in) plain round cutter

large paintbrush

Tip

☆ *The cake board looks effective covered with metallic gold or deep coloured wrapping paper.*

---

1 Twist the three pieces of liquorice together into a rope, then secure the ends under two weights to maintain the shape until needed.

2 Level the surface of the cake by cutting off any peak that formed during baking. Cut the cake horizontally in half and place the layers, side by side, on the cake board. Brush the layers all over with the apricot glaze.

3 Reserve 125g (4oz) sugarpaste (rolled fondant). Roll out the remainder on a surface dusted with cornflour (cornstarch) to a 43 x 23cm (17 x 9in) rectangle. Lay this over the cakes, then smooth around the sides, easing to fit. (Do not shape the icing into the cracks between the cakes. Instead, let the icing fall naturally.) Trim off excess icing around the base of the cake and reserve.

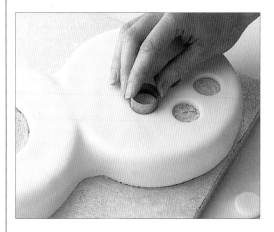

4 Dip the large round cutter in cornflour, then cut out the centre of the sugarpaste on one side of the cake. Use the small cutter to cut out four circles on the other side of the cake.

5 Using a large paintbrush, brush all over the cake with black food colouring, diluting the colouring with a little water if it is too thick.

6 Colour a little sugarpaste grey using black paste food colouring. Roll out and cut out a circle with the large cutter. Position in the centre of the large cut-out circle.

7 Colour a little more sugarpaste red and roll out thickly. Cut out a cross shape, reserving the trimmings, and position over the grey circle. Using the tip of a knife, mark an arrow pointing outwards on each arm of the cross. Use the end of a wooden spoon or paintbrush to impress a decorative pattern in the black icing around the large circle.

8 Colour half of the remaining sugarpaste blue and half green. Press a flattened ball of each of the primary colours, and the grey, into each of the small cut-out circles.

9 Finish the cake by adding other small sugarpaste controls, such as an ON/OFF control.

10 Press one end of the liquorice 'rope' into the side of the cake, leaving the other end trailing. Trim the board with ribbon. Add candles, if wished.

Boy Racers

For boys (or girls) who like a little fast action on the track.

CAKE AND DECORATION

CAKE AND DECORATION

25cm (10in) square Madeira (pound) cake (see page 16)

strawberry jam (conserve), lemon curd or buttercream (see page 18) for filling

250g (8oz/1 cup) royal icing (see page 17)

125ml (4fl oz/½ cup) apricot glaze (see page 21)

1kg (2lb) sugarpaste (rolled fondant)

Christmas green and red, black, berry blue, melon yellow, mint green and tangerine paste food colourings

silver lustre powder (petal dust/blossom tint)

1.25m (1¼yd) red ribbon for board edge

EQUIPMENT

25cm (10in) square cake board

no. 1 paintbrush

paper piping bag

no. 3 piping tube (tip)

1 Trim the cake, if necessary, so that it sits level. Slice it into two layers and sandwich with the filling of your choice. Attach to the board with a little royal icing, then coat with apricot glaze.

2 Colour 375g (12oz) sugarpaste (rolled fondant) pale Christmas green. Roll out to 5mm (¼in) thick and cover the cake (see page 22).

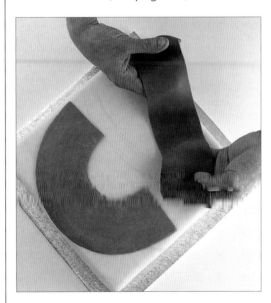

3 Colour 125g (4oz) sugarpaste grey. Roll the paste out thinly and cut two 30 x 6cm (12 x 2¼in) strips. Dampen the surface of the cake with a little water. Lay the strips on top of the cake, curving them as shown, to form the race track. Trim off the excess.

4 Colour 60g (2oz) sugarpaste dark grey. Roll the paste into 5mm (¼in) thick sausage shapes and cut into 7.5cm (3in) lengths. Stick three pieces together

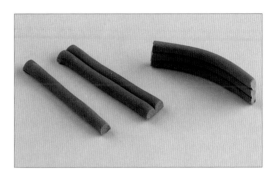

with a little water and curve to form crash barriers for the corners of the race track. Paint with silver arrows when dry.

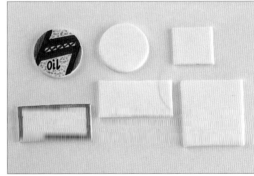

5 Roll out a small piece of white sugarpaste thinly and cut out small oblongs and squares for advertising hoardings and to make a chequered flag. Leave to dry, then paint the details as illustrated.

6 Divide the remaining sugarpaste into five pieces and colour each piece differently: red, blue, yellow, green and orange. Using the templates on page 128, cut two front pieces and one back piece for each car. Model five helmets and windscreens and five graduated pieces which sit behind the driver. Stick

the pieces together with icing or water. Assemble all the cars, sticking the various pieces together with a little royal icing or water.

7 Make four wheels for each car and mark the criss-cross tread pattern with a knife. Attach to the cars.

8 Colour a little royal icing green and spread it thinly around the edge of the race track. Stipple the icing to represent grass by dabbing it with a paintbrush held vertically. Decorate the cake board in the same way, if wished.

9 Pipe a line of shells to neaten the bottom edge of the cake, using a no. 3 piping tube (tip) and green royal icing. Trim the edge of the board with the red ribbon.

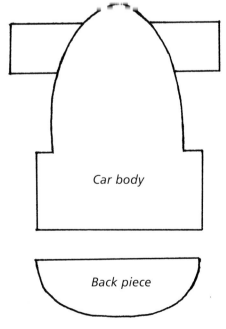

Car body

Back piece

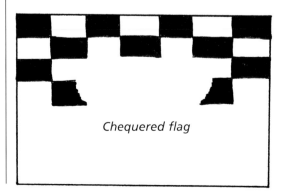

Chequered flag

Red Aeroplane

A colourful novelty cake that will suit boys or aspiring pilots of all ages. Change the colours to suit the recipient.

1 Colour 315g (10oz) sugarpaste (rolled fondant) blue, roll out and cover the cake board (see page 24). Roll out 125g (4oz) white paste to the same thickness. Use the cloud template (see page 130) to cut out shapes from the blue paste in a random fashion over the board. Replace with white clouds and smooth the joins.

2 Using a sharp knife dipped in warm water, shape the cake as shown to form the body of the aeroplane. (To make cutting easier and neater, chill or part-freeze the cake prior to shaping.) Remove the cockpit using the oval cutter. Cover the cake with buttercream or jam (conserve).

CAKE AND DECORATION

500g (1lb) Madeira (pound) cake (see page 16), baked in a 500g (1lb) loaf tin (pan)*

750g (1½lb) sugarpaste (rolled fondant)

blue, red, black and egg yellow paste food colourings

buttercream (see page 18) or jam (conserve) for filling and covering

small piece each red and black card

1 modelled marzipan (almond paste) or plastic pilot figure

1.25m (1¼yd) blue ribbon for board edge

EQUIPMENT

28cm (11in) square

oval cutter

*Double the cake mixture and tin size if required – remember to double filling and sugarpaste, too

Tip

☆ This attractive novelty cake can be personalized by adding the age of the recipient to the wing tips, either by piping directly or using readily available edible or plastic numerals.

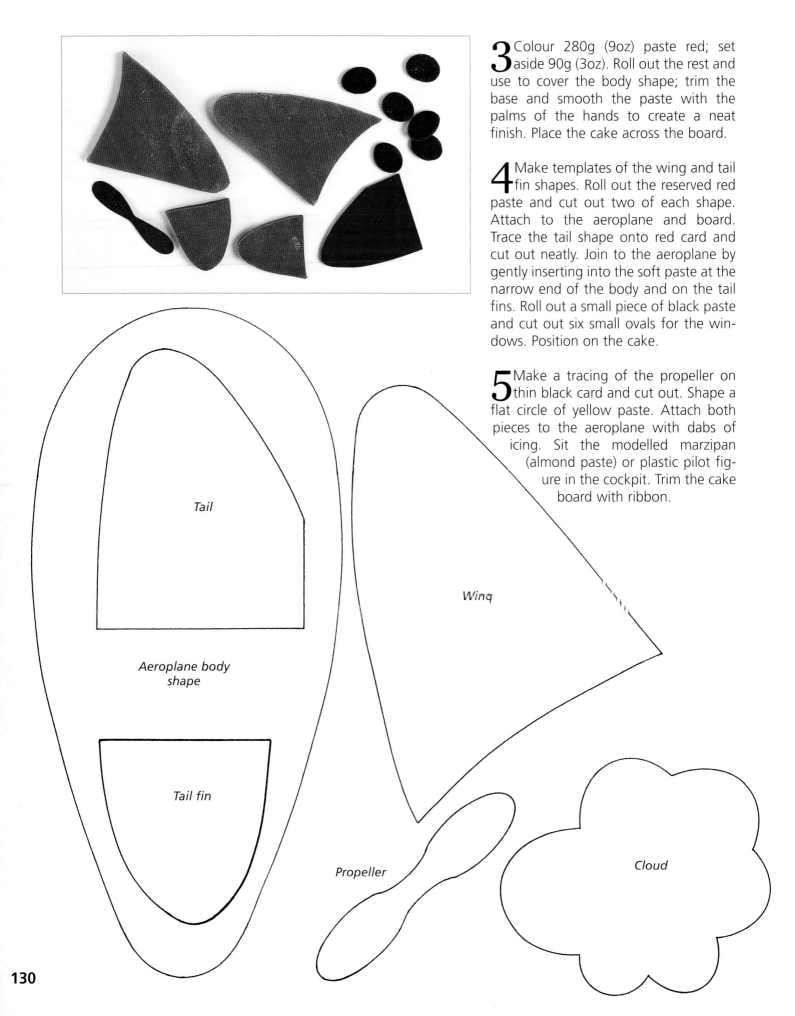

3 Colour 280g (9oz) paste red; set aside 90g (3oz). Roll out the rest and use to cover the body shape; trim the base and smooth the paste with the palms of the hands to create a neat finish. Place the cake across the board.

4 Make templates of the wing and tail fin shapes. Roll out the reserved red paste and cut out two of each shape. Attach to the aeroplane and board. Trace the tail shape onto red card and cut out neatly. Join to the aeroplane by gently inserting into the soft paste at the narrow end of the body and on the tail fins. Roll out a small piece of black paste and cut out six small ovals for the windows. Position on the cake.

5 Make a tracing of the propeller on thin black card and cut out. Shape a flat circle of yellow paste. Attach both pieces to the aeroplane with dabs of icing. Sit the modelled marzipan (almond paste) or plastic pilot figure in the cockpit. Trim the cake board with ribbon.

Tail

Aeroplane body shape

Tail fin

Wing

Propeller

Cloud

Planetarium

CAKE AND DECORATION

Madeira (pound) cake mixture for 18cm (7in) round tin (pan) (see page 16)

125g (4oz/½ cup) buttercream (see page 18)

1.5kg (3lb) sugarpaste (rolled fondant)

dark blue, silver and black food colourings

3 tbsp apricot glaze (see page 21)

red, pale blue, orange and green paste food colourings

candles

0.5m (½yd) dark blue ribbon for board edge

EQUIPMENT

1.4 litre (2½ pint/6 cup) ovenproof mixing bowl

33cm (13in) round silver cake board

large paintbrush

15cm (6in) round silver cake card

fine paintbrush

This is one of the simplest yet most effective novelty cakes, ideal for a boy's party. The large planet sits on a small tumbler or bowl to give it extra height.

1 Preheat the oven to 160°C (325°F/Gas 3). Grease and line the base of the mixing bowl. Spoon the cake mixture into the bowl and level the surface. Bake in the oven for 1¼–1½ hours or until firm. Turn out onto a wire rack and leave to cool.

2 Level the surface of the cake to lie flat on its widest end. Cut the cake horizontally into three, then sandwich it back together with the buttercream.

3 Lightly brush the surface of the large cake board with water. Roll out 315g (10oz) sugarpaste (rolled fondant) on a surface dusted with cornflour (cornstarch). Lay the icing over the board and smooth out, using hands dusted with cornflour. Trim off the excess around the edge. Using a large paintbrush, completely cover the iced board with dark blue food colouring.

4 Using a fine paintbrush, flick the board with silver food colouring until lightly speckled all over.

5 Brush the cake with apricot glaze and position on the cake card. Rest the cake on a small bowl, ready for covering.

6 Reserve 125g (4oz) of the remaining white sugarpaste. Roughly knead a little black food colouring into the remainder until lightly marbled with colour (see page 23). Roll out the marbled icing to a 28cm (11in) round and place over the cake, smoothing the icing around the side to eliminate creases. Trim off the excess icing around the base. Using the bowl of a measuring spoon dusted with cornflour, press 'craters' into the icing. Accentuate the edges of the craters by pinching between thumb and forefinger.

7 Colour small amounts of the remaining sugarpaste red, blue, orange and green, and use to shape small planets. Arrange over the board. Shape and paint small 'spaceships' from trimmings or buy plastic craft (see TIP). Press candles into the icing around the edge of the board and trim the board with ribbon.

Tip

☆ *Instead of using sugarpaste trimmings painted silver, buy small plastic space-craft from a cake-decorating or toy shop. A few extras could be bought for filling party bags, particularly if the party has a space theme.*

Tip

☆ *If you do not have a very dark blue for the 'space' background, use a brighter blue, deepening the colour by mixing in a little black colour before painting.*

Yellow Dinosaur

This multi-coloured species would certainly draw attention on a party table.

CAKE AND DECORATION

18cm (7in) round Madeira (pound) cake (see page 16)

½ 500g (1lb) Madeira loaf cake

buttercream (see page 18) or jam (conserve) for filling and covering

1.25kg (2½lb) lemon sugarpaste (rolled fondant)

375g (12oz) white sugarpaste

blue, claret and black paste food colourings

1.5m (1½yd) purple ribbon for board edge

EQUIPMENT

45.5 x 20cm (18 x 8in) oblong cake board covered in black paper (see TIP page 188)

1 Split and sandwich the round cake with chosen filling, then cut in half to form two semi-circles. Sandwich the two halves together, side by side, to form the basic body shape of the dinosaur. Shape the smaller cake into a cube for the head. Split and sandwich the cube of cake and arrange on the cake board with the body in a curved position. Cover the cake with buttercream or jam (conserve).

2 For the tail, take about 90g (3oz) lemon sugarpaste (rolled fondant), form a long carrot shape and attach to the body.

3 Reserve about 125g (4oz) lemon sugarpaste. Roll out the remaining paste and cover the cake (see page 22). Place on the cake board. While still soft, indent the surface of the paste all over using the fingertips lightly pressed in.

4 Colour 60g (2oz) white sugarpaste blue and make balls of varying sizes. Flatten them, then press into the body and tail of the dinosaur.

5 Colour 280g (9oz) paste claret, roll into a long sausage and cut into pieces, graduating in size from small to large then back to small. Roll each piece into a ball, then shape into a squat carrot shape. Flatten the shape to form a spike. Attach to the body and tail in sequence of size.

6 For the legs, divide the reserved lemon paste into four pieces and shape as shown. Attach to the body.

7 Attach four flattened balls of yellow paste to the head, two for the eyes and two for the nostrils. Indent the nostrils with a fingertip. Roll 22g (¾oz) white paste into two ball shapes and attach to the eyes. Attach two smaller balls of black paste to the eyes. Make the mouth from a long thin strip of black paste and attach to the head. Trim the cake board with ribbon.

Jolly Pirate

Any boy will treasure memories of a party featuring this novel face cake, complete with spotted scarf and eye patch.

CAKE AND DECORATION

23 x 18cm (9 x 7in) oval Madeira (pound) cake*

buttercream (see page 18) or jam (conserve) for filling and covering

410g (13oz) peachy-pink sugarpaste (rolled fondant)

375g (12oz) white sugarpaste

purple, lemon, black and brown paste food colourings

EQUIPMENT

28 x 23cm (11 x 9in) oval cake board, covered with decorative paper (see TIP page 188)

oval cutter

* Use Madeira mixture for a 20cm (8in) square cake (see page 16)

1 Split and sandwich the cake with chosen filling (see page 15) and cover with buttercream or jam (conserve).

2 Reserving a little for the nose, roll out the peachy-pink sugarpaste (rolled fondant) and cover the cake (see page 22). Place on the cake board.

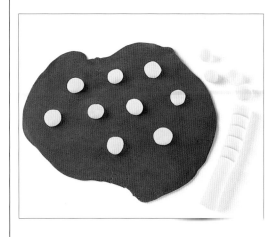

3 Colour 140g (4½oz) white sugarpaste purple and roll out thinly. Colour 60g (2oz) paste lemon, flatten into balls and attach to the purple paste

to form a regular pattern. Continue rolling the paste for a smooth, spotted 'material' effect. Attach to the top of the face as a scarf. Cut the sugarpaste trimmings to form a tied knot.

4 Use cutters to make the eyes from 45g (1½oz) each white and black paste. Shape the nose from reserved paste. Use templates for the mouth and eye patch. Attach to the cake. For the tufts of hair, model short pointed shapes of brown paste.

Tip

☆ *Don't worry if you don't have an oval tin to make this cake, it looks equally attractive made using a round sponge as the base – this also applies to the Rag Dolly (see page 114).*

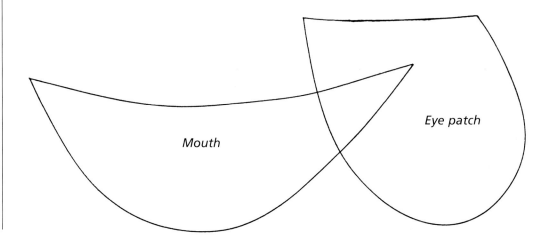

Mouth

Eye patch

Trophy Cake

This cake will be a real winner for any achievement celebration and can easily be adapted to suit the occasion.

CAKE AND DECORATION

18cm (7in) round Madeira (pound) cake (see page 16)

18cm (7in) square Madeira (pound) cake (see page 16)

buttercream (see page 18) or jam (conserve) for filling and covering

790g (1lb 9½oz) sugarpaste (rolled fondant)

black and red food colourings

30g (1oz/2 tbsp) royal icing (see page 17)

EQUIPMENT

38 x 36cm (15 x 14in) oblong cake board

Garrett frill cutter or round fluted cutter and small round cutter

cocktail stick (toothpick)

no. 2 piping tube (tip)

Tip

☆ *Don't worry if you haven't got a Garrett frill cutter to hand. You can make the basic rosette shape using a large scone cutter or by making a card template of a fluted circle to cut around.*

1 Cut the round cake in half and sand-wich with filling to make a semi-circle. Cut the square cake as shown and attach the large piece to the semi-circle with buttercream or jam. Join the remaining pieces with buttercream or jam and cut to form the plinth shape. Cover both cakes with buttercream or jam. Colour 545g (1lb 1½oz) of the sugarpaste (rolled fondant) grey, using black food colouring. Then roll out 220g (7oz) of it and cover the cup (see page 22). Colour 185g (6oz) sugarpaste black, roll out and cover the plinth. Position the two cakes on the cake board.

2 Divide the remaining grey sugar-paste into three. Roll two pieces into long tapering ropes and curve them to make two handles. Model the stem shape from the third piece of paste. Attach all pieces to the cup and plinth with water. Roll out the black sugarpaste trimmings, cut out a narrow strip for the plinth detail and attach with water.

3 Colour 60g (2oz) sugarpaste red, roll out and cut two pieces to represent ribbon tails for the rosette. Also, cut out a fluted circle and a smaller circle. Place a cocktail stick (toothpick) on the edge of the circle, press gently and roll the stick from side to side to frill the edge of the paste. Attach the tails to the cup with water, followed by the fluted circle and finally the small circle. Using a no. 2 tube (tip) and white royal icing, pipe on the '1st' lettering.

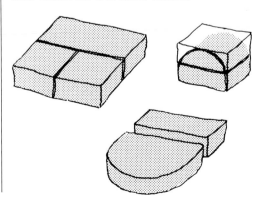

Green Monster

Not too frightening, this novelty cake would make an ideal centrepiece for a boy's theme party.

CAKE AND DECORATION

15cm (6in) shallow round and 15cm (6in) square Madeira (pound) cake (see page 16)

buttercream (see page 18) or jam (conserve) for filling and covering

345g (11oz) green sugarpaste (rolled fondant)

125g (4oz) white sugarpaste

navy, black and green paste food colourings

30g (1oz/2 tbsp) royal icing (see page 17)

EQUIPMENT

30 x 25cm (12 x 10in) oblong cake board, covered in decorative paper (see TIP page 188)

paintbrush

paper piping bag

no. 2 piping tube (tip)

Tip

☆ *To avoid using two separate cake shapes, cut the monster's face out of an oblong cake.*

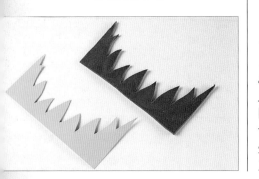

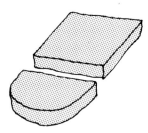

1 Cut the round cake in half and sandwich with filling. Split the square cake and sandwich with filling (see page 15). Join the cakes as shown and cover with buttercream or jam (conserve). Cover the prepared shape with the green sugarpaste (rolled fondant) (see page 22) and place on the cake board.

2 Colour 60g (2oz) sugarpaste navy. Using the template on page 252, cut out the hair and attach to the head. Texture the hair with lines using the rounded tip of a paintbrush handle.

3 Make the ears, eyebrows, lip and nose from green trimmings. Make eyes, teeth and mouth from 30g (1oz) each white and black using templates on page 252. Make 2 dark green eyeballs.

4 Attach all parts to the cake with water. Pipe an outline around the eyes and corners of the mouth with the no. 2 tube (tip) and black royal icing.

Birthday Express

A dream come true for any young boy hoping to be a train driver.

CAKE AND DECORATION

20cm (8in) square Madeira (pound) cake (see page 16)

buttercream (see page 18) or jam (conserve) for filling and covering

470g (15oz) navy sugarpaste (rolled fondant)

440g (14oz) white sugarpaste

small jam-filled Swiss (jelly) roll

60g (2oz/¼cup) royal icing (see page 17)

black, yellow, red and grey paste food colourings

coloured sweets (candies)

gold plastic bell

2 plastic 'Happy Birthday' writings

EQUIPMENT

30 x 20cm (12 x 8in) oblong cake board, covered with black paper (see TIP page 188)

assorted round cutters

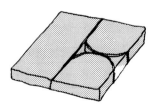

1 Cut the cake in half and sandwich with filling (see page 15). Cut out as shown and assemble to form the basic shape, joining the parts together with buttercream or jam (conserve).

2 Cover the prepared engine shape with navy sugarpaste (rolled fondant) (see page 22) and place on the cake board.

3 Cut the Swiss (jelly) roll to the required length, about 9cm (3¾in). If necessary, unroll the cake until the desired diameter of about 5.5cm (2¼in) is obtained. Cover the Swiss roll with

Tip

☆ As there are a lot of off-pieces and shapes to make for this cake, a short cut could be to use large sweets (candies) or shop-bought chocolate or icing-covered biscuits (cookies) for the wheels.

navy sugarpaste and attach to the engine with royal icing.

4 Colour 185g (6oz) sugarpaste black and roll out to about 2.5mm (⅛in) thick. Cut out a rectangle to form the roof, allowing about 5mm (¼in) overhang all the way around the roof. Attach to the cabin with royal icing.

5 Roll out the remaining black sugarpaste to 1cm (½in) thick and cut out eight small and two large wheels, using template below. Colour 60g (2oz) sugarpaste grey, roll out to a similar thickness and cut out two long bar shapes. Colour 45g (1½oz) sugarpaste

yellow and cut out the window shapes and the front plate. Make the boiler front from a circle of 60g (2oz) red sugarpaste; use the remaining red paste to model the funnel.

6 Attach the various parts to the train with royal icing, waiting a few minutes to allow each part to set a little.

7 Attach coloured sweets (candies) to the front of the train and to each wheel with royal icing. Attach the plastic bell behind the funnel and finish off with the plastic 'Happy Birthday' writings, attached to each side of the boiler with royal icing.

Wheels

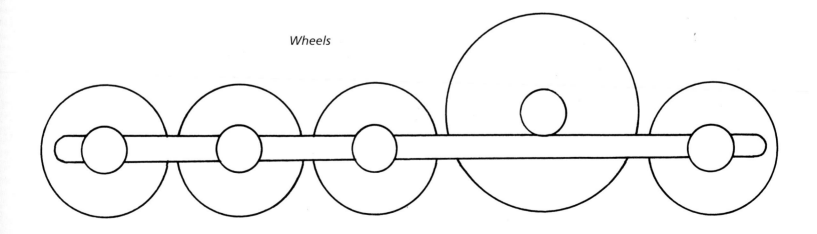

Party Cakes FOR OLDER CHILDREN

Beetle Mania

A young person's dream is to own a car just like this one. Change the colour of the sugarpaste for a boy.

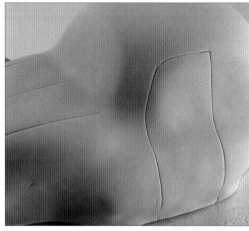

4 Mark lines for the door, bonnet and boot immediately, with a sharp knife, as shown. Do not cut all the way through the sugarpaste.

5 Using two pieces of pink sugarpaste the size of table tennis balls, model the front and back wings. Roll the sugarpaste into sausages, tapering them at one end. Lay in position, flattening the front end as you work. This is where the headlights will be positioned. Cut oblongs of thin white modelling paste for windows and windscreens, rounding

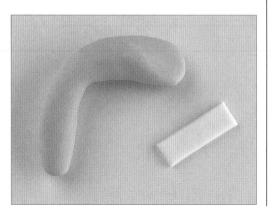

1 Turn the square cake upside down on a board and place the basin cake upside down on top. Carve the cakes to shape as illustrated. The sides should be slightly sloping, so that the car appears to be narrower at the top than the bottom.

2 Cut holes in the sides, near the front and rear, for the wheels. Slice the pieces of cake into layers and sandwich with the filling of your choice (see page 15), then assemble and attach to the cake board with a little royal icing. Coat with apricot glaze.

3 Colour 1kg (2lb) sugarpaste (rolled fondant) shocking pink, roll out and cover the cake (see page 22). Ease the paste gently over and into the curves, lifting out and smoothing away pleats and folds as you work.

CAKE AND DECORATION

25cm (10in) square Madeira (pound) cake (see page 16)

15cm (6in) diameter bowl-shaped Madeira (pound) cake*

strawberry jam (conserve), lemon curd or buttercream (see page 18) for filling

250ml (8fl oz/1 cup) apricot glaze (see page 21)

1.25kg (2½ lb) sugarpaste (rolled fondant)

pink, berry blue, yellow and liquorice black paste food colourings

125g (4oz) bought modelling paste

125g (4oz/½ cup) royal icing (see page 17)

cornflour (cornstarch) for dusting

silver lustre powder (petal dust/blossom tint)

1.5m (1½ yd) pink ribbon for board edge

EQUIPMENT

35cm (14in) round cake board

paper piping bag

no. 2 piping tube (tip)

plastic smoother

no. 1 paintbrush

ball modelling tool

cocktail stick (toothpick)

*Use the 15cm (6in) square Madeira mixture (see page 16)

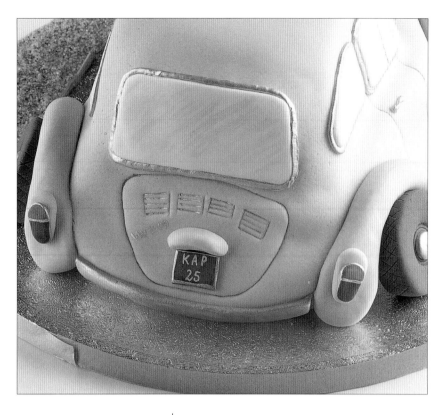

6 Pipe royal icing windscreen wipers and window rims on waxed paper using the no. 2 piping tube (tip). Paint silver when dry. Attach to windows and windscreen. Colour 175g (6oz) sugarpaste black and model four tyres, headlight bulbs, two bumpers and back numberplate. Colour the bumpers if liked. Attach all the pieces to the car. Paint on the car number. Mark the tyres with a criss-cross pattern to represent the tread. Mark on the radiator grilles (see picture left). Cut out the back lights using white modelling paste; attach and paint when dry.

7 To finish, paint on any other details, such as a VW sign on a small disk of modelling paste. Pipe royal icing door handles with the no. 2 piping tube. Paint silver when dry. Decorate the cake board with 'gravel' if liked (see page 28). Trim the edge of the board with pink ribbon.

off corners (see below), and front numberplate. Attach to cake. Measure the width of the car wings, cut out yellow sugarpaste headlights and mark lightly with a criss-cross pattern (see diagram below).

Tips

☆ *Always start with two equal-sized balls of sugarpaste (rolled fondant) when modelling identical items, so that both end up the same size.*

☆ *Always support unstable sugarpaste additions with pieces of foam sponge until they are thoroughly dried. For example, the wings of the car should be supported until the paste has dried.*

Headlight guide

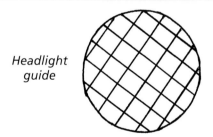

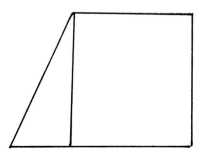

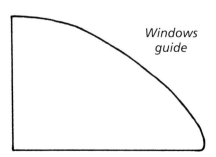

Windows guide

Chess Set

With the 'wood effect' borders and simplified pieces, this novel cake looks strikingly realistic – the ideal present for any chess enthusiast.

1 Preheat the oven to 140°C (275°F/Gas 1). Grease and line the base and sides of the cake tin (pan). Make up the cake mixture, turn it into the tin and level the surface. Bake in the oven for about 3 hours or until a skewer inserted in the centre comes out clean. Leave to cool in the tin.

2 Remove the cake from the tin and level the top by cutting off any peaks formed during baking. Invert the cake onto the cake board, positioning it at an angle. Brush the cake with apricot glaze, ~~then cover with marzipan (almond paste), then position some strips of~~ marzipan around the sides (see page 21).

3 Colour 375g (12oz) sugarpaste (rolled fondant) black. Thinly roll out the paste on a surface dusted with cornflour (cornstarch). Thinly roll out 375g (12oz) white sugarpaste. From each colour, cut out 32 squares, each measur-

ing 3cm (1¼in), for the chessboard. A pizza cutter gives a good cut as it does not 'drag' the paste out of shape.

4 Lay the squares over the cake, alternating colours as on a chessboard and leaving an even border around the sides.

5 Colour another 500g (1lb) of the sugarpaste brown, using the marbling technique described on page 23. Roll out the paste and cut out four strips, each 30cm (12in) long and as ~~wide as the depth of the cake. Fix the~~ strips around the sides of the cake. Use more brown icing to cover the top edges of the cake, securing with a dampened paintbrush and cutting the corners diagonally to neaten.

6 Knead the trimmings of brown sugarpaste with another 250g (8oz) sugarpaste, adding a little black, brown and red food colourings to produce a different-coloured wood effect.

7 Dampen the surface of the board around the base of the cake. Thinly roll out the icing and cut it into triangular pieces. Use to cover one side of the cake board at a time, smoothing the icing together at the joins and trimming off the excess from around the edges of the board.

8 Colour another 250g (8oz) sugarpaste dark grey, using black food colouring. To shape pawns, take 60g

CAKE AND DECORATION

rich fruit cake mixture for 23cm (9in) square cake tin (pan) (see page 16) baked in a 30cm (12in) square cake tin

3 tbsp apricot glaze (see page 21)

1kg (2lb) marzipan (almond paste)

icing (confectioners') sugar for dusting

2kg (4lb) sugarpaste (rolled fondant)

black, brown and red paste food colourings

cornflour (cornstarch) for dusting

EQUIPMENT

38cm (15in) square silver ~~board~~

large and fine paintbrushes

(2oz) grey sugarpaste and shape eight tiny balls, each the size of a pea. Divide the remainder of the 60g (2oz) piece into eight equal pieces. Shape into cones and position a small rolled ball on top of each.

9 Take another 125g (4oz) grey paste and cut into six equal pieces. Shape two into bishops, two into rooks, and two into knights, using the photograph below as a guide. Use actual chess pieces if possible to perfect shapes and details.

10 Use another 30g (1oz) grey sugarpaste for the queen and the remaining 30g (1oz) for the king. For both king and queen, roll and shape the crowns separately, then wrap them around the top of the cones, securing with a dampened paintbrush.

11 Make the white pieces in exactly the same way. Place the pieces on a sheet of greaseproof (parchment) or non-stick paper, or foil, to harden overnight, then arrange on and around the chessboard.

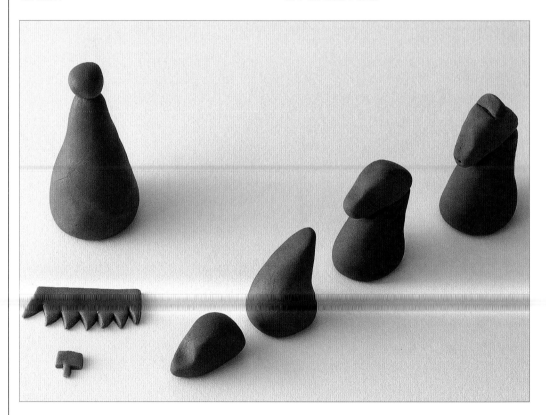

Tips

☆ *A Madeira (pound) cake mixture can easily be substituted for the rich fruit cake, if preferred. Use the same quantity of mixture and tin (pan) size as for the fruit cake to create a shallow sponge.*

☆ *The chess pieces are surprisingly easy to make. Each is shaped from a basic 'cone', but completed in a different way.*

Fishing Trip

A fun cake design to draw the attention of any young fishing enthusiast.

CAKE AND DECORATION

23cm (9in) round Madeira (pound) cake (see page 16)

7 tbsp raspberry or strawberry jam (conserve)

250g (8oz/1 cup) buttercream (see page 18)

1.5kg (3lb) sugarpaste (rolled fondant)

blue, brown, red, green and yellow food colourings

cornflour (cornstarch) for dusting

small piece of thread

1m (1yd) green ribbon, about 1cm (½in) wide

EQUIPMENT

28cm (11in) round silver cake board

fine paintbrush

cocktail sticks (toothpicks)

paper piping bag

no. 2 piping tube (tip)

Tip

☆ *Make the fisherman in his boat at least 24 hours before assembling the cake to allow time for the items to harden.*

1 Level the surface of the cake by cutting off any peaks, then cut it horizontally in half (see page 15). Spread the bottom layer with 4 tablespoons of the jam (conserve). Reserve 2 tablespoons of the buttercream and spread the rest over the jam. Cover with the top cake layer and place the cake on the board.

2 Sieve the remaining jam, then brush it over the cake top and side.

3 Colour 1kg (2lb) sugarpaste (rolled fondant) blue. Roll it out on a surface dusted with cornflour (cornstarch) and use to cover the cake (see page 22).

4 Colour another 60g (2oz) sugarpaste brown. Thinly roll out a little and cut out a leaf shape 7.5cm (3in) long and 2.5cm (1in) at its widest point. Cut two more strips, each 10cm (4in) long and 2cm (¾in) wide. Dampen the edges of the leaf shape, then secure the strips around it, pinching the ends together for the sides of a boat. Trim off any excess. Place on a piece of greaseproof (parchment) or non-stick paper.

5 Colour another 60g (2oz) paste pink using a dot of red colouring. Roll a small ball out for the fisherman's head. Shape an 8.5cm (3½in) sausage from the remaining pink paste, tapering it at the ends. Cut a 2.5cm (1in) slit from each end towards the centre. Open out one end and shape to resemble bent arms; cross the pieces at the other end for legs. Place in the boat. Position the fisherman's head as if resting on his

arms as he lies in the boat. (If necessary, prop up the sides of the boat with crumpled absorbent kitchen paper (paper towels) while the sugarpaste hardens.)

6 Colour another 250g (8oz) sugarpaste green. Roll it out thinly and cut out leaves in various sizes. Using a dampened paintbrush, secure them all around the side of the cake.

7 Press several cocktail sticks (toothpicks) at intervals into the cake side. Thread a small sausage of brown icing over the end of each for bulrushes.

8 Once the fisherman has hardened, paint on his clothes using different food colourings and a fine paintbrush. If liked, add icing hair, a hat, boots, hook etc. Secure the boat to the cake.

9 Push a cocktail stick into the base of the boat for a fishing rod. Tie thread on for a dangling line. Paint the rod brown or red. From the remaining paste, shape small fish heads and position on the water. Shape a small piece of sugarpaste on the fishing rod to resemble a reel.

10 Place the reserved buttercream in a piping bag fitted with the no. 2 piping tube (tip) and pipe ripples of water around the line, fish and boat.

11 Wrap the ribbon around the base of the cake, securing with a little buttercream. When serving this cake, remember to remove the bulrushes. Trim the board with ribbon.

Sewing Box

CAKE AND DECORATION

20 x 15cm (6 x 8in) oval Madeira (pound) cake*

1kg (2lb) sugarpaste (rolled fondant)

chestnut, claret, pink, violet and black paste food colourings, plus a selection for buttons and material

500g (1lb/2 cups) royal icing (see page 17)

confectioners' varnish

90g (3oz) pastillage (see page 17)

silver food colouring

75g (2½oz/¼cup) jam (conserve) for filling

250g (8oz/1cup) buttercream (see page 18)

625g (1lb 4oz) marzipan (almond paste)

1m (1yd) deep pink ribbon for board edge

EQUIPMENT

35 x 30cm (14 x 12in) oval cake board

ribbed rolling pin

paper piping bag

nos. 1, 2, 3, 13, 22 and 43 piping tubes (tips)

round cutters

crimper

straight frill cutter (optional)

* use the 18cm (7in) square Madeira mixture (see page 16)

As a personal touch, pipe a suitable inscription and name in stitch effect on this beautiful life-like cake.

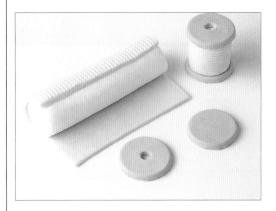

1 Roll 220g (7oz) sugarpaste (rolled fondant) into a sausage shape to make the cotton reel centres. Colour 60g (2oz) pale chestnut for the cotton reel tops, then divide and colour the remainder for the cotton colours. Roll out and form as shown, using a ribbed rolling pin to create the thread effect. Join all parts by moistening with water. Pipe a loose thread using the no. 1 piping tube (tip) and royal icing.

2 Roll out various colours of sugarpaste and use different-sized round cutters to make buttons. Use nos. 1 and 2 tubes to make holes in the buttons. Leave to dry, then glaze with confectioners' varnish.

3 Use the pastillage to model a small pair of scissors; have a real pair to hand to copy the proportions and shapes. Leave to dry, then paint with silver and pale chestnut colouring.

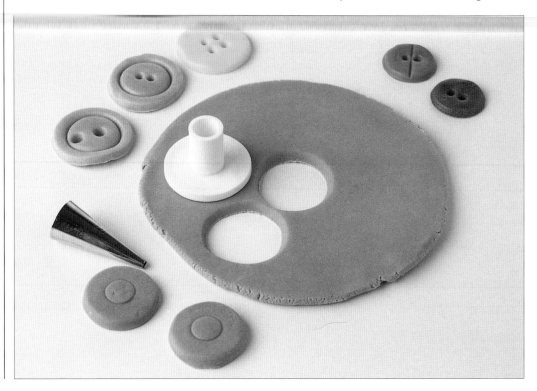

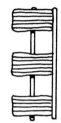

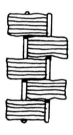

4 Prepare and layer the cake (see page 15). Cover the cake completely with a thin spreading of buttercream.

5 Roll out the marzipan (almond paste) and cover the cake (see page 21). Place the cake on a waxed paper-lined workboard ready to decorate.

6 Colour 250g (8oz/1 cup) royal icing dark claret and use 100g (3½oz/½cup) to fill a piping bag fitted with a no. 3 tube. Colour the remaining icing light claret and use some to fill a piping bag fitted with a no 22. basketwork tube. Pipe the basketwork onto the cake side as shown in the technique photograph, referring to the illustration left (see also page 31). Practise piping the basketwork technique on card first. Using the no. 3 tube, pipe a vertical line. With the basketwork tube, pipe short horizontal bands. The distance between each band should be the width of the basketwork tube. Ensure the bands are all the same length. Pipe a second vertical line just

resting on the edge of the bands. Again pipe short horizontal bands, this time between the first piped ones. Repeat the technique to complete the basketwork.

7 Make a template of the oval lid shape and cover with waxed paper on a flat board. Pipe the basketwork as described above. Leave to dry, then edge with a line piped using the no. 43 tube and the reserved dark claret icing. Pipe a small curved handle onto waxed paper using the no. 13 tube and dark claret icing. When dry, attach to the lid.

8 Take 500g (1lb) sugarpaste and colour half violet and half pink. Roll out the pink and violet pastes separately and cut into narrow strips. Moisten the cake board with water and lay alternate coloured strips to cover the board. Trim off the excess sugarpaste and then crimp the edge (see page 24).

9 Remove the prepared cake from the waxed paper and position on the prepared board, securing with a dab of icing. Pipe a small line border around the top and base edge using tube no. 43 and dark claret icing. Leave to dry.

10 Roll out two colours of the remaining sugarpaste very thinly and cut into squares for the material. Fancy edges can be created using a straight frill cutter. Arrange the material pieces quickly into folds and drapes before they set, tucking some inside and resting some on top of the prepared lid. Attach the lid and pieces with icing. Trim the board with ribbon.

11 Arrange and attach the prepared cotton reels, buttons and scissors with dabs of icing. Make the needles by piping onto waxed paper using the no. 1 piping tube and white icing. Leave to dry, then paint with silver colouring. Attach the needles with dabs of icing and pipe thread using the no. 1 piping tube and black royal icing. Pipe an inscription on the cake, if liked.

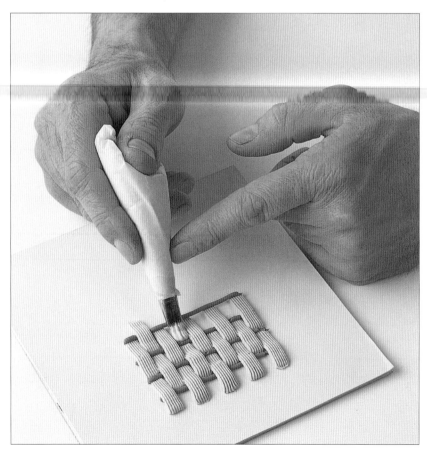

Greenhouse

To create a realistic glass effect, cut out shapes of leaf gelatine to fit the various greenhouse panes.

CAKE AND DECORATION

three 20cm (8in) square Madeira (pound) cakes (see page 16)

90g (3oz) pastillage (see page 17)

yellow, blue, paprika, peach, red, violet, orange, brown and green paste food colourings

yellow, orange and red dusting powders (petal dusts/blossom tints)

orange and black food colouring pens

315g (10oz/1cup) jam (conserve) for filling

470g (15oz/2 cups) buttercream (see page 18)

fondant)

200g (7oz/¾ cup) royal icing (see page 17)

1.5m (1½yd) green ribbon for board edge

EQUIPMENT

33cm (13in) square cake board

petal cutter

small round cutter

scriber

nos. 1 and 2 sable paintbrushes

brickwork rolling pin

small piece of foam sponge for stippling

paper piping bag

no. 2 piping tube (tip)

1 Make the sunshine design using the template and cutters. Reserve 7g (¼oz) white pastillage and colour the remainder yellow. Roll out the pastillage thinly and cut the three-quarter circle and petal shapes. Lay the circle on a waxed paper-lined board, moisten the edge and attach the petal shapes.

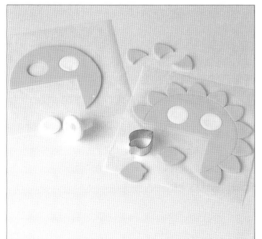

2 Using a small round cutter, remove two holes for the eyes. Roll out the white pastillage and cut out two circles to fill the holes. Smooth with the fingers to conceal the join. Leave to dry, then colour with yellow and orange dusting powders (petal dusts/blossom tints). Use orange and black food colour pens to draw the nose, eyes and mouth.

3 Prepare the cakes, cutting and shaping as shown on page 158 to form the basic house shape. Layer the

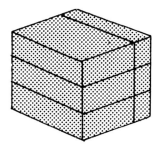

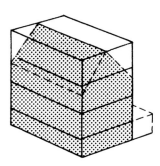

cakes as described on page 15. Cover the cake completely with a thin spreading of buttercream.

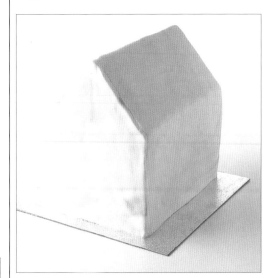

4 Reserve 1kg 60g (2lb 2oz) sugarpaste (rolled fondant) for later use. Colour 45g (1½oz) sugarpaste blue and knead through the remaining white sugarpaste; do not mix thoroughly. Roll out to create a streaked appearance and use to cover the cake (see page 22). Take care with the corners, smoothing with the fingers to create neat joins. The streaked effect will help convey the effect of glass in the finished greenhouse (see also the introduction to this recipe).

5 Use a ruler and scriber to mark the positions of the frame on the greenhouse. Make templates of the flower designs below and, using a scriber, pinprick onto the cake. Paint the

flowers, foliage, seed boxes and plant pots using fine paintbrushes and colourings. Outline the flowers and pots with a food colouring pen. Leave to dry.

6 Colour 280g (9oz) of the reserved sugarpaste with paprika and peach colourings. Roll out the sugarpaste and texture with the brickwork rolling pin. Cut the prepared paste into the required shapes, moisten the lower half of the cake and attach the shapes to make the wall. Leave a gap for the door. Leave to dry, then tint with orange and red dusting powders.

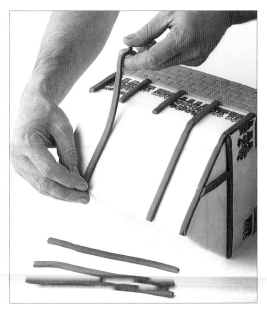

7 Colour 155g (5oz) of the reserved sugarpaste brown for the frame. Roll out and cut into long strips. Attach to the cake by moistening with water, using the pre-marked lines as a guide.

8 Colour the remaining sugarpaste green and cover the board (see page 24). Colour 60g (2oz) royal icing green and, using a small piece of foam sponge, stipple the board to create a grass effect. Leave to dry, then place the cake on the board and secure with dabs of icing. Using sugarpaste trimmings, make a path following the method for gravel described on page 28. Attach the prepared pastillage sunshine with a line of royal icing piped using the no. 2 tube (tip). Cover the board edge with ribbon.

Tip

☆ A door and roof window could be made in advance from pastillage and allowed to dry on waxed paper. The prepared pieces would then be attached to the cake with royal icing to appear as if they were ajar.

Golf Bag

For budding golfing fanatics when they're off the green, this is an ideal cake and will be much admired.

CAKE AND DECORATION

20 x 10cm (8 x 4in) Swiss (jelly) roll (see page 14)

155g (5oz/⅔ cup) buttercream (see page 18)

cake trimmings/off-cuts

2kg (4lb) sugarpaste (rolled fondant)

green, brown, chestnut, red, yellow and blue paste food colourings

250g (8oz) pastillage (see page 17)

silver food colouring

185g (6oz/¾ cup) royal icing (see page 17)

90g (3oz/⅓ cup) chocolate, melted (see page 32)

1m (1yd) yellow ribbon for board edge

EQUIPMENT

36cm (14in) petal shaped cake board

small piece of foam sponge for stippling

ball modelling tool

no. 3 sable paintbrush

paper piping bag

no. 1 piping tube (tip)

1 Prepare the cake (see page 14), reserving any trimmings, then stand as shown. Cover the cake with buttercream.

2 Arrange the cake trimmings on the board to form a mound, attaching with dabs of buttercream. Colour 1.1kg (2lb 2oz) sugarpaste (rolled fondant) green and cover the board (see page 24). Stipple the sugarpaste with browny-green royal icing (see page 27).

3 Colour 60g (2oz) pastillage brown and roll out. Cut out a long narrow

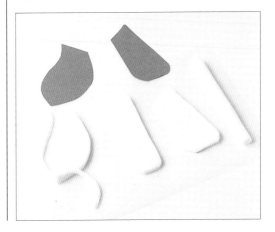

strip for the handle and leave to dry on crumpled foil to create a natural shape. Cut out three golf club heads from remaining pastillage using templates on page 251. Add the markings using a knife. Also roll out three handles. Leave to dry. Attach the heads to the handles. When dry, paint with silver food colouring.

4 Use the remaining white pastillage to model a golf ball, indenting the surface with a ball modelling tool. Also model some tees. Leave to dry, then paint with food colourings.

5 Colour the remaining sugarpaste brown. Roll out and cover the cake (see page 22), forming a shallow collar around the top. Use trimmings to model the pocket, moisten and attach. Secure the cake to the board with royal icing. Attach the prepared handle with brown icing. Pipe on stitching using a no. 1 piping tube (tip) and pale brown icing.

6 Pour melted chocolate into the top of the golf bag then insert the golf clubs. Arrange the tees and ball and attach with icing. Trim the board with yellow ribbon.

Tip

☆ *As an alternative to using Swiss (jelly) roll to create the golf bag shape, use three 10cm (4in) round Madeira (pound) cakes (see page 16, using half the 20cm (8in) round cake mixture) sandwiched on top of each other.*

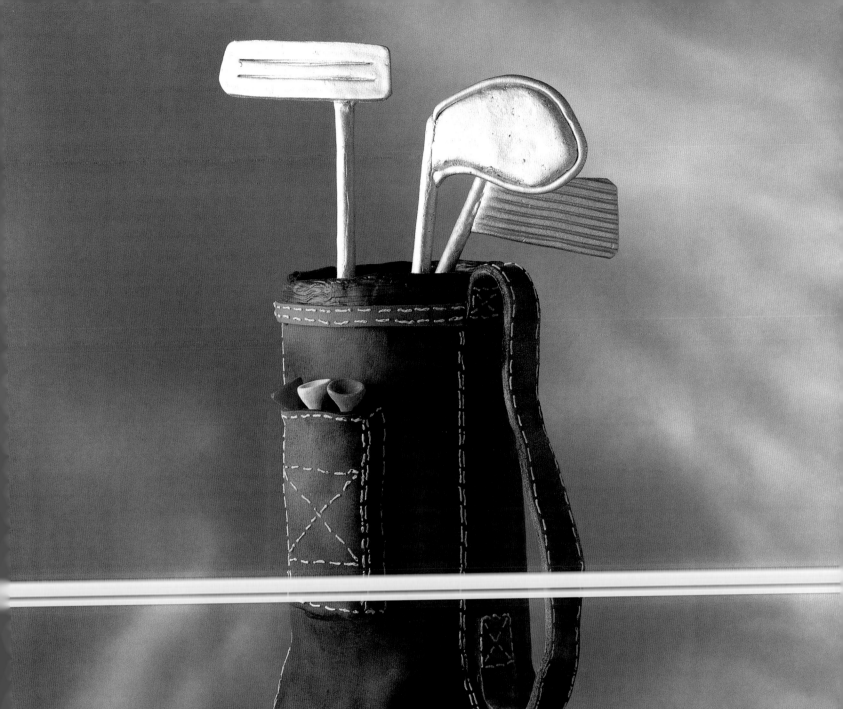

Computer

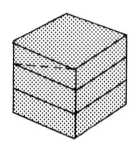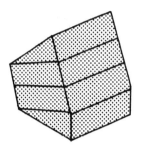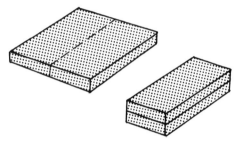

Anyone with an interest in computers, whether for homework or games, would be delighted with this realistic novelty cake.

CAKE AND DECORATION

three 18cm (7in) square Madeira (pound) cakes (see page 16)

20cm (8in) square Madeira cake

185g (6oz) pastillage (see page 17)

yellow, blue, red and cream dusting powders (petal dusts/blossom tints)

black food colouring pen

140g (4½oz/scant ½ cup) jam (conserve) for filling

500g (1lb/2 cups) buttercream (see page 18)

2.1kg (4lb 4oz) white sugarpaste (rolled fondant)

2.5m (2½yd) white ribbon for board edge

black and green paste food colourings

liquorice 'lace'

185g (6oz/¾ cup) royal icing (see page 17)

EQUIPMENT

cardboard tube

38cm (15in) square cake board

paper piping bag

nos. 1 and 3 piping tubes (tips)

short length of wooden dowel

wooden skewer

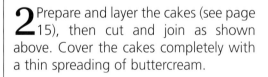

1 Prepare in advance the pencil holder, pencils, sheet of note paper and notepad, giving them time to dry adequately. Model each item from white pastillage, shaping the pencil holder around a cardboard tube to be removed later. The sheet of note paper is thinly rolled pastillage with a row of holes removed using the no. 3 piping tube (tin), dried over crumpled foil. Make the notepad from a thick rectangle of pastillage and punch out a row of holes. When dry, colour the items using dusting powders (petal dusts/blossom tints). Add detail with a black food colouring pen.

2 Prepare and layer the cakes (see page 15), then cut and join as shown above. Cover the cakes completely with a thin spreading of buttercream.

3 Roll out 750g (1lb 8oz) sugarpaste (rolled fondant) and use to cover the board (see page 24). Trim with ribbon.

4 Colour 125g (4oz) sugarpaste black and reserve. Using a small amount of black food colouring, colour the

remaining sugarpaste grey. Roll out 185g (6oz) and cut into small squares as shown to make the keys. Leave to dry on a waxed paper-lined tray.

5 Roll out the remaining grey sugarpaste and cover both cakes (see page 22). Roll out the black sugarpaste thinly and cut out a rectangle for the screen. Moisten the grey sugarpaste and attach the shape. Roll out some grey trimmings and cut into strips. Moisten the edges of the black screen and attach the strips to create a frame.

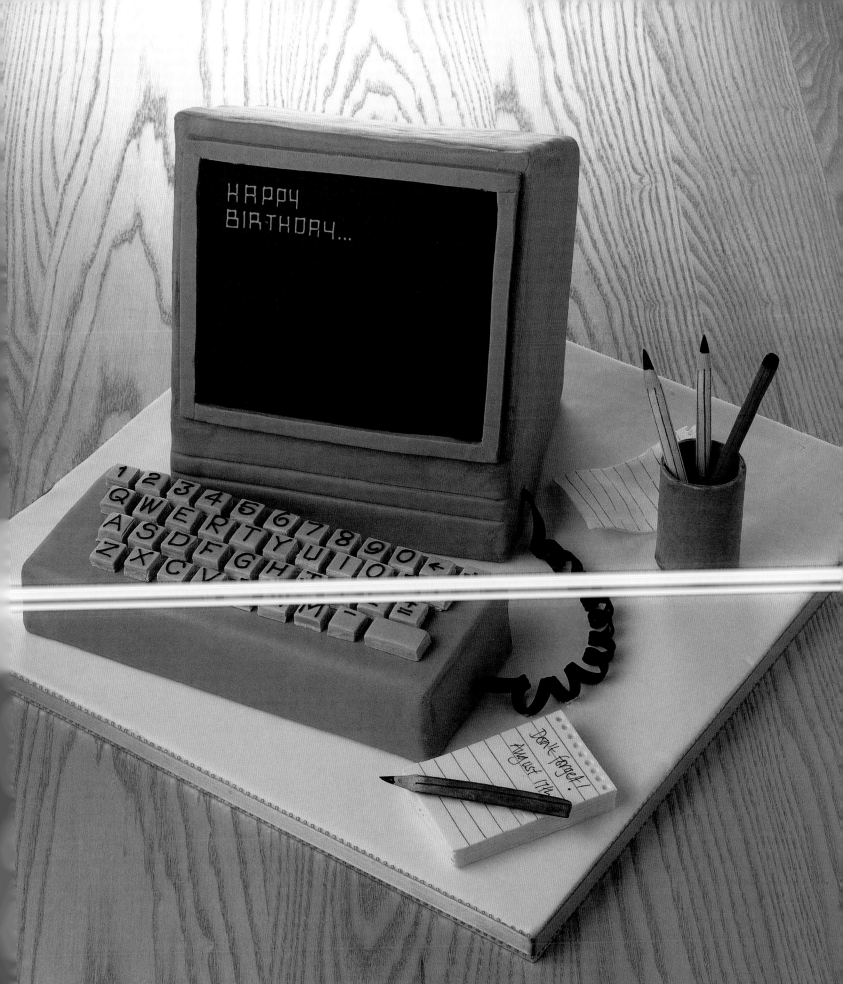

HAPPY BIRTHDAY

8 Colour 45g (1½oz/¼ cup) royal icing green and, using the no. 1 piping tube, pipe the inscription in 'digital' style lettering on the black screen. (See TIP for other inscriptions or message ideas.)

9 Position the screen and keyboard cakes on the prepared board and secure with dabs of the remaining royal icing. Make a small hole in the side of each cake using a wooden skewer. Link the two cakes together by inserting the prepared liquorice coil into the holes. Arrange the pencil holder, pencils, paper and notepad on the board, securing each with dabs of royal icing.

Tip

☆ *To personalize this cake creatively, simply alter the inscription or message on the screen and also include the recipient's name. The date written on the notepad could be the birthday or anniversary of the individual.*

6 Unravel the liquorice and wind neatly around a short length of greased dowel. Place on a waxed paper-lined tray and bake at 160°C (325°F/Gas 3) for about 6 minutes. Remove from the oven, cool slightly and then carefully unwind from the dowel.

7 Colour 45g (1½oz/⅓ cup) royal icing black and, using the no. 1 tube, pipe the letters and numerals onto the prepared grey sugarpaste keys. Set aside to dry. Attach to the prepared keyboard cake with dabs of royal icing.

Desert Island

Here's a cake to remind someone of a great holiday or for anyone who would love their very own treasure island.

1 Colour the caster (superfine) sugar with paprika colouring to create the sand. Spread the coloured sugar on a greaseproof (parchment) or non-stick paper-lined tray and leave to dry naturally for use later.

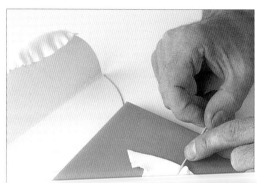

2 Roll out thinly 60g (2oz) pastillage. Make a template of the design left and cut out seven palm fronds. Use a cocktail stick (toothpick) as shown above to frill the edges. Mark the vein detail using the back of a knife and cut a few slits. Allow the shapes to dry over a former as shown.

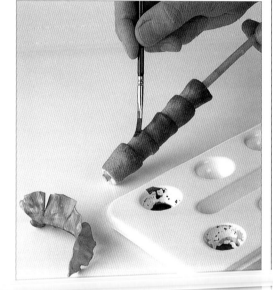

3 For the trunk of the palm tree, colour 60g (2oz) pastillage mustard-coloured (yellow and brown). Roll out on a surface dusted with a cornflour (cornstarch) and cut into strips. Wrap a strip around the dowel, moisten the end and secure. Repeat the method, overlapping each strip until the dowel is almost fully covered, leaving 7.5cm (3in) exposed. Leave to dry. Paint the palm fronds green.

Tip

☆ To make this cake more suited to a sun worshipper or for a happy holiday cake, make pastillage sunshine as described for the Greenhouse cake (see page 157) and attach to the back of the board to peep over the island.

CAKE AND DECORATION

two 15cm (6in) round Madeira (pound) cakes (see page 16)

60g (2oz/¼ cup) caster (superfine) sugar

paprika, yellow, brown, green, red, tangerine, blueberry, blue and peach paste food colourings

220g (7oz) pastillage (see page 17)

cornflour (cornstarch) for dusting

155g (5oz/⅔ cup) royal icing (see page 17)

orange and brown dusting powders (petal dusts/blossom tints)

940g (1lb 14oz)

1m (1yd) white ribbon for board edge

60g (2oz/scant ¼ cup) jam (conserve) for filling

185g (6oz/¾ cup) buttercream (see page 18)

clear alcohol (gin or vodka)

EQUIPMENT

cocktail stick (toothpick)

curved former

plastic or wooden dowel

no. 2 sable paintbrush

30cm (12in) round cake board

165

4 Make templates of the designs left for the star fish, shells and leaping fish. Roll out the remaining pastillage and cut out the shapes. Mark the detail on the pastillage while still soft. Leave the pieces to dry. Model the body of the crab and claws. Leave to dry, then join parts together with royal icing.

5 When all the shaped pieces are fully set, add the detail and effects using food colourings and petal dusts (dusting powders/blossom tints).

6 Colour 470g (15oz) sugarpaste (rolled fondant) blue and use to cover the cake board (see page 24). To create a sea effect see page 18. Attach the ribbon to the board edge.

7 Prepare and layer the cakes (see page 15) then, using a small serrated knife, cut away small, irregular-shaped pieces from the top edge of the cake. Position the pieces around the cake at random, attaching to the main cake with buttercream – this will create the basic island shape. Alternatively, truffle paste (see page 20) can be used to make the rugged island shape. Cover the cake completely with a thin spreading of buttercream.

8 Colour 470g (15oz) sugarpaste peach. Roll out the sugarpaste and use to cover the cake (see page 22), pressing the sugarpaste gently into the contoured surface.

9 Brush the sugarpaste lightly with alcohol and sprinkle with the prepared coloured caster sugar to create a sand effect. Remove excess sugar. Position the cake off-centre on the cake board, securing with a dab of royal icing.

10 Position the tree trunk on the cake, securing with a little royal icing. Leave to set. Attach the leaves individually with royal icing, leaving each one to set before adding another. Position and attach the shells, star fish, crab and leaping fish as shown.

Wallet Cake

CAKE AND DECORATION

15cm (6in) square Madeira (pound) cake mixture (see page 16), baked in a 23cm (9in) square cake tin (pan)

4 tbsp apricot glaze (see page 21)

1.5kg (3lb) sugarpaste (rolled fondant)

black, brown and gold food colourings

cornflour (cornstarch) for dusting

football or other collecting cards

1 bag gold chocolate coins

1 bag silver chocolate coins

EQUIPMENT

30cm (12in) square gold cake board

polythene bag

fine paintbrush

Gold and silver chocolate coins are now available from supermarkets most of the year. Tumbling out of a simply moulded 'wallet', they make an effective cake for an older child.

1 Preheat the oven to 160°C (325°F/Gas 3). Grease and line the cake tin (pan). Spoon the cake mixture into the tin and level the surface. Bake in the oven for about 40 minutes or until firm. Turn out onto a wire rack and leave to cool.

2 Level the surface of the cake by cutting off any peak that formed during baking. Invert the cake onto the cake board and brush with apricot glaze.

3 Colour 1.1kg (2¼lb) sugarpaste (rolled fondant) pale grey, using black food colouring. Roll it out on a surface dusted with cornflour (cornstarch) and use to cover the cake (see page 22).

4 Colour the remaining sugarpaste brown. Roll out two-thirds and cut out a 20cm (8in) square. Lay this over the cake.

5 Crumple up a polythene bag, then slightly uncrumple it and lay it on top of the brown icing. Roll lightly with a rolling pin to give the icing a textured finish. Remove the bag. Using a knife, make several horizontal cuts down one side of the wallet and insert the cards.

6 Scatter some coins over the other side of the icing, then dampen the edges of the sugarpaste with water. Roll more brown icing to a 21 x 10cm (8¼ x 4in) rectangle. Use the polythene bag to texture it in the same way, then lay it

over the coins, pressing the edges gently together to secure.

7 Paint the teeth of a zip along the edge of the icing. Shape a small zip end from trimmings, position this on the cake and paint it gold.

8 Using black food colouring, paint 'stitches' around the wallet. Trim the cake board edge, if liked.

Tip

☆ *Before inserting the cards, dust them with cornflour (cornstarch) so they can easily be pulled out before the cake is cut.*

Witches' Cauldron

CAKE AND DECORATION

18cm (7in) round Madeira (pound) cake mixture (see page 16)

125g (4oz/½ cup) buttercream (see page 18)

4 tbsp raspberry or strawberry jam (conserve)

1.5kg (3lb) sugarpaste (rolled fondant)

green, orange, black, red and silver food colourings

cornflour (cornstarch) for dusting

3 large chocolate flake bars

250g (8oz/1 cup) royal icing (see page 17)

EQUIPMENT

850ml (1½ pt) ovenproof mixing bowl

30cm (12in) round silver cake board

large paintbrush

fine paintbrush

Tip

☆ The 'spell book' is made by cutting a rectangle of black paste trimmings, adding white pages, and finishing with painted symbols. The edges of the pages are brushed with diluted black colouring to give an old, wrinkled appearance.

This fun scary cake allows you to get really carried away when making the contents of the cauldron!

1 Preheat the oven to 160°C (325°F/Gas 3). Grease and line the base of the mixing bowl. Spoon the cake mixture into the bowl and level the surface. Bake in the oven for 1¼–1½ hours or until firm. Turn out onto a wire rack and leave to cool.

2 Level the surface of the cake by cutting off any peak that formed during baking. Cut the cake horizontally into three, then reassemble it, sandwiching the layers together with the buttercream and jam (conserve).

3 Colour 315g (10oz) sugarpaste (rolled fondant) dark green and 90g (3oz) a paler green. Colour another 125g (4oz) orange. Leave 90g (3oz) of the remainder white, and colour the rest black.

4 Lightly brush the surface of the cake board with water. Roll out the dark green sugarpaste on a surface dusted with cornflour (cornstarch). Lay the icing over the board and smooth it out using hands dusted with cornflour. Trim off the excess around the edge of the board.

5 Place the cake, widest side down, on a sheet of greaseproof (parchment) or non-stick paper. Reserve 185g (6oz) of the black paste. Roll out the remainder and use it to cover the cake (see page 22), smoothing the icing around the side to eliminate creases. Trim off the excess around the base and reserve the trimmings. Carefully turn the cake the other way up and position it to one side of the cake board.

6 Cut the chocolate flake bars into chunks and arrange around the side of the cauldron. Shape long, pointed 'flames' of orange paste and tuck them around the base of the cauldron, securing with a dampened paintbrush. Roll a long, thin sausage of black paste and position it around the top of the cauldron to make a rim. Secure with water.

7 Use the remaining black paste and the paler green paste to shape the contents of the cauldron. Add two white 'eyeballs'.

8 Colour the royal icing green and pour over the top of the cake so the contents of the cauldron show above the surface. Shape any remaining green sugarpaste into 'bubbles' and position around the edge. Paint details on the 'eyeballs' using a fine paintbrush and black, red and silver colourings. Trim the board with black ribbon, if wished.

Barge Cake

CAKE AND DECORATION

25cm (10in) square Madeira (pound) cake (see page 16)

strawberry jam (conserve), lemon curd or buttercream (see page 18) for filling

8 tbsp apricot glaze (see page 21)

1.25kg (2½lb) sugarpaste (rolled fondant)

liquorice black, berry blue, mint green, Christmas red, melon yellow, tangerine and dark brown paste food colourings

250g (8oz/1 cup) royal icing (see page 17)

125g (4oz) bought modelling paste

raspberry pink liquid food colouring

1.25m (4ft) blue ribbon for board edge

EQUIPMENT

30cm (12in) square cake board

nos. 1 and 2 paintbrushes

ball modelling tool

pieces of foam sponge

paper piping bag

Almost all children love boats and boating with their lure of endless adventures.

1 Using the template on page 252, cut the basic shape of the barge, as shown. Cut a 10 x 7.5cm (4 x 3in) oblong from the remaining sponge for the cabin. Cut the oblong so that it is slightly narrower than the width of the barge and approximately 7.5cm (3in) long. Place a 2.5cm (1in) strip of sponge cake along the back end of the cabin. Slice the cakes in two layers and sandwich with the filling of your choice (see page 15). Attach to the board with royal icing and assemble as shown.

2 Hollow out the front and back of the barge down to approximately 5mm (¼in) in depth, as illustrated. Take care to keep the sides even and not to cut right through the cake. Remove the cabin from the barge; this will be covered separately. Coat the cakes with apricot glaze.

3 Roll out 500g (1lb) sugarpaste (rolled fondant) and cover the barge (see page 22). Colour 125g (4oz) sugarpaste red, roll out and cover the cabin, then attach to the barge with a little royal icing.

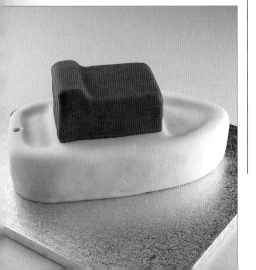

6 Use modelling paste to make a tiller, rail, bucket, lifebelt and duck. Leave to dry, then paint on any details and attach the pieces to the barge with a little royal icing.

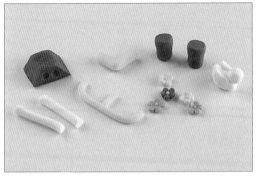

7 Colour some royal icing blue and spread it on the board around the barge with a paddling motion, using a palette knife (metal spatula) to produce a rough watery effect. Add swirls of darker blue and white royal icing to give a little more depth.

8 Paint any final details on the barge, such as a name. Place a little blue royal icing in a greaseproof (parchment) paper piping bag without a piping tube (tip) and cut off the tip of the bag roughly to the size of a no. 3 piping tube. Pipe some water ripples along the bottom edge of the barge. Trim the edge of the cake board with blue ribbon.

Tip

☆ *The barge can be decorated as simply or with as colourful a pattern as you please. Plant pots on barges usually have a black background with bright flowers. Always paint the flowers first, then outline them with black food colouring and fill in the background.*

4 Colour several pieces of sugarpaste in bright colours. Roll out and cut strips or other shapes to decorate the sides of the barge. Follow the ideas used on the cake illustrated or vary them according to your requirements.

5 Colour a plum-sized piece of modelling paste chocolate brown. Model the bargeman's body, arms and legs (see above). Model a head and hands using flesh-coloured modelling paste. Model a flat cap in brown paste. Make a scarf and paint it when dry.

Bucket

Rail

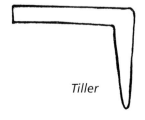

Tiller

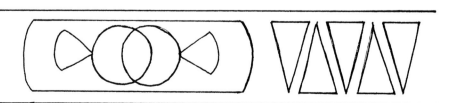

Barge side

174

Special Occasion CAKES

Moulded Fruits Cake

CAKE AND DECORATION

25cm (10in) round Madeira (pound) cake mixture (see page 16) baked in a 25cm (10in) petal-shaped tin (pan)

250g (8oz/1cup) butter-cream (see page 18)

juice of 2 oranges

4 tbsp apricot glaze (see page 21)

1.5kg (3lb) sugarpaste (rolled fondant)

yellow, red, blue, black, green food colourings

cornflour (cornstarch) for dusting

500g (1lb) marzipan (almond paste)

250g (8oz/1cup) royal icing (see page 17)

2m (2¼yd) soft red ribbon, about 2.5cm (1in) wide

EQUIPMENT

33cm (13in) round or petal-shaped silver cake board

scalloped crimping tool

fine paintbrush

small five-point star or calyx cutter

paper piping bag

no. 0/1 piping tube (tip)

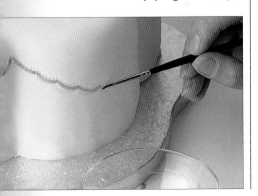

This cake is decorated with marzipan (almond paste) 'soft' fruits rather than the more usual apples, pears, etc. Perfect for a summer celebration.

1 Level the surface of the cake by cutting off any peak that formed during baking. Slice the cake horizontally in half and sandwich the layers together again with the buttercream. Place the cake on the cake board. Drizzle the orange juice over the cake. Brush the cake with apricot glaze.

2 Colour the sugarpaste (rolled fondant) yellow. Roll it out on a surface dusted with cornflour (cornstarch) and use to cover the cake, following the method for covering a round cake on page 22. Press the icing into the flutes of the petal shape. Trim off excess around the base of the cake and reserve for making strawberry calyxes.

3 Trace the template on page 251 onto greaseproof (parchment) or non-stick paper. Cut out the shape and place it against one of the rounded sides of the cake. Mark the curved outline on the cake with a pin. Repeat all round the cake.

4 Using a scalloped crimping tool, make a decorative pattern over the template line (see page 28).

5 Dilute a little red food colouring with water and use to paint the crimped line with a fine paintbrush. The crimped line stands out well once it is painted.

6 Use the food colourings, marzipan (almond paste) and reserved sugarpaste to make the moulded soft fruits (see page 29). You will need 16–18

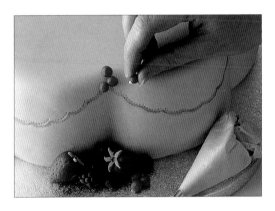

strawberries and blackberries, about 60 blueberries and about 120 redcurrants.

7 Put the royal icing in a paper piping bag fitted with a piping tube (tip), and use to secure the fruits to the cake. Start by piling up one or two strawberries and blackberries at the base of each tier, then continue adding the smaller fruits, finishing with a cluster of redcurrants at the top. You only need a tiny dot of royal icing to secure each redcurrant to the cake.

8 Arrange the ribbon and remaining fruits over the top of the cake and trim the board with ribbon if wished.

Tip

☆ *For the cake top, try and use decorative ribbon with a central thread that you can pull up to gather it. Or, loop ordinary ribbon, securing it to the cake with dots of royal icing. The moulded soft fruits, piled up on top, hide the piping.*

Ribbons and Rose Cake

CAKE AND DECORATION

25cm (10in) round rich fruit cake (see page 16)

4 tbsp apricot glaze (see page 21)

1.5kg (3lb) marzipan (almond paste)

icing (confectioners') sugar for dusting

2kg (4lb) sugarpaste (rolled fondant)

cornflour (cornstarch) for dusting

pale pink, deep pink and gold food colourings

1m (1yd) pale pink ribbon, about 1cm (½in) wide

250g (8oz/1 cup) royal icing (see page 17)

pink dusting powder (petal dust/blossom tint)

30cm (12in) fine gold cord

EQUIPMENT

30cm (12in) round silver cake board

small piece of foam sponge

paper piping bag

nos. 1 and 2 piping tubes (tips)

fine paintbrush

Tip

☆ *Before stippling the cake's surface, practise on a square piece of icing. The colour should be well diluted to give a pale finish; the sponge should not be saturated.*

With its two-tone pink colourings and stippled surface, this would make an ideal cake for a young lady on a very special birthday.

1 Brush the cake with apricot glaze and cover with marzipan (almond paste) (see page 21). Place on the cake board.

2 Reserve 500g (1lb) of the sugarpaste (rolled fondant). Roll out the remainder and use to cover the cake (see page 22).

3 Dilute a little pale pink colouring with water on a plate. Dip the foam sponge in the colour, then gently dab the surface of the cake so that it becomes lightly stippled. Repeat until the top and side of the cake is evenly stippled, then leave to dry. (See also TIP.)

4 Use a little sugarpaste to make a large white rose (see page 25) and leave to harden. Reserve 125g (4oz) of the remaining sugarpaste and colour the rest with the two shades of pink colouring, using the marbling technique described on page 23.

5 Thinly roll out the marbled sugarpaste on a surface dusted with cornflour (cornstarch) and cut into strips 5cm (2in) wide; reserving the trimmings. Trim the ends of the strips neatly, either square or at an angle, then drape them across the cake, looping them to give a ribbon effect. Secure the undersides of the strips to the cake with a dampened paintbrush and let the ends hang down the side of the cake.

6 Knead the marbled pink trimmings until evenly coloured, adding more

deep pink if necessary. Use them to cover the cake board around the cake (see page 23).

7 Roll out the reserved white sugarpaste and cut into strips 1cm (½in) wide. Arrange these over the top of the cake.

8 Wrap the pink ribbon around the base of the cake, securing it with a dot of royal icing. Place royal icing in a paper piping bag fitted with a no. 2 piping tube (tip) and use to pipe small shells around the base of the cake.

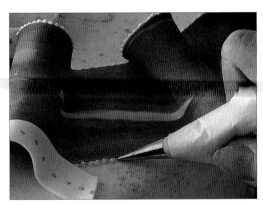

9 Using a fine paintbrush and gold food colouring, paint small dots along the white icing ribbon. Using pink dusting powder (petal dust/blossom tint) and a paintbrush, lightly colour the inner areas of the rose.

10 Tie the gold cord into a bow and secure with the rose on the top of the cake. Place more royal icing in a bag fitted with a no. 1 piping tube and pipe dots along the edges of the icing ribbons.

Fuchsia Cake

A triangular cake is eye-catchingly different and its shape is enhanced by the elegance of a fuchsia's hanging blooms.

CAKE AND DECORATION

25 x 20cm (10 x 8in) Madeira (pound) cake*

685g (1lb 6oz) sugarpaste (rolled fondant)

pale pink paste food colouring

buttercream (see page 18) or jam (conserve) for filling and covering

125g (4oz/½ cup) royal icing (see page 17)

lavender, pink, violet and green food colourings

1m (1yd) narrow fuchsia ribbon

1m (1yd) fuchsia ribbon for board edge

EQUIPMENT

triangular cake board

large carnation cutter or 3.5cm (1⅛in) fluted round cutter

paper piping bag

no. 1 piping tube (tip)

paintbrush

*use the 25cm (10in) square Madeira mixture (see page 16)

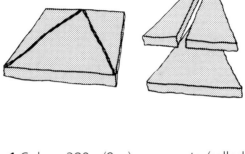

1 Colour 280g (9oz) sugarpaste (rolled fondant) pale pink. Roll out and cover the cake board, trimming the edges neatly (see page 24). Cut the cake as shown and join together with buttercream or jam (conserve) to make a triangular shape. Cover the top and sides with buttercream or jam. Roll out 345g (11oz) pink sugarpaste and cover the cake (see page 22). Place the cake on the prepared board.

2 Roll out the remaining sugarpaste and use the carnation cutter or small fluted round cutter to cut out several fluted circles to make the border pieces. Cut each circle neatly in half with a small sharp knife. Make three circles with a 'v' shape cut out to fit the angle of the pointed corners. Attach the pieces to the cake board with water.

3 Using a no. 1 piping tube (tip) with lavender-coloured royal icing, pipe a small, plain shell border around the base of the cake where the fluted semi-circles join the cake sides.

4 Attach the narrow ribbon and a bow around the cake, securing the join at the back with a dab of royal icing.

5 Trace the stencil design on page 182 and place on the cake top. Using a small palette knife (metal spatula), spread royal icing across all the cut-outs – carefully remove the stencil. Trim the board edge with ribbon.

6 Make a tracing of the inscription on page 182 and pin-prick onto the cake top. Pipe the inscription using the same lavender icing and tube as before. Using a fine brush with food colourings,

> ## Tip
>
> ☆ To ensure a neat and professional finish is achieved, it is worth taking the time to arrange the cut-out border shapes alongside the cake to check the spacing between each piece is equal, before sticking them to the board.

paint in the coloured detail on the raised icing of the stencilled motif.
Note: The lettering shown on the cake is piped using a no. 1.5 tube (tip) with slightly softened royal icing (see page 31).

As an alternative, choose from the wide range of plastic lettering available from cake-decorating shops.

Fuchsia design stencil

Lettering

With Love X

Broderie Anglaise Cake

With its delicate piping and decorations, this pretty cake would make the perfect centrepiece for any special occasion.

1 Brush the cake with apricot glaze and cover with marzipan (almond paste) (see page 21). Place on the cake board.

2 Colour 1kg (2lb/4 cups) royal icing the palest shade of yellow and use to apply two or three coats of flat icing (see page 30). Leave the last coat overnight to harden.

3 Cut out a 28cm (11in) circle of greaseproof (parchment) or non-stick paper. Fold it in half, then into quarters. Fold once again to create a cone of eight layers of paper. Trace the

4 Open out the outer template and lay it on the board around the cake. Secure it in place with pins. Place a little decorative icing in a paper piping bag fitted with a no. 1 piping tube (tip) and pipe scallops on the board, around the template. Remove the template.

5 Unfold the small template and lay it on top of the cake. Secure with pins. Mark the scalloped border with icing in the same way. Remove the template. Pipe a line of icing 5mm (¼in) inside the top edge of the cake.

one of the end sections of the cone. Cut out the shaded areas of the template through all the layers of paper. (The outer shaded area forms the template for the board; the inner shaded area is the template for the top of the cake.)

intervals around the top of the cake in groups of three, then pipe further individual circles between the groups. Repeat on the cake board within the marked scallops, to make a similar design around the base of the cake.

CAKE AND DECORATION

20cm (8in) round rich fruit cake (see page 16)

3 tbsp apricot glaze (see page 21)

1kg (2lb) marzipan (almond paste)

icing (confectioners') sugar for dusting

1kg (2lb/4 cups) royal icing for flat icing (see page 17)

yellow food colouring

500g (1lb/2 cups) royal icing for decoration (see page 17)

60cm (24in) yellow ribbon, about 3cm (1¼in) wide

8 small yellow silk or fabric roses

8 small yellow bows

EQUIPMENT

28cm (11in) round silver cake board

icing ruler

icing scraper

paper piping bag

no. 1 piping tube (tip)

medium star tube

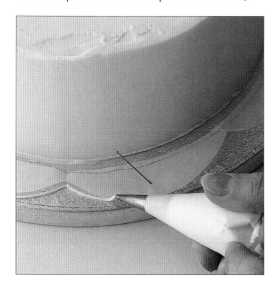

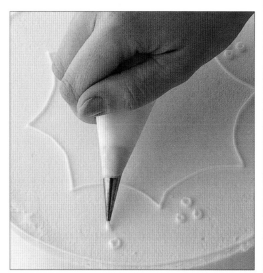

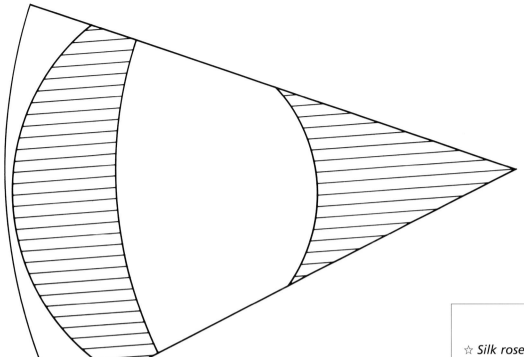

7 Place half of the remaining icing in a bowl and thin with a little beaten egg white or water until it becomes completely level when left to settle in the bowl for several seconds. Colour the icing using a slightly darker shade of yellow. Using the technique described on page 31, flood the scalloped areas around the base and on top of the cake. Leave the icing for several hours to harden.

Tips

☆ *Silk roses and yellow bows are available from cake-decorating shops. Alternatively make homemade bows using 2.5mm (⅛in) wide ribbon, and mould small roses in yellow sugarpaste (rolled fondant) (see page 25).*

☆ *When flooding a large area with icing, work on 10cm (4in) sections at a time so that the icing does not form a crust before you have had time to ease it into the corners.*

8 Place a little white icing in a piping bag fitted with the piping tube and pipe small circles to emphasize the broderie anglaise work. Finish off with leaf outlines.

9 Pipe decorative loops of icing around the scalloped edges.

10 Put more white icing in a piping bag fitted with the medium star tube. Use to pipe a shell border around the top and base of the cake.

11 Wrap the yellow ribbon around the cake and secure with a dot of icing. Place the roses and bows at the point of each scallop around the top and side of the cake, securing with dots of icing.

Pink Rose Heart

CAKE AND DECORATION

20cm (8in) heart-shaped rich fruit cake* covered with marzipan (almond paste) (see page 21)

1.1kg (2lb 2oz) sugarpaste (rolled fondant)

pink and claret food colourings

clear alcohol (gin/vodka)

1m (1yd) pink ribbon for board edge

7 pink wafer roses

pink dusting powder (petal dust/blossom tint)

5 green fabric leaves

plastic 'With Love' words

15g (½oz/1tbsp) royal icing (see page 17)

This is a simple cake but looks exquisite and could be used for various occasions other than birthdays, such as special parties and celebrations.

1 Colour 1kg (2lb) sugarpaste (rolled fondant) pale pink. Brush the marzipan (almond paste) with alcohol and cover with the sugarpaste (see page 22). Use the remainder to cover the cake board (see page 24).

2 On a plate, mix a small amount of pink food colouring with a little clear alcohol. Scrunch up a small piece of cloth and dip into the mixed colour. Lightly dab the cloth gently on the sugarpasted board in a random pattern to create a 'ragging' effect. Repeat the technique with the claret colour. Colour the sugarpasted cake in the same way.

shape slightly smaller than the cake. Immediately after cutting out the shape, and before the paste begins to crust, use the small crimper to create a decorative edge around the heart shape. Attach to the cake top with a little water.

5 Brush the edges of the wafer rose petals with pink dusting powder (petal dust/blossom tint). Remove the outer petals from two flowers to create buds. Arrange the flowers, leaves and plastic writing on the cake and attach with royal icing.

EQUIPMENT

small piece of cloth

28cm (11in) heart-shaped cake board

small and large crimpers

paintbrush

*Use the 20cm (8in) round rich fruit cake mixture (see page 16)

3 Place the cake on the board. Trim the board edge with ribbon. Roll out the pink sugarpaste trimmings into a long narrow rope and attach to the base of the cake with water. Use the large crimping tool to make a decorative pattern on the rope.

4 Roll out the white sugarpaste and use a template to cut out a heart

---

Tip

☆ *If you think the ragging technique may be too time-consuming for you, cover the cake and cake board with marbled sugarpaste (see page 23).*

Black and White Cake

CAKE AND DECORATION

20cm (8in) square rich fruit cake (see page 16) covered with marzipan (almond paste) (see page 21)

685g (1lb 6oz) sugarpaste (rolled fondant)

black paste food colouring

clear alcohol (gin or vodka)

30g (1oz/2 tbsp) grey royal icing (see page 17)

150 silver dragees

30cm (12in) ribbon for champagne glass

champagne glass

pink foil-covered chocolate truffles

EQUIPMENT

20cm (8in) square thin cake card

28cm (11in) square cake board

paper piping bag

no. 1 piping tube (tip)

Something different ... this cake could be used as a centrepiece for a party table for an 18th birthday.

1 Colour 105g (3½oz) sugarpaste (rolled fondant) black. Reserve 60g (2oz) each of white and black sugarpaste. Divide the white in half and shape each piece into a rough oblong. Shape the black into an oblong and sandwich between the two pieces of white. Roll up Swiss-roll (jelly roll) fashion and cut into slices. Group the pieces together in a random fashion and roll out on a surface dusted with icing (confectioners') sugar to give a streaky, marbled effect.

2 Brush the cake with alcohol and cover with the prepared sugarpaste (see page 22). Place the cake on the thin cake card, then position centrally on the larger cake board, covered with decorative paper (see Tip).

3 Take the reserved white and black sugarpaste and roll each out into two long narrow ropes, twist together and roll slightly to neaten. Attach the twisted rope to the base of the cake with water, trim and join neatly at the back.

4 Using a no. 1 piping tube (tip) and grey royal icing, pipe random groups of three small dots and single dots over the top and sides of the cake, attaching a silver dragee to each dot. Pipe a few at a time otherwise the icing may dry before you have attached the dragee.

5 Tie the ribbon in a bow around the stem of the glass. Position the glass on the cake and pile with truffles.

Tips

☆ *The silver dragees used as part of the decoration on this cake are quite small to handle – you will probably find them easier to pick up and position more accurately using tweezers.*

☆ *If you cover cake boards with decorative foils or gift wrapping paper, first place the cake on a cake card or waxed paper to avoid contact.*

Garlands and Bows

Flowers always look good especially on such an attractive petal-shaped cake, here garlanded with bows.

CAKE AND DECORATION

20cm (8in) petal-shaped rich fruit cake (see page 16) covered with marzipan (almond paste) (see page 21)

1kg (2lb) sugarpaste (rolled fondant)

ivory and lavender paste food colourings

clear alcohol (gin or vodka)

1.5m (1⅔yd) lavender ribbon for board edge

90g (3oz/⅓ cup) royal icing (see page 17)

plastic posy spike

wired posy of fabric flowers and ribbon loops

EQUIPMENT

30cm (12in) petal-shaped cake board

clay gun/sugar shaper with clover leaf-shaped blade

paper piping bag

no 2. piping tube (tip)

1 Colour 875g (1¾lb) sugarpaste (rolled fondant) ivory. Brush the marzipan (almond paste) with clear alcohol and cover with the sugarpaste (see page 22). Trim away any excess paste. Cover the cake board with sugarpaste and place the cake in the centre (see page 24). Trim the board edge with ribbon.

2 Using the ivory sugarpaste trimmings, fill the clay gun and fit the clover leaf-shaped blade. Squeeze out a short length of paste and, whilst still soft, twist neatly and attach to the cake with water to form a curved garland effect. Repeat around the cake. Alternatively, roll out two thin lengths of sugarpaste and twist together.

3 Using the no. 2 piping tube (tip) and ivory royal icing, pipe a plain shell border around the base of the cake.

4 Colour the remaining sugarpaste lavender and roll out thinly on a board dusted with icing (confectioners') sugar. Use your own templates to cut out the bow and tail shapes. Moisten the centre of the bow with a little water and fold in the two ends. Cover the join with a small rectangle of sugarpaste. Attach two tails to the back of the bow and then attach the bow to the cake with water at the join of the garlands. Repeat around the cake.

5 Press the plastic posy spike into the cake and then insert the flower arrangement, securing it with a little royal icing.

Tip

☆ *Most of the time making this cake will be spent covering the intricate petal shape with sugarpaste (rolled fondant). To cut down decorating time, you may prefer to use ready-made ribbon bows instead of the hand-made sugarpaste ones.*

Stack of Presents

If stuck for a teenager's birthday cake idea, this pile of presents might be the solution, particularly if the teenager has 'outgrown' kids' cakes and has no particular hobby.

CAKE AND DECORATION

Madeira (pound) cake mixture for a 23cm (9in) square tin (pan) baked in a 25cm (10in) square cake tin (see page 16)

250g (8oz/1 cup) butter-cream (see page 18)

2kg (4lb) sugarpaste (rolled fondant)

6 tbsp apricot glaze (see page 21)

cornflour (cornstarch) for dusting

250g (8oz/1 cup) royal icing (see page 17)

blue and green food colourings

gold, green or blue lustre food dusting powders (petal dusts/ blossom tints)

2m (2¼yd) navy ribbon, about 1cm (½in) wide

EQUIPMENT

20cm (8in) square silver cake board

small shaped cutter, e.g., crescent, star, heart

paper piping bag

no. 2 piping tube (tip)

large and fine paintbrushes

Tip

☆ *For an effective colour scheme, use two rich, bold colours. 'Lustre' dusting powder has a pretty sheen and comes in many colours.*

---

1 Grease and line the base and sides of the cake tin (pan). Make up the Madeira (pound) cake mixture, turn it into the tin and level the surface. Bake in the oven for about 1¾ hours or until a skewer inserted in the centre comes out clean. Turn out onto a wire rack to cool.

2 Trim off the outer edges of the cake and level the surface by cutting off any peak formed during baking. Cut the cake into two pieces, one 15cm (6in) across, the other 10cm (4in) across. Cut the large portion in half and sandwich the two pieces with buttercream, to make the largest parcel.

3 Cut the remaining cake into two pieces, one 18cm (7in) long, the other 7.5cm (3in) long. Cut each in half and sandwich with buttercream to make the second and third parcels.

4 Fill in the gaps around the sandwiched cakes with pieces of sugarpaste (rolled fondant), so the surfaces are quite smooth. Brush all the cakes with apricot glaze and place the largest cake on the board.

5 Roll out 875g (1¾lb) sugarpaste on a surface dusted with cornflour (cornstarch) and use to cover the large cake, a side at a time (see page 22). Use 625g (1¼lb) to cover the second cake, and 375g (12oz) to cover the third. Shape the remaining 125g (4oz) sugar-paste into a small cube for the smallest parcel.

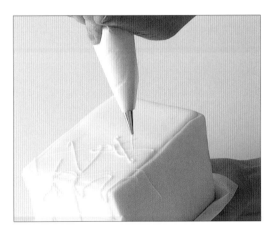

6 Dip the shaped cutter in cornflour, then impress the surfaces of two of the parcels with the shape. Put the royal icing in a piping bag fitted with a no. 2 piping tube (tip). Use to pipe squiggly lines over the top and sides of the two remaining parcels. Support the cake on your hand, turning so lines can be piped over the edges and sides. Carefully stack the parcels and leave them overnight to harden before the next stage.

7 Using a large paintbrush, paint the largest and third parcel blue and the second and fourth greeny gold (carefully painting over the piping). Leave to dry.

8 Using a fine, dry paintbrush, dust the cutter-impressed areas and the raised piped areas with dusting powder (petal dust/blossom tint).

9 Halve the ribbon. Slide one end of each ribbon under opposite sides of the large cake. Bring the ribbons up and over the cakes and tie on top.

Daisy Cake

Small, foil-wrapped chocolate eggs, half-hidden under clusters of moulded flowers, make a pretty decoration for a spring or Easter birthday cake.

CAKE AND DECORATION

23cm (9in) round Madeira (pound) cake (see page 16)

60g (2oz) petal paste (see page 26)

cornflour (cornstarch) for dusting

1.5kg (3lb) sugarpaste (rolled fondant)

yellow food colouring

3 tbsp apricot glaze (see page 21)

1kg (2lb) marzipan (almond paste)

icing (confectioners') sugar for dusting

10–12 mini chocolate eggs

gold foil

1 tbsp icing (confectioners') sugar

1m (1yd) purple ribbon, about 5cm (2in) wide

a small square of tulle

EQUIPMENT

small and large daisy or simple flower cutters

piece of tulle

fine paintbrush

30cm (12in) round gold or silver cake board

Tips

☆ *If preferred, substitute a spicy Simnel cake for the Madeira (pound) and omit the sugarpaste, leaving the more traditional covering of marzipan alone. If so, use yellow marzipan (almond paste), rather than white.*

☆ *Save gold foil from chocolate bars for wrapping the mini eggs.*

1 To make the daisies, roll out the petal paste as thinly as possible on a surface dusted with cornflour (cornstarch). Cut out shapes with daisy or flower cutters. You will need about eight large flowers and 24 small. Cup the flowers slightly between your fingers, then place on a piece of crumpled foil and leave to harden for several hours.

2 Colour 60g (2oz) sugarpaste (rolled fondant) deep yellow. Roll a small piece into a ball and press it against a piece of tulle until the netting leaves an impression on the icing. This gives a realistic textured appearance. Pull away the tulle. Using a fine paintbrush and a

little water, lightly dampen the centre of a flower, then position the yellow ball in it. Repeat with the remainder.

3 Level the surface of the cake, brush with apricot glaze and cover with marzipan (almond paste) (see page 21). Place on the cake board. Reserve 125g (4oz) of the remaining white sugarpaste and colour the rest pale yellow. Use to cover the cake (see page 22).

4 Using the remaining white sugarpaste, cover the cake board around the cake (see page 23). Use the remaining deep yellow sugarpaste to make a 'twist' border around the base of the cake (see page 25).

5 Wrap the eggs in gold foil. Using a dampened paintbrush, secure the daisies and eggs to the cake. To secure the ribbon, make a paste with the icing (confectioners') sugar and a dash of water. Wrap the ribbon around the cake and secure the ends with a dot of paste.

Peach Dragee Cake

The gold dragees on the quilting pattern add a special sparkle to this delicately coloured cake.

CAKE AND DECORATION

20cm (8in) hexagonal rich fruit cake (see page 16) covered with marzipan (almond paste) (see page 21)

4 tbsp apricot glaze (see page 21)

125g (4oz) marzipan (almond paste)

625g (1¼ lb) sugarpaste (rolled fondant)

peach paste food colouring

clear alcohol (gin/vodka)

60g (2oz/¼ cup) peach royal icing (see page 17)

about 100 gold dragees

about 1m (1yd) each peach ribbon and lace for board edge

wired spray of fabric peach flowers and ribbon loops

EQUIPMENT

plastic ruler

paper piping bag

nos. 1 and 2 piping tubes (tips)

tweezers (optional)

25cm (10in) hexagonal cake board

Tip

☆ *If you need to stop before the quilted pattern markings are complete, keep the cake in a sealed polythene bag to prevent the sugarpaste skinning over.*

1 Use the ruler to indent lines from point to point on the cake top by pressing gently. Take a sharp knife and cleanly cut any one of the six sections. Remove the wedge to leave a space. (The removed wedge can be sliced and wrapped to make extra portions.) Brush the exposed cut surfaces of the cake with apricot glaze and cover with the 125g (4oz) marzipan (almond paste), carefully neatening the joins and edges (see page 21).

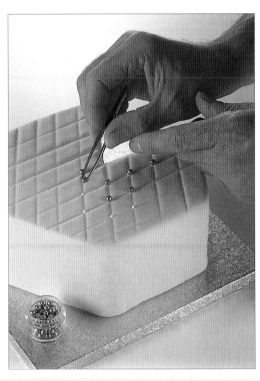

2 Colour the sugarpaste peach. Brush the marzipan with alcohol and cover the cake with the sugarpaste (rolled fondant) (see page 22). Whilst the paste is still soft, mark the diagonal quiltwork pattern carefully and accurately with the ruler on the top and sides of the cake as shown above. (Make a template first if preferred.)

3 Using a no. 1 piping tube (tip), pipe tiny dots of peach royal icing where the quiltwork lines cross and attach a gold dragee on each – if you find the dragees difficult to pick up and position, use tweezers. Position the dragees before the icing sets.

4 Roll out the remaining sugarpaste to cover the cake board (see page 24), position the cake and trim the board edge with ribbon and lace.

5 Pipe a small, plain shell border around the base of the cake using a no. 2 tube and peach royal icing. Attach the spray of peach flowers and ribbon loops in the cut-away area with a spot of royal icing.

Gold Drape Cake

The unusual colour scheme gives a really rich and sophisticated look to this stylish party cake.

CAKE AND DECORATION

25cm (10in) round rich fruit cake (see page 16) covered with marzipan (almond paste) (see page 21)

1.1kg (2lb 2oz) sugarpaste (rolled fondant)

cream and navy paste food colourings

clear alcohol (gin or vodka)

1m (1yd) navy ribbon for board edge

185g (6oz) pastillage (see page 17)

gold dusting powder (petal dust/blossom tint)

confectioners' varnish (glaze)

small plastic vase (see step 6)

6 navy ribbon bows

30g (1oz/2 tbsp) royal icing (see page 17)

wired arrangement of **cream flowers and navy ribbon loops**

EQUIPMENT

33cm (13in) round cake board

paintbrush

1 Colour 410g (13oz) sugarpaste (rolled fondant) cream and 625g (1¼lb) navy blue. Brush the marzipan (almond paste) with alcohol and cover the top of the cake with a large circle of cream sugarpaste. Make the circle large enough to curve over onto the top of the cake side. Roll out 280g (9oz) navy sugarpaste into a long narrow strip to cover the side of the cake. Attach to the cake and neaten the join where the two colours meet.

2 Cover the cake board with the remaining navy sugarpaste and position the cake (see page 24). Trim the board edge with ribbon, then mark the cake's circumference into six equal parts.

3 Very thinly roll out a sixth of the white pastillage and cut into a 13.5 x 9.5cm (5¼ x 3¾in) rectangle using a template.

4 Without delay and working quickly, brush both short sides with a little water and fold the piece, concertina fashion, to form neat pleats.

5 Pinch the two ends firmly and attach to the cake with water before the paste starts to crust, arranging the drape to form a nice curved shape. Repeat around the cake with the five remaining portions of pastillage.

6 If the atmosphere is dry, the pastillage will set quickly. If in doubt, dry under the warmth of a desk lamp. Mix gold dusting powder (petal dust/blossom tint) with confectioners' varnish (glaze) to a creamy consistency and paint the drapes. If you wish, paint the vase.

7 Attach the ribbon bows to the drapes with royal icing. Fix the flowers securely into the vase and position on the cake.

Tip

☆ *To achieve a good golden colour and make painting easier, mix the gold dusting powder (petal dust/blossom tint) to a creamy consistency with confectioners' varnish and use immediately.*

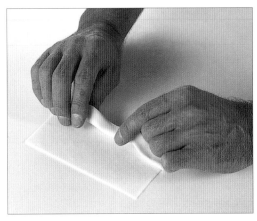

Posy of Flowers

A small posy of artificial or sugar flowers, tucked into a sugarpaste 'wrapping', makes a novel cake decoration.

CAKE AND DECORATION

25 x 20cm (10 x 8in) oval rich fruit or Madeira (pound) cake, made using mixture for 23cm (9in) round tin (pan) (see page 16)

3 tbsp apricot glaze (see page 21)

1kg (2lb) marzipan (almond paste)

icing (confectioners') sugar for dusting

1.5kg (3lb) sugarpaste (rolled fondant)

green and yellow food colourings

cornflour (cornstarch) for dusting

1m (1yd) green ribbon, about 5cm (2in) wide

1 tbsp icing (confectioners') sugar

small posy of silk flowers

1m (1yd) green ribbon for board edge

EQUIPMENT

30 x 25cm (12 x 10in) oval silver cake board

fine paintbrush

Tip

☆ *This cake works particularly well in an oval-shaped cake tin (pan) which can be bought or hired from most cake-decorating shops. If preferred, use a 23cm (9in) round cake tin.*

1 Level the surface of the cake by cutting off any peak formed during baking. Brush the cake with apricot glaze and cover with marzipan (almond paste) (see page 21). Place on the cake board. Colour 185g (6oz) sugarpaste (rolled fondant) green and set aside. Reserve another 125g (4oz) sugarpaste.

2 Marble the remaining sugarpaste with yellow colouring (see page 23), and use to cover the cake (see page 22).

3 Roll out the green sugarpaste on a surface dusted with cornflour (cornstarch) and use to cover the cake board around the base of the cake (see page 23). Roll out the remaining green sugarpaste and cut out a strip about 1cm (½ in) wide. Lay this strip over the iced board with one edge against the side of the cake, making a decorative 'step'.

4 Trace the flower wrapping template on page 251 onto greaseproof (parchment) or non-stick paper and cut out the shape. Thinly roll out the reserved white sugarpaste. Lay the template over the sugarpaste and cut around it.

5 Dampen the centre of the top of the cake with water. Lay the white icing on the cake and fold the straight sides over so that they just overlap,

dampening one edge with a paintbrush and pressing together to secure. Tuck some crumpled absorbent kitchen paper (paper towels) inside to keep the icing raised as it hardens. Leave the flower wrapping to dry overnight.

6 Dilute a little green food colouring and use to paint stripes on the sugarpaste posy wrapping.

7 Wrap the green ribbon around the cake and secure with a dot of paste made by mixing about 1 tablespoon icing (confectioners') sugar with a dash of water.

8 Just before serving the cake, remove the absorbent kitchen paper from inside the wrapping and tuck the artificial or sugar flowers into position. Trim the board with ribbon.

Cream Roses Cake

The beautiful cream roses that adorn this cake have a fabric effect. Fortunately they are surprisingly easy to make.

CAKE AND DECORATION

28cm (11in) square rich fruit cake (see page 16)

3 tbsp apricot glaze (see page 21)

1.5kg (3lb) marzipan (almond paste)

icing (confectioners') sugar for dusting

2kg (4lb) sugarpaste (rolled fondant)

cream food colouring

cornflour (cornstarch) for dusting

250g (8oz/1 cup) royal icing (see page 17)

EQUIPMENT

36cm (14in) square silver cake board

large paintbrush

paper piping bag

no. 2 piping tube (tip)

1 Brush the cake with apricot glaze and cover with marzipan (almond paste) (see page 21). Place on the cake board.

2 Colour the sugarpaste (rolled fondant) cream. Reserve 500g (1lb) of the sugarpaste and use the remainder to cover the cake (see page 22). Use a little more to cover the cake board around the base of the cake (see page 23).

3 Roll out a little more cream sugarpaste as thinly as possible on a surface dusted with cornflour (cornstarch)

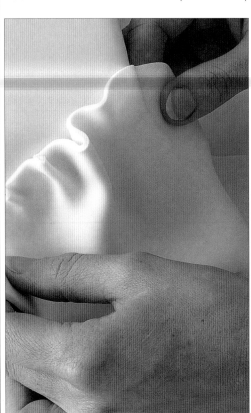

and cut out a 23cm (9in) round. Cut the round into two semi-circles. Dampen the curved edge of one semi-circle, then lift it onto the cake so that the widest part of the semi-circle rests on one corner. Using your fingers, gently gather up the curved edge of the semi-circle on either side of the corner and press onto the sides of the cake so that the points of the semi-circle can be tucked against the base of the cake.

4 Use the remaining semi-circle on another corner of the cake. Cut out another 23cm (9in) round of cream sugarpaste and apply semi-circles to the remaining corners in the same way.

5 Cut out a 14cm (5½in) circle of greaseproof (parchment) or non-stick paper and lay it in the centre of the top of the cake. Using a pin, mark the surface of the cake all around the paper. Remove the paper.

6 To make the flowers, thinly roll out a little cream sugarpaste and cut out a

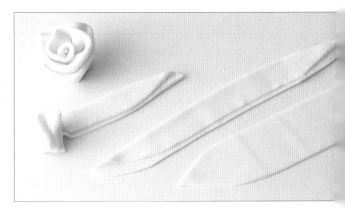

15cm (6in) strip that is 3.5cm (1½in) wide but which tapers to a point at each end. Lightly dampen one long edge of the strip, then fold it lengthways in half. Starting at one end, roll up the strip, gathering it slightly at intervals to resemble a simple rose.

7 Cut off any excess icing around the base of the flower, then dampen the underside and push it onto the top of one corner of the cake, hiding the edges of the gathered icing. (If necessary, push the end of a paintbrush between the layers or 'petals' of the flower to secure it firmly to the cake without crushing the flower.)

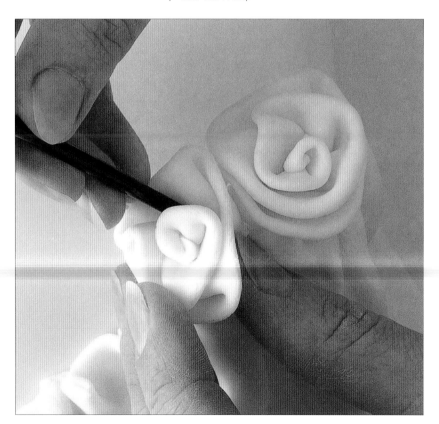

Tip

☆ *If you find the royal icing difficult to pipe out of the narrow tube, thin it with a little water so that it flows from the bag more easily.*

---

8 Make more flowers to complete the corner of the cake, making each rose slightly smaller as you work away from the first central one. Cover the remaining corners in the same way.

9 Make eight more small roses and position them in a ring in the centre of the cake. Make one or two slightly larger roses and place them very gently in the centre.

10 Colour the royal icing the same shade of cream as the cake and place in a paper piping bag fitted with a no. 2 piping tube (tip). Pipe long continuous curvy lines over the cake, keeping the tube about 1cm (½in) above the cake and breaking off frequently to rest your hand and change position. Do not pipe in the central circle on top of the cake.

11 Pipe diagonal lines of royal icing, about 2.5mm (⅛in) apart, on the cake board. Trim with ribbon, if liked.

12 Pipe tiny dots or scrolls of icing around the base of the cake and along the edges of the gathered corners. Pipe further dots or scrolls around the edge of the marked circle on the top of the cake.

Coming-of-Age Cake

CAKE AND DECORATION

28cm (11in) square rich fruit cake (see page 16)

4 tbsp apricot glaze (see page 21)

1.5kg (3lb) marzipan (almond paste)

icing (confectioners') sugar for dusting

cornflour (cornstarch) for dusting

2kg (4lb) sugarpaste (rolled fondant)

blue, green and gold food colourings

500g (1lb/2 cups) royal icing (see page 17)

2m (2¼yd) gold or coloured ribbon, about 3cm (1¼in) wide

EQUIPMENT

33cm (13in) square gold cake board

2 paper piping bags

no.1 piping tube (tip)

medium star piping tube

fine paintbrush

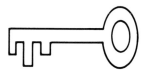

Gold-edged filigree work gives an interesting finish to this 18th or 21st birthday celebration cake.

1 Brush the cake with apricot glaze and cover with marzipan (almond paste) (see page 21). Place on the cake board and dust the top surface of the marzipan, to within 2.5cm (1in) of the edges, with cornflour (cornstarch). Cut out a 23cm (9in) square greaseproof (parchment) or non-stick paper.

2 Roll out the sugarpaste on a surface dusted with cornflour and use to cover the cake (see page 22). Reserve the trimmings. Once the sugarpaste is completely smoothed around the edges and sides of the cake, lay the square of greaseproof or non-stick paper over the top, securing it at the corners with pins. Using a sharp knife, cut right through the paste around the paper. Lift out the central square of white paste. Remove the paper and pins.

3 Knead the white paste square and trimmings together and colour with equal quantities of blue and green colourings. Roll out and cut a 23cm (9in) square, reserving the trimmings. Lay the square over the top of the cake, so that the edges meet the edges of the white paste. Smooth down lightly.

4 Use the coloured paste trimmings to make the key using the template (left) to cut out the shape. Leave overnight to harden.

5 Put a little royal icing in a paper piping bag fitted with a no.1 piping tube (tip) and pipe thin wavy lines over two-thirds of the coloured paste. This is

done by piping long, continuous, curvy lines, keeping the tube about 1cm (½ in) above the cake and breaking off the icing frequently to rest your hand and change position.

6 Using more royal icing and a medium star tube, pipe a shell border around the edge of the coloured paste and around the base of the cake. Leave overnight to harden.

7 Using gold food colouring and a fine paintbrush, carefully paint over the piped icing. Paint the edges of the key with a little gold colouring. Leave to dry for several hours.

8 Wrap the ribbon around the sides of the cake, cutting off the excess and securing with a dot of royal icing. Shape the remaining ribbon into a bow and position it on top of the cake. Lay the key over the bow (see overleaf). The bow and key can be fixed in position with a small dot of royal icing.

Tips

☆ The deep colour of part of the sugarpaste (rolled fondant) on this cake is made by mixing together equal quantities of blue and green food colourings. Other rich colours, such as cerise or deep yellow, would look equally effective.

☆ The little key is made from sugarpaste, using a template to cut out the shape. Alternatively, a small key can be bought from a cake-decorating shop.

Chocolate
& CREAMY
CAKES

White Chocolate Box

The 'paper' cases are made from white chocolate; favourite chocolates and sweets make delicious fillings.

CAKE AND DECORATION

3-egg chocolate-flavoured Genoese Sponge mixture (see page 12)

440g (14oz/14 squares) white chocolate

16 large Brazil nuts

470ml (¾pt/2 cups) double (heavy) cream

10–12 truffles rolled in grated white chocolate

12 silver sugared almonds

12 gold sugared almonds

1m (1yd) gold- or silver-trimmed pink ribbon, about 1cm (½in) wide

EQUIPMENT

18cm (7in) square cake tin (pan)

paper sweet cases (candy cups)

Note: This cake is not suitable for young children or people allergic to nuts.

1 Preheat the oven to 180°C (350°F/ Gas 4). Spoon the cake mixture into the base lined and greased square cake tin (pan) and bake in the oven for about 25 minutes. Cool on a wire rack.

2 Draw a 23 x 18.5cm (9 x 7¼ in) rect-angle on a sheet of waxed paper. Melt half of the white chocolate, spoon it onto the paper and spread with a palette knife (metal spatula) to just cover the marked rectangle. Shake the paper to level the chocolate. Leave until set.

3 Melt the remaining white chocolate and use some to dip the Brazil nuts. Use the rest to make 12 chocolate *petit four* cases (see page 35). Leave to set.

4 Using a long serrated knife, cut the cake horizontally in half. Place one half on a flat serving plate. Whip the cream in a mixing bowl to soft peaks. Spread about a third of the cream over the cake. Gently rest the second half on top.

Use a palette knife to spread more cream thickly over the sides of the cake. Spread the remaining cream over the top, smoothing it lightly.

5 Trim the white chocolate rectangle to precisely 23 x 18.5cm (9 x 7¼in), using a clean ruler and sharp knife. Cut the rectangle into four equal panels, each measuring 5.5 x 18.5cm (2¼ x 7¼in). Carefully peel the paper away from the chocolate panels. Place one panel against the side of the cake and press gently into place. Complete the box effect by fixing the remaining panels in place so that the edges meet neatly at the corners.

6 Scatter most of the chocolate-coated Brazil nuts, truffles and chocolate cases over the top of the cake. Arrange silver and gold sugared almonds over the chocolate decorations in a random but neat arrangement.

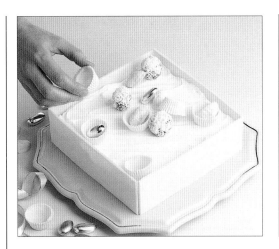

Tips

☆ *Make the cake, chocolate box panels and decorations several days in advance, but do not assemble the cake until the day of serving or the cream will deteriorate.*

☆ *For a quick version, use bought white chocolates, arranging them uniformly in chocolate or paper cases – a delectable gift for a chocolate-lover.*

7 Scatter the remaining truffles, chocolate cases and Brazil nuts beside the cake on the plate if liked. Tie the ribbon neatly around the cake, securing it with a dot of melted chocolate. Keep the cake cool until required, but always serve the same day it is completed.

Chequered Parcel

*Everything on this parcel cake is edible, even the ribbon!
Allow plenty of time for the decoration.*

1 Preheat the oven to 160°C (325°F/Gas 3). Beat the chocolate chips (bits) into the cake mixture. Bake in the base-lined and greased loaf tin (pan) for 1¼–1½ hours or until a skewer inserted into the centre comes out clean. Cool on a wire rack. This cake will probably 'dome' in the centre during baking. Slice the top level once the cake has cooled to create the parcel shape. Using a palette knife (metal spatula) completely cover the cake with buttercream, making the the coating slightly thicker at the top of the sloping sides to give as square a shape as possible. Smooth down gently.

2 Melt the plain (semisweet) and white chocolate in separate mixing bowls. Spread on separate sheets of waxed paper as described on page 33. Leave to set. Cut out a panel from the dark chocolate, exactly the same size as one long side of the cake. Cut the same in white. Repeat this process for the remaining long side, both ends and top of the cake. Cut all the panels into even-sized squares.

3 Using appropriate panels for each cake side, peel off squares as

required and secure to the cake in a chequered design, making sure the squares line up neatly along the edges. Continue the design until the cake is completely covered in chocolate squares.

CAKE AND DECORATION

60g (2oz/⅓ cup) plain (semisweet) chocolate chips (bits)

Madeira (pound) cake mixture for a 20cm (8in) round tin (pan) or 18cm (7in) square tin (see page 16)

¾ quantity buttercream (see page 18)

125g (4oz/4 squares) plain (semisweet) chocolate

125g (4oz/4 squares) white chocolate

½ quantity modelling chocolate made with plain chocolate (see page 34)

½ quantity modelling chocolate made with white chocolate

icing (confectioners') sugar for dusting

EQUIPMENT

1kg (2lb) loaf tin (pan)

fine paintbrush

211

Leftover chocolate squares can be used to make boxes (see page 33), if liked.

4 Lightly knead both pieces of modelling chocolate. On a surface dusted with icing (confectioners') sugar, thinly roll each to a long strip. Using a sharp knife, cut out thin strips from both colours, each about 5mm (¼in) wide. Lightly dampen the edges of a white strip with a fine paintbrush dipped in water; sandwich between two dark strips to make a striped ribbon. Press the strips together firmly. Use the remaining chocolate icing to make more chocolate ribbon in the same way.

5 Measure the distance from the centre of the top of the cake to the base on each side. Cut four strips of striped chocolate ribbon of appropriate length. For the bow, cut two 13cm (5in) lengths of chocolate ribbon and pinch the ends together to make loops. Cut two shorter lengths for the ribbon ends, pinching one end of each together and

cutting out a 'v' from the opposite ends. Finally position the four lengths of modelling chocolate ribbon so that they meet on top of the cake, brushing ends lightly with water to seal. Fix the bow loops in position and add the ends. Neaten the centre of the bow with a small knot of 'ribbon'.

Tips

☆ *A square tin (pan) could be used for a parcel of a different shape. For a novelty parcel cover the cake completely with plain (semisweet) chocolate and use fancy cutters to shape animal, star or crescent white chocolate cut-outs for securing to the cake.*

☆ *Modelling chocolate will keep in a cool place for several weeks if tightly wrapped in a polythene bag. Break off pieces as required, kneading them lightly until pliable.*

Chocolate Heart

Decorated with chocolate leaves and luxurious candied fruits, this moist rich chocolate cake is perfect for a special occasion.

CAKE AND DECORATION

2-egg moist rich chocolate cake mixture (see page 15)

apricot glaze (see page 21)

500g (1lb) marzipan (almond paste)

icing (confectioners') sugar for dusting

315g (10oz/10 squares) plain (semisweet) chocolate

125g (4oz/4 squares) milk (German sweet) chocolate

185g (6oz) mixed candied (glacé) fruit

EQUIPMENT

25cm (10in) heart-shaped tin (pan)

heart-shaped board (optional)

paper piping bag

no. 2 piping tube (tip)

1 Preheat the oven to 160°C (325°F/ Gas 3). Grease and base-line the heart-shaped tin (pan). Spoon in the cake mixture and bake in the oven for about 1½ hours or until a skewer inserted into the centre comes out clean. Cool on a wire rack.

2 Invert the cake onto a large flat serving plate or heart-shaped cake board.

3 Brush apricot glaze over the top and sides of the cake. Roll out the marzipan (almond paste) to a round, 30cm (12in) in diameter, on a surface lightly dusted with icing (confectioners') sugar. Lift over the cake and ease to fit around the sides. Trim off the excess marzipan around the base of the cake.

4 Melt the plain (semisweet) chocolate and pour over the cake; spread to cover the top and sides (see page 32). Keep in a cool place until set.

5 Melt the milk (German sweet) chocolate and place a little in a piping bag fitted with a no. 2 piping tube (tip). Holding the piping bag about 5cm (2in) above the cake, pipe continuous fine lacy lines by moving your hand quickly over the cake. To cover the sides, tilt the plate or board slightly with your free hand and work with the bag nearer the surface of the cake.

6 Use the remaining melted milk chocolate to half-dip fruits (see page 35) and to make about eight chocolate rose leaves (see page 34). When the chocolate has set, arrange the fruit and leaves over the top of the cake.

Tips

☆ *The moist rich chocolate cake should be baked immediately after mixing as soda is activated when combined with liquid.*

☆ *Fresh fruits may be used instead of candied, if preferred, but should only be added just before serving.*

Chocolate Fudge Cake

CAKE AND DECORATION

20cm (8in) round chocolate fudge cake (see page 13)

155ml (¼ pint/⅔ cup) double (heavy) cream

2 tsp icing (confectioners') sugar, plus extra for dusting

1 quantity chocolate fudge icing (see page 19)

1 quantity chocolate caraque (see page 32)

Children will eagerly dive into this deliciously rich and tasty cake, made from a traditional recipe.

1 Using a long serrated knife, split the cake in half horizontally. Place the bottom half on a flat serving plate. Combine the cream and icing (confectioners') sugar in a bowl and whip to soft peaks. Sandwich the cake together.

2 Using a palette knife (metal spatula), spread about half of the chocolate fudge icing around the side of the cake. Spoon the remaining icing over the top. Spread the icing to cover the cake evenly, then use the tip of a palette knife to mark a diagonal line from the centre top of the cake down to the base. Repeat at 1cm (½ in) intervals all around the cake to give a neat finish.

3 Carefully arrange some of the chocolate caraque on top of the cake. Add the remaining pieces, placing them at different angles to create an informal but symmetrical effect.

4 Cut three strips of greaseproof (parchment) or non-stick paper, each about 2.5cm (1in) wide. Lightly lay strips over the caraque then sift a little icing sugar heavily over the top of the cake. Carefully lift off the greaseproof paper strips to reveal contrast between dusted and plain areas.

Tips

☆ *To save time, coarsely grated chocolate can be used instead of caraque. To ensure that chocolate curls stick to icing, position them while the icing is still soft.*

☆ *Removing greaseproof (parchment) paper strips from the cake requires steady hands. Lift the strips off one by one.*

☆ *Try to avoid moving the cake once dusted with icing (confectioners') sugar. If you have to transport it, take the paper and sugar with you and complete the cake when you reach your destination.*

Mocha Gâteau

This cake uses a Genoese cake base but a moist rich chocolate cake could be used instead.

CAKE AND DECORATION

4-egg mocha-flavoured Genoese sponge mixture (see page 12)

155ml (¼ pint/⅔ cup) double (heavy) cream

1 tbsp icing (confectioners') sugar

¼ tsp vanilla essence (extract)

1 tbsp instant coffee powder

2 tsp boiling water

1 quantity ganache (see page 18)

60g (2oz/2 squares) plain (semisweet) chocolate

1m (1yd) cream ribbon, about 4cm (1½ in) wide

1m (1yd) brown ribbon, about 1.5cm (¾ in) wide

EQUIPMENT

2 x 20cm (8in) round cake tins (pans)

paper piping bag

no. 1 piping tube (tip)

1 Preheat the oven to 180°C (350°F/Gas 4). Spoon the cake mixture into the base-lined and greased round cake tins (pans) and bake in the oven for 20 minutes. Cool on a wire rack. Remove the lining paper.

2 In a mixing bowl, whip the cream to soft peaks, then continue whipping while gradually adding the icing (confectioners') sugar and vanilla. Use to sandwich the cakes together. Place on a flat serving plate.

3 Dissolve the coffee powder in the measured boiling water in a cup. Make the ganache mixture, adding the coffee after the cream. Leave until the mixture is thickened but remains level in the bowl.

4 Pour the ganache over the cake and smooth down the side using a palette knife (metal spatula). Leave in a cool place to set.

5 To make the chocolate lace motifs, make several tracings of the template on page 254 on the same piece of paper. You will need about 35 motifs, allowing for a few breakages. Secure the tracings to a flat surface with a smooth piece of waxed paper on top. Melt the chocolate, put it in a paper piping bag fitted with a no. 1 piping tube (tip) and quickly pipe over the lace motif outlines. Leave to set.

6 Using an upturned bowl, cutter or pan, about 18cm (7in) in diameter and with a very fine rim, carefully mark a central circle on top of the cake. To decorate the cake top with chocolate motifs, first carefully peel the paper away from the chocolate lace. Gently press the motifs into the marked circle, tilting each backwards and spacing them slightly apart. Chill until set.

7 Just before serving, wrap the ribbons around the cake as illustrated.

Tip

☆ *The coffee flavouring added to both sponge and icing can be omitted if a dark chocolate gâteau is preferred.*

Woodcutter's Cottage

CAKE AND DECORATION

315g (10oz/2½ cups)
plain (all-purpose) flour

60g (2oz/½ cup) cocoa
(unsweetened cocoa
powder)

½ tsp baking powder

185g (6oz/¾ cup) butter,
softened

185g (6oz/1 cup) soft
dark brown sugar

2 tbsp black treacle
(molasses or dark
corn syrup)

2 eggs

250g (8oz/8 squares)
plain (semisweet)
chocolate

125g (4oz/4 squares)
white chocolate

¾ quantity chocolate-
flavoured buttercream
(see page 18)

30g (1oz/1 square) milk
(German sweet)
chocolate

60g (2oz) chocolate
marzipan (almond paste)
(see page 20)

4 large flaky chocolate
bars

several chocolate
buttons

icing (confectioners')
sugar for dusting

EQUIPMENT

25cm (10in) round cake
board

paper piping bag

no. 1 piping tube (tip)

This chocolate variation on the familiar gingerbread house theme makes a good centrepiece for a party tea.

1 Sift the flour, cocoa and baking powder together. Beat the butter and sugar together in a mixing bowl until just softened. Add the treacle (molasses or dark corn syrup) and eggs with the flour mixture. Mix to a soft dough. Knead lightly, wrap in greaseproof (parchment) or non-stick paper and chill for about 30 minutes until firm.

2 Trace the cottage walls and roof on pages 252–253 on non-stick paper. Cut out the templates.

3 Preheat the oven to 190°C (375°F/Gas 5). Roll out some of the dough on a lightly floured surface and lay it on a baking sheet. Cut around each template, using a small sharp knife. Remember to remove windows. Lift away excess dough. You will need two roof shapes, two end walls and one of each long wall. Bake the shapes for about 10 minutes or until beginning to colour around the edges. Leave on the baking sheets for 5 minutes, then transfer to a wire rack to cool completely.

4 Trace the tree sections on page 253. You will need 5 tracings of the large tree and 10 each of medium and small trees. On a separate piece of paper trace 12 window shutters and 1 door, using the templates on page 253. Secure the tracings to a flat surface with a smooth piece of waxed paper on top. Melt the plain (semisweet) chocolate and make runouts of trees, shutters and doors, (see page 35). Leave to set.

5 Melt the white chocolate. Spoon a little onto the cottage walls. Spread

Tips

☆ *For a tiled roof effect omit the flaky chocolate bars and use some chocolate buttons instead.*

☆ *Chocolate runouts seldom break, but it is worth making a few extra tree and shutter runouts just in case!*

☆ *Position three bears – made from modelling chocolate – at the front door to recall the story of Goldilocks. Although the cottage is hollow, it could be filled with a buttercream-covered rectangular chocolate cake to provide more servings.*

with a palette knife (metal spatula), then make a swirled pattern over the chocolate with the tip of the knife. Leave to set.

6 Roughly spread a little of the butter-cream all over the surface of the cake board.

7 Assemble the house, generously spreading the inner ends of each

wall with buttercream. Fix the four walls together, siting the cottage towards the back of the cake board with the door facing the front. Gently rest one roof section in position so that the point at the top of the walls is level with the top of the roof. Repeat on the other side.

8 Melt the milk (German sweet) chocolate, put it in a piping bag fitted with a no. 1 piping tube (tip) and pipe handles on the runout door and shutters. Shape a small chimney from chocolate marzipan (almond paste). Carefully spread the roof with butter-cream and position the chimney. Cut the chocolate bars into 2.5cm (1in) pieces. Cut each lengthways into three or four flat sections. Starting from the bottom of the roof, secure the sections in position, with the chocolate overlapping.

9 Place 3 tablespoons of the remaining buttercream in a paper piping bag fitted with a piping tube. Peel the runout shutters and doors away from the paper. Pipe a little buttercream on the back of each shutter runout and fix them in place. Finally add the door, using buttercream as mortar, and fixing it slightly ajar.

10 Peel the runout trees from the paper. Pipe several lines of butter-cream up the straight edge of one tree section. Holding this vertically, secure four more tree sections to the first, then transfer the tree to the cake board. Make

the remaining trees in the same way. Make a path from the chocolate buttons, then sift icing (confectioners') sugar over the cake and board.

Box of Chocs

This luxurious edible box of confections must be a choc-aholic's dream; alter the inscription to suit the occasion.

1 Roll out the black sugarpaste (rolled fondant) and cover the cake board (see page 24). Cut the cake in half and sandwich with buttercream. Make a 15cm (6in) square template from thin card or paper and place centrally on top of the cake. Use a sharp knife to chamfer the cake at an angle from the template edge to the outside base edge of the cake. Reserve the template for later use. Spread the top and sides of the cake with buttercream and place on the prepared cake board.

2 Make a template of the side of the cake. Roll out the ivory pastillage and texture the surface using the ribbed rolling pin. Cut out four side

shapes, ensuring the ribbing runs in the same direction on all four sides. Attach to the cake and, if possible, try to extend the sides about 5mm (¼ in) above the height of the cake to create a box effect. Cut out a square lid from the textured paste using the cake cutting template.

3 Roll out the ivory pastillage trimmings thinly and cut out a rect-

CAKE AND DECORATION

18cm (7in) square chocolate Genoese sponge (layer) cake (see page 12)

200g (6½oz) black sugarpaste (rolled fondant)

buttercream (see page 18) for filling and covering

440g (14oz) ivory pastillage (see page 17)

185g (6oz) plain (semisweet) chocolate, melted

30g (1oz/2 tbsp) royal icing (see page 17)

black food colouring

10cm (4in) gold thread

125g (4oz) pink pastillage

assortment of luxury chocolates

1.25m (1⅓yd) pink ribbon for board edge and bow

EQUIPMENT

28cm (11in) square cake board

ribbed rolling pin

paper piping bag

nos. 1, 4 and 43 piping tubes (tips)

angle for the gift tag. Cut a hole in the tag, using a no. 4 tube (tip), for the tie.

4 Add a few drops of cold water to the melted chocolate to thicken it slightly. Using a no. 43 piping tube and the prepared chocolate, pipe a shell border around the top and base edges and corners of the box. Pipe around the edge of the box lid.

5 Using a no. 1 piping tube and black royal icing, pipe an inscription of your choice onto the prepared gift tag. Knot the gold thread through the hole.

6 Roll out the pink pastillage thinly and cut out a square using the reserved cake top template. Lay the square crossways on top of the cake to look like tissue paper lining. Arrange the chocolates in the box and attach the prepared gift tag and a pink bow with melted chocolate. Trim the cake board with ribbon.

Tip

☆ *To make this cake even more enjoyable for the recipient, replace the chocolate assortment with their favourite toffee, fudge or jellies.*

Polka Dot Boxes

Little boxes decorated with contrasting spots of chocolate make a mouth-watering treat, and are especially popular with children as they can choose their own.

CAKE AND DECORATION

½ quantity whisked sponge cake (see page 11)

125g (4oz/4 squares) white chocolate

315g (10oz/10 squares) plain (semisweet) chocolate

150ml (¼ pint/⅔ cup) double (heavy) cream

2 tbsp icing (confectioners') sugar

220g (7oz) mascarpone cream cheese

small frosted flowers (see page 29)

EQUIPMENT

15cm (6in) square cake tin (pan)

paper piping bag

large star cream piping tube (tip)

Tips

☆ *The sponge trimmings soaked in fruit juice and topped with whipped cream make a simple dessert.*

☆ *When spreading the plain (semisweet) chocolate over the white dots, work gently and quickly so that the white dots do not blend into the plain chocolate.*

1 Preheat the oven to 180°C (350°F/ Gas 4). Grease and line the base of the cake tin (pan). Spoon the whisked sponge mixture into the tin. Bake in the oven for 10–12 minutes or until just firm. Turn out onto a wire rack and leave to cool.

2 Break up the white chocolate and place it in a heatproof bowl over a saucepan of gently simmering water. Leave until melted, then stir until smooth. Melt the plain (semisweet) chocolate in a separate bowl in the same way.

3 Cut out a rectangle of greaseproof (parchment) or non-stick paper measuring 36 x 25cm (14 x 10in). Put the melted white chocolate in a paper piping bag and snip off the smallest tip. Pipe white chocolate dots, 1cm (½in) apart, all over the paper to within 2.5cm (1in) of the edges. Chill for 15 minutes.

4 Quickly spread the plain chocolate over the paper with a palette knife (metal spatula), completely covering the white dots. Leave until almost set, then cut the chocolate into 5cm (2in) squares. Leave to set completely.

5 Cut the sponge cake into six 4cm (1¾in) cubes, trimming as necessary. Whip the cream with the icing (confectioners') sugar until it just forms soft peaks. Lightly beat the mascarpone cheese, then fold it into the whipped cream.

6 Place half of the cream mixture in a large nylon piping bag fitted with a large star tube (tip). Use the remainder to coat the sides of the sponges.

7 Carefully peel the paper away from the chocolate squares and position four squares around the sides of each cream-covered sponge. Pipe the cream mixture over the top of the sponges. Decorate the boxes with frosted flowers.

Variation

For rich chocolate boxes make the cases as above, but use plain (semi-sweet) chocolate only. Once the chocolate has been spread onto the paper, swirl with a palette knife (metal spatula) to give a decorative surface. Use piped chocolate ganache (see page 18) to cover the sponges, and decorate with frosted fruits (see page 29).

Jolly Clown Cake

A perfect cake for a small child's birthday.

CAKE AND DECORATION

double quantity quick mix sponge cake (see page 12)

200g (7oz/7 squares) plain (semisweet) chocolate

375g (12oz) marzipan (almond paste)

peach, yellow, blue, red and green food colourings

¾ quantity buttercream (see page 18)

1 quantity chocolate moulding icing (see page 18) made with milk (German sweet) chocolate

cornflour (cornstarch) for dusting

4 chocolate buttons

white chocolate chips (bits)

1 liquorice 'lace'

milk (German sweet) chocolate chips

EQUIPMENT

2 x 1.1 litre (2pt/5 cup) pudding basins

315ml (½pt/1¼ cup) pudding basin

1.4 litre (2½pt/6¼ cup) pudding basin

23cm (9in) square cake board

paintbrush

cocktail stick (toothpick)

paper piping bag

no.1 piping tube (tip)

1 Preheat the oven to 160°C (325°F/ Gas 3). Grease the two 1.1 litre (2pt/ 5 cup) pudding basins and one 315ml (½ pt/1¼ cup) pudding basin. Base line the basins with circles of greaseproof (parchment) or non-stick paper.

2 Spoon the cake mixture into the basins and bake in the oven, allowing 35 minutes for the small basin and 1 hour 10 minutes for the large basins. Invert onto wire racks to cool. Trim off the top of the cake baked in the small basin to give a rounded shape for the clown's head.

3 Melt the plain (semisweet) choco-late (see page 32). Cover the outside of the 1.4 litre (2½ pt/ 6¼ cup) pudding basin with foil, tucking the ends neatly inside the bowl and pressing the creases as flat as possible. Spread the melted chocolate over the foil to within 5mm (¼ in) of the basin rim. Leave to set.

4 Carefully lift away the foil tucked inside the bowl. Twist the bowl and remove it completely. With one hand gently resting in the base of the chocolate bowl, carefully peel away the foil lining to leave a chocolate case.

5 Colour half of the marzipan (almond paste) peach and two-thirds of the rest yellow. Colour some of remaining pieces red and some blue, leaving a small piece plain. Shape two-thirds of yellow marzipan into two flat boots. Position towards the front of the cake board.

6 Reserve 3 tablespoons of the butter-cream for piping. Generously spread the rounded top of one large cake with

buttercream. Gently drop it into the chocolate case. Position the case on the cake board, behind the feet. Spread the cake with buttercream and place the second large cake on top (see TIP).

7 Cut off one-third of the chocolate moulding icing; reserve a small piece, about the size of a plum. Divide the rest in half for arms. Roll into thick sausage shapes on a surface dusted with cornflour (cornstarch), tapering each 'sausage' at the end. Flatten slightly, then bend for arms. Neatly cut off the thin ends for cuffs, referring to the photograph below left.

8 Still keep the plum-sized piece of moulding icing aside. Use the rest to cover the clown's body. On a surface dusted with cornflour, roll out the remaining chocolate moulding icing into a 25cm (10in) round. Place over the top of the cake, tucking the ends inside the chocolate bowl. Ease the icing to fit around the back of the clown.

9 Secure the arms in position using a dampened paintbrush. Use a cocktail stick (toothpick) to mark elbow creases. Press chocolate buttons onto the front of the clown to make shirt buttons. Dot the shirt with white chocolate chips (bits).

10 Roll a little of the peach marzipan into two balls for hands. Flatten slightly, then cut four slits for fingers, using a sharp knife. Attach the clown's left hand to the shirt cuff.

11 Roll out the remaining marzipan to a circle about 18cm (7in) in diameter. Wrap around the reserved small pudding cake, easing the paste and smoothing the ends underneath. Secure to the cake to form the clown's head. Colour the reserved buttercream green and place in a paper piping bag fitted with a no. 1 piping tube (tip). Starting from the top of the head, pipe vertical lines of buttercream hair, short at the front for a fringe and longer around the neck.

12 Shape the reserved chocolate moulding icing into a small hat. Decorate the hat with a liquorice 'lace' band and a small flower made from red and blue marzipan. Fix the hat on top of the clown's head.

13 To make braces, roll out two strips of blue marzipan, each about 28cm (11in) long and 5mm (¼in wide). Secure over the clown's shoulders so the ends just overhang the trousers. Press a milk (German sweet) chocolate chip into each end. Position the second hand clutching the brace. Roll out the remaining yellow marzipan and cut out a wide collar. Position around the clown's neck and finish with a blue marzipan bow tie. Shape the mouth and nose from red marzipan.

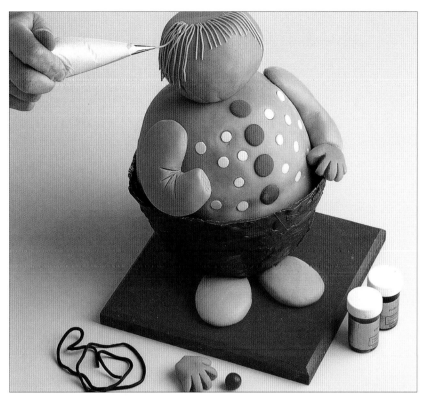

Tips

☆ *When positioning the second basin cake to make clown's body, place it towards the back of the chocolate bowl so that it almost touches the bowl, emphasising the 'baggy' trousers effect from around the front.*

☆ *When chocolate moulding icing is placed over the cake, the excess will fall in folds. Make sure this is at the back of the cake. Trim off the excess icing with a sharp knife, then gently smooth down the icing, using hands dusted with cornflour (cornstarch) to remove creases.*

☆ *The easiest way to pipe buttercream 'hair' is to begin with a few guidelines to frame the face area, then fill in and build up with plenty of piped lines.*

☆ *If you wish to add candles, press them into small balls of chocolate moulding icing. Attach them to the cake board.*

14 For the eyes use plain marzipan rounds, pressing a milk chocolate chip into the centre of each.

15 Cut the remaining liquorice 'lace' into short lengths and press into the boots for laces.

Ultra Choc-Chip Cake

Indulge someone with the chocolate dream of a cake.

CAKE AND DECORATION

125g (4oz/½ cup) butter

125g (4oz/⅔ cup) soft brown sugar

1 tbsp instant coffee powder (optional)

2 eggs, lightly beaten

1 tsp vanilla essence (extract)

40g (1⅓ oz/⅓ cup) self-raising flour

125g (4oz/1 cup) plain (all-purpose) flour

1 tsp bicarbonate of soda (baking soda)

60g (2oz/½ cup) cocoa (unsweetened cocoa powder)

185ml (6fl oz/¾ cup) buttermilk

200g (6½oz/1 cup) plain (semisweet) chocolate chips (bits)

100g (3½oz/scant ½cup) unsalted butter

100g (3½ oz/3½ squares) plain (semisweet) chocolate, chopped

EQUIPMENT

20cm (8in) round deep cake tin (pan)

paper piping bag

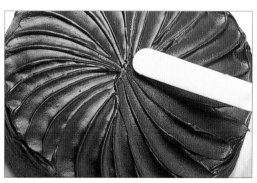

smooth the surface. Bake for 50–60 minutes or until a skewer inserted into the centre of the cake comes out clean. Leave the cake in the tin for 30 minutes, then turn onto a wire rack to cool.

1 Preheat the oven to 180°C (350°F/Gas 4). Brush the cake tin (pan) with melted butter or oil. Line the base and side with greaseproof (parchment) or non-stick paper. Using electric beaters, beat the butter and sugar until light and creamy. Add the coffee powder if using, and beat until combined. Add the eggs gradually, beating well after each addition; add the vanilla.

2 Transfer the mixture to a mixing bowl. Using a metal spoon, fold in the sifted flours, soda and cocoa alternately with the buttermilk. Stir until combined and smooth. Stir through half of the chocolate chips (bits). Pour the mixture into the prepared tin and

3 To make the icing, melt the (unsalted) butter and plain (semisweet) chocolate in a small heatproof bowl. Stand the bowl over a pan of simmering water until the chocolate is smooth and glossy. When cool, spread the icing evenly over the top of the cake using a palette knife (metal spatula). Decorate with chocolate zigzags, if desired (see below).

4 To make zigzags, place the remaining chocolate chips in a heatproof bowl. Stand the bowl over a pan of simmering water and stir until the chocolate has melted and the mixture is smooth. Pour into a paper piping bag, seal the end and snip off the tip. Drizzle the chocolate over greaseproof (parchment) or non-stick paper in zigzag patterns. When set, carefully lift off with a flat-bladed knife. Store in an airtight container in the refrigerator, between sheets of greaseproof or non-stick paper.

Tip

☆ *The cake can be made up to 3 days ahead. Store in an airtight container.*

Spotted Collar Cake

A child will go dotty over this delicious delight.

CAKE AND DECORATION

125g (4oz/½ cup) butter

125g (4oz/½ cup) caster (superfine) sugar

1 tsp vanilla essence (extract)

2 eggs

160g (5¼oz/⅓ cup) strawberry jam (conserve)

40g (1⅓ oz/⅓ cup) self-raising flour

125g (4oz/1 cup) plain (all-purpose) flour

1 tsp bicarbonate of soda (baking soda)

60g (2oz/½ cup) cocoa (unsweetened cocoa powder), plus extra for dusting

185ml (6fl oz/¾ cup) buttermilk

ICING

150g (4¾ oz/¾ cup) white chocolate chips (bits)

125g (4oz/½ cup) butter

80ml (2¾ fl oz/⅓ cup) single (light) cream

COLLAR

40g (1⅓oz/¼ cup) white chocolate chips, melted

80g (2⅔oz/½ cup) plain (semisweet) chocolate chips, melted

EQUIPMENT

23cm (9in) round cake tin (pan)

1 Preheat the oven to 180°C (350°F/Gas 4). Brush the cake tin (pan) with melted butter or oil. Line the base and side with greaseproof (parchment) or non-stick paper. Using electric beaters, beat the butter, sugar and vanilla in a small mixing bowl until light and creamy. Add the eggs gradually, beating well after each addition. Add the jam (conserve) and beat until smooth.

2 Transfer the mixture to a mixing bowl. Using a metal spoon, fold in the sifted flours, soda and cocoa alternately with the buttermilk. Stir until smooth. Pour the mixture into the prepared tin. Bake for 45 minutes or until a skewer inserted into the centre of the cake comes out clean. Leave the cake in the tin for 5 minutes, then turn out onto a wire rack to cool.

3 To make the chocolate icing, combine the white chocolate, butter and cream in a small pan; stir over a low heat until the chocolate and butter have melted and the mixture is smooth. Remove from the heat. Transfer to a bowl and leave to cool, stirring occasionally.

4 Place the cake on a serving plate; spread the side and top evenly with the chocolate icing.

5 To make the chocolate collar, measure the height of the cake – it should be about 6 cm/2½in high. Cut a long rectangular strip 75 x 6.5cm (30 x 2½in) out of greaseproof or non-stick paper. Drop dots of melted white chocolate randomly over the strip. Leave until just set, then spread a layer of melted plain (semisweet) chocolate over the entire strip. Working quickly, wrap the paper, chocolate-side in, around the cake.

6 Hold the paper strip in place until the chocolate sets, then carefully peel away the paper. Refrigerate the cake until ready to serve. Just before serving, dust the cake heavily with sifted cocoa.

Milky Marble Cake

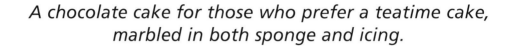

A chocolate cake for those who prefer a teatime cake, marbled in both sponge and icing.

CAKE AND DECORATION

Madeira (pound) cake mixture for 20cm (8in) round tin (pan) (see page 16)

2 tbsp cocoa (unsweetened cocoa powder)

1 tbsp boiling water

1 tsp vanilla essence (extract)

grated rind of 1 lemon

220g (7oz/7 squares) milk (German sweet) chocolate

125g (4oz/¾ cup) icing (confectioners') sugar

1 tbsp lemon juice

EQUIPMENT

20cm (8in) round cake tin (pan)

cocktail stick (toothpick)

1 Preheat the oven to 160°C (325°F /Gas 3). Base-line and grease the cake tin (pan).

2 Divide the cake mixture between two mixing bowls. Beat the cocoa and boiling water together and add to one bowl. Stir the vanilla essence (extract) and lemon rind into the remaining bowl.

3 Put alternate spoonsful of chocolate and lemon-flavoured mixture into the tin, occasionally drawing a skewer through the mixture. Bake for about 1½ hours or until a skewer inserted into the centre of the cake comes out clean. Cool on a wire rack.

4 Using 90g (3oz/3 squares) of the chocolate, make curls, using a potato peeler or grater. Spread the curls out thickly on a sheet of greaseproof (parchment) or non-stick paper. Melt the remaining chocolate and set 2 tablespoons aside. Spread the rest of the melted chocolate around the side of the cake.

5 While the chocolate is still soft, coat the side of the cake in chocolate curls. The easiest way to do this is to place one hand palm down on top of the cake and the other palm underneath it. Turn the cake and roll it lightly in the chocolate curls. Do not press heavily or the cake will be unevenly coated.

6 Place the cake on a serving plate. Sift the icing (confectioners') sugar into a bowl. Add the lemon juice and mix the glacé icing to the consistency of pouring cream. Spoon the icing onto the top of the cake and spread to the edge. Drizzle the reserved 2 tablespoons melted chocolate over the icing. While still soft, run the tip of a cocktail stick (toothpick) through the chocolate and icing to create the marbled effect.

Devil's Food Cake

CAKE AND DECORATION

165g (5½oz/1⅓ cups) plain (all-purpose) flour

85g (2⅔oz/⅔ cup) cocoa (unsweetened cocoa powder)

1 tsp bicarbonate of soda (baking soda)

250g (8oz/1 cup) caster (superfine) sugar

2 eggs, lightly beaten

250ml (8fl oz/1 cup) buttermilk

1 tsp vanilla essence (extract)

125g (4oz/½ cup) butter, softened

125ml (4fl oz/½ cup) double (heavy) cream, whipped

60g (2oz/2 squares) white chocolate, coarsely chopped

ICING

60g (2oz/¼ cup) unsalted **butter**

60g (2oz/2 squares) plain (semisweet) chocolate, melted

EQUIPMENT

20cm (8in) round cake tin (pan)

paper piping bag

An ultra 'wicked' cake for a special occasion or for sheer indulgence.

☆ Store for three days unfilled in an airtight container or up to three months in the freezer, unfilled and un-iced. The filled cake is best assembled and eaten on the same day.

1 Preheat the oven to 180°C (350°F/Gas 4). Brush the cake tin (pan) with melted butter or oil, line the base and side with greaseproof (parchment) or non-stick paper. Sift the flour, cocoa and soda into a large mixing bowl. Add the sugar. Pour the combined eggs, buttermilk, essence and butter onto the dry ingredients. Using electric beaters, beat on low speed for 3 minutes or until just moistened.

2 Beat the mixture on high speed for 5 minutes or until the mixture is free of lumps and increased in volume. Pour the mixture into the prepared tin and smooth the surface. Bake for 40–50 minutes or until a skewer inserted into the centre of the cake comes out clean. Leave the cake in the tin for 15 minutes, then turn out onto a wire rack to cool.

3 To make the icing, combine the butter and chocolate in a small pan; stir over a low heat until melted, then remove from the heat. Cool. Trim the cake if necessary to level the surface.

Cut the cake in half horizontally. Spread the whipped cream over the trimmed half of the cake. Sandwich with the other layer. Spread the icing over the top using a palette knife (metal spatula). Place the white chocolate in a small mixing bowl. Stir over barely simmering water until melted; remove from the heat. Cool slightly.

4 Spoon the melted chocolate into a small paper piping bag. Seal the open end, snip off the tip and pipe eight to ten small to large circles around the top of the cake. Drag a skewer from the centre circle to the outside of the cake. Clean the skewer and repeat this process, working around the cake in wedges. Decorate with rounds of chocolate if liked.

White Choc Cream Cake

CAKE AND DECORATION

125g (4oz/½cup) cream cheese

60g (2oz/¼cup) butter

185g (6oz/¾cup) caster (superfine) sugar

2 eggs, lightly beaten

100g (3½oz/3½squares) plain (semisweet) chocolate, melted

250g (8oz/2 cups) plain (all-purpose) flour

30g (1oz/¼cup) cocoa (unsweetened cocoa powder)

1 tsp bicarbonate of soda (baking soda)

185ml (6fl oz/¾cup) water

strawberries, raspberries or young berries

WHITE CHOCOLATE CREAM

125g (4oz) white chocolate chips (bits)

60ml (2fl oz/¼ cup) single (light) cream

500ml (16fl oz/2 cups) double (heavy) cream, whipped

250g (8oz/1⅔cups) strawberries or raspberries, quartered

EQUIPMENT

20cm (8in) round cake tin (pan)

Tip

☆ *The basic cake can be made several days ahead. Store in the refrigerator.*

Combine the freshness of berries with white chocolate to create this superb layered cake.

1 Preheat the oven to 180°C (350°F/ Gas 4). Brush the cake tin (pan) with melted butter or oil. Line the base and side with greaseproof (parchment) or non-stick paper. Using electric beaters, beat the cream cheese, butter and sugar in a small bowl until light and creamy. Add the eggs gradually, beating thoroughly after each addition. Add the melted chocolate and beat until smooth.

2 Transfer the mixture to a large mixing bowl. Using a metal spoon, fold in the sifted flour, cocoa and soda alternately with the water. Stir until combined and the mixture is smooth. Pour evenly into the prepared tin and smooth the surface. Bake for 45–50 minutes or until a skewer inserted into the centre of the cake comes out clean. Leave the cake in the tin for 5–10 minutes, then turn out onto a wire rack to cool.

3 To make the white chocolate cream, combine the white chocolate and single (light) cream in a small heatproof bowl. Stand the bowl over a pan of simmering water and stir until the chocolate has melted and the mixture is smooth. Cool in the refrigerator until spreadable, stirring occasionally.

4 Cut the cake horizontally into three even layers. Place the base layer on a serving plate. Spread with half of the white chocolate cream, top with one-fifth of the whipped cream, then half of the berries. Top with the second layer of cake and repeat the layering with the remaining white chocolate cream, a quarter of the whipped cream and the remaining berries. Top with the last layer of cake. Spread the cake side and top evenly with the remaining whipped cream. Decorate the cake with berries.

Summer Fruits Cake

CAKE AND DECORATION

1 quantity orange-flavoured whisked sponge cake (see page 11)

315ml (10fl oz/1¼ cups) double (heavy) cream

155g (5oz/¾cup) strawberry yogurt

double quantity white chocolate modelling paste (clay) (see page 34)

icing (confectioners') sugar for dusting

500g (1lb) strawberries

185g (6oz) redcurrants

5 tsp redcurrant jelly

8 white chocolate leaves (see page 34)

EQUIPMENT

23cm (9in) round cake tin (pan)

large paintbrush

Prettily pleated with white chocolate modelling paste (clay) and piled high with soft fruits, this special-occasion cake makes a mouth-watering centrepiece.

1 Preheat the oven to 180°C (350°F/Gas 4). Grease and line the base of the cake tin (pan). Spoon the whisked sponge mixture into the tin. Bake in the oven for 20 minutes or until just firm to the touch. Turn out onto a wire rack and leave to cool completely.

2 Cut the cake in half horizontally. Put the cream in a large bowl with the strawberry yogurt, and whip until the mixture forms soft peaks.

3 Place one-half of the cake on a large serving plate. Spread with a third of the cream mixture and cover with the second cake layer. Using a palette knife (metal spatula), cover the top and side of the cake with the remaining cream mixture.

4 Divide the modelling paste (clay) into six pieces. Roll out one piece on a surface dusted with icing (confectioners') sugar and cut into a strip slightly deeper than the cake and about 20cm (8in) long. Using your fingers, gently pleat the strip into loose folds. Position it around the side of the cake. Cut, shape and position more strips of modelling paste until the side of the cake is completely covered.

5 Hull the strawberries and halve any large ones. Arrange over the top of the cake, then fill in the gaps with the redcurrants.

6 Melt the redcurrant jelly with 2 tablespoons water in a small saucepan. Cool slightly, then use a large paintbrush to brush the glaze over the fruits. Finish with white chocolate leaves. Store in a cool place until ready to serve.

Tips

☆ *Any other soft fruits, such as raspberries, blackcurrants, blackberries or blueberries can be substituted for the strawberries and redcurrants.*
☆ *The cake, with cream and chocolate pleating, can be assembled up to a day in advance, but pile up the fruits and glaze them no more than 2–3 hours before serving.*

Raspberry Vanilla Delight

Relish the tastes of summer with this sensational cake.

CAKE AND DECORATION

150g (5oz/⅔ cup) unsalted butter

175g (6oz/¾ cup) caster (superfine) sugar

2 eggs, lightly beaten

2 tsp vanilla essence (extract)

1 tbsp liquid glucose

175g (6oz/1½ cups) self-raising flour

125ml (4fl oz/½ cup) buttermilk

100g (3½ oz/3½ squares) white chocolate, chopped

2 x 300g (10oz) packets frozen raspberries, drained, or 2 punnets fresh raspberries

VANILLA CREAM

500ml (16fl oz/2 cups) double (heavy) cream

2 tbsp icing (confectioners') sugar

½ tsp vanilla essence

EQUIPMENT

23cm (9in) round cake tin (pan)

1 Preheat the oven to 180°C (350°F/ Gas 4). Brush the cake tin (pan) with melted butter or oil, line the base and side with greaseproof (parchment) or non-stick paper. Using electric beaters, beat the butter and sugar in a small mixing bowl until light and creamy. Add the eggs gradually, beating thoroughly after each addition. Add the essence and glucose and beat until combined. Transfer the mixture to a large mixing bowl. Using a metal spoon, fold in the sifted flour alternately with the buttermilk. Stir until just combined and the mixture is almost smooth.

2 Pour the mixture evenly into the prepared tin and smooth the surface. Bake for 40 minutes or until a skewer inserted into the centre of the cake comes out clean. Leave the cake in the tin for 15 minutes, then turn out onto a wire rack to cool.

3 Place the chocolate in a heatproof bowl. Stir over barely simmering water until melted; remove from the heat. Pour the chocolate onto a marble board or cool work surface in a 4cm

(1½in) wide strip. Smooth the surface and leave the chocolate to set. Shave off strips with a vegetable peeler and set aside. (If the weather is very warm, refrigeration may be necessary.)

4 To make vanilla cream, place the cream in a small mixing bowl. Using electric beaters, beat until soft peaks form. Add the sifted icing (confectioners') sugar and essence. Continue beating until firm peaks form.

5 Cut the cake in half horizontally. Place one half on a serving plate. Top with raspberries, slightly squashing onto the cake with a fork; reserve a few for decoration. Sandwich with the other half. Spread vanilla cream over the top and side of the cake using a palette knife (metal spatula). Smooth the surface. Cover the cake with reserved white chocolate shavings and top with the remaining raspberries.

Passionfruit Torte

A creamy party cake with tropical tangy fruit.

CAKE AND DECORATION

200g (7oz/⅞ cup) unsalted butter

250g (8oz/1 cup) caster (superfine) sugar

3 eggs, lightly beaten

60g (2oz/¼ cup) fresh passionfruit pulp

300g (10oz/2½ cups) self-raising flour

155ml (¼pt/⅔ cup) milk

250ml (8fl oz/1¼ cups) double (heavy) cream, whipped

3 kiwifruit, sliced, and mint leaves to decorate (optional)

FILLING

125g (4oz/½ cup) caster sugar

60g (2oz/¼ cup) fresh passionfruit pulp

2 egg whites

EQUIPMENT

23cm (9in) round cake tin (pan)

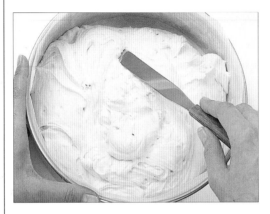

1 Preheat the oven to 180°C (350°F/ Gas 4). Brush the cake tin (pan) with melted butter or oil. Line the base and side with greaseproof (parchment) or non-stick paper. Using electric beaters, beat the butter and sugar in a small mixing bowl until light and creamy. Add the eggs gradually, beating thoroughly after each addition. Add the passionfruit pulp and beat until combined. Transfer the mixture to a large mixing bowl. Using a metal spoon, fold in the sifted flour alternately with the milk. Stir until just combined and the mixture is smooth. Spoon the mixture evenly into the prepared tin; smooth the surface. Bake for 50 minutes or until a skewer inserted into the centre of the cake comes out clean. Leave the cake in the tin for 15 minutes, then turn out onto a wire rack to cool.

2 To make the filling, combine the sugar and passionfruit pulp in a small pan. Stir constantly over a low heat until the mixture boils and the sugar has dissolved. Simmer without stirring, uncovered, for 3 minutes; remove from the heat. Using electric beaters, beat the egg whites in a clean, dry mixing bowl until stiff peaks form. Pour the hot passionfruit mixture in a thin stream over the egg whites, beating constantly until the cream is thick, glossy and increased in volume.

3 Turn the cake upside down and cut horizontally into four layers (see page 15). Divide the passionfruit cream into three even portions. Place one cake layer on a serving plate and spread with the filling. Continue layering with the remaining cake and filling, ending with cake. Using a palette knife (metal spatula), spread the whipped cream over the top and side of the cake. If liked, decorate with a piped border of cream, sliced kiwifruit and mint leaves.

Tip

☆ *This is best assembled and eaten on the day it is made. It can be decorated up to 3 hours before serving. Store, uncovered, in the refrigerator.*

Chocolate Truffle Cake

CAKE AND DECORATION

125g (4oz/½ cup) cream cheese, softened

60g (2oz/¼ cup) butter

175g (6oz/¾ cup) caster (superfine) sugar

2 eggs, lightly beaten

1 tsp vanilla essence

¼ tsp red food colouring

60g (2oz/2 squares) chocolate, melted

250g (8oz/2 cups) plain (all-purpose) flour

30g (1oz/¼ cup) cocoa

1 tsp bicarbonate of soda

FILLING

250g (8oz/8 squares) plain (semisweet) chocolate, chopped

90ml (3fl oz/⅓ cup) cream

2 egg yolks

ICING

125g (4oz/4 squares) plain (semisweet) chocolate, chopped

125g (4oz/½ cup) unsalted butter

TRUFFLES (makes 20)

150g (5oz/5 squares) plain (semisweet) chocolate, chopped

60g (2oz/¼ cup) unsalted butter

2 tbsp cream

30g (1oz/¼ cup) icing (confectioners') sugar

2 tsp orange juice

30g (1oz/¼ cup) cocoa

30g (1oz/¼ cup) drinking chocolate

list continues page 250

A spectacular cake with the addition of home-made truffle topping which all children will love.

1 Preheat the oven to 180°C (350°F/ Gas 4). Grease the cake tins (pans), line the bases and sides with grease-proof (parchment) or non-stick paper. Using electric beaters, beat the cream cheese, butter and sugar in a bowl until light and creamy. Add the eggs gradually, beating thoroughly after each addition. Add the vanilla, colouring and melted chocolate; beat until combined. Transfer to a large bowl. Using a metal spoon, fold in the sifted flour, cocoa and soda alternately with 175ml (6fl oz/¾ cup) water. Stir until just combined. Pour the mixture evenly into the prepared tins and smooth the surface. Bake the cakes for 30–35 minutes or until a skewer inserted into the cake comes out clean. Leave in the tins for 10 minutes, then turn out onto a wire rack to cool.

2 To make the filling, combine the chocolate and cream in a small pan. Stir over a low heat until the chocolate has melted; remove from the heat. Whisk in the egg yolks until smooth.

3 To make the icing, place the chocolate in a heatproof bowl. Stir over barely simmering water until melted; remove from the heat. Beat the butter in a small mixing bowl until light and creamy. Add the chocolate, beating for 1 minute or until the mixture is glossy and smooth.

4 To make the truffles, combine the chocolate, butter, cream, sifted icing sugar and the orange juice in a small

WEDGES

150g (5oz/5 squares)
plain (semisweet)
chocolate, melted

EQUIPMENT

two 20cm (8in) round
cake tins (pans)

pan. Stir over a low heat until the chocolate and butter have melted; remove from the heat. Transfer the mixture to a medium mixing bowl. Refrigerate for 15 minutes or until semi-set. Using electric beaters, beat the mixture until creamy. Roll heaped teaspoons of the mixture into balls; roll in the combined sifted cocoa and drinking chocolate to coat. Refrigerate until firm.

5 To make the chocolate wedges, cover the base of a cake tin with foil. Spread the melted chocolate evenly over the foil; refrigerate until it is semi-set. Using a sharp palette knife (metal spatula), carefully mark the chocolate into 12 wedges. Return to the refrigerator until the chocolate is completely set.

6 To assemble, cut the domes off both the cakes to give a level surface. Cut each cake in half horizontally. Place one cake layer on a serving plate and spread with one third of the filling. Continue layering the remaining cake and filling, ending with cake. Spread the icing evenly over the top and side of the cake using a palette knife. Place 12 truffles around the edge of the cake. Position the chocolate wedges on the cake, resting each one on a truffle.

Tip

☆ *Store up to 4 days in the refrigerator. Have the cream cheese at room temperature to make it easier to work.*

Templates

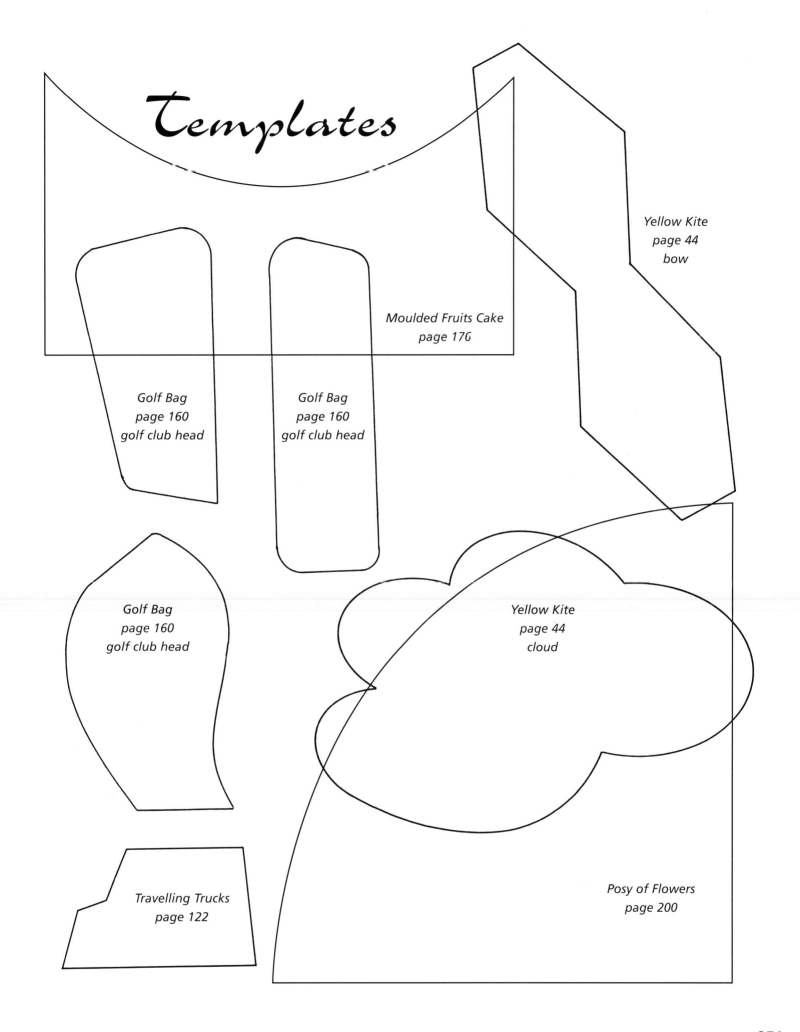

Yellow Kite
page 44
bow

Moulded Fruits Cake
page 176

Golf Bag
page 160
golf club head

Golf Bag
page 160
golf club head

Golf Bag
page 160
golf club head

Yellow Kite
page 44
cloud

Travelling Trucks
page 122

Posy of Flowers
page 200

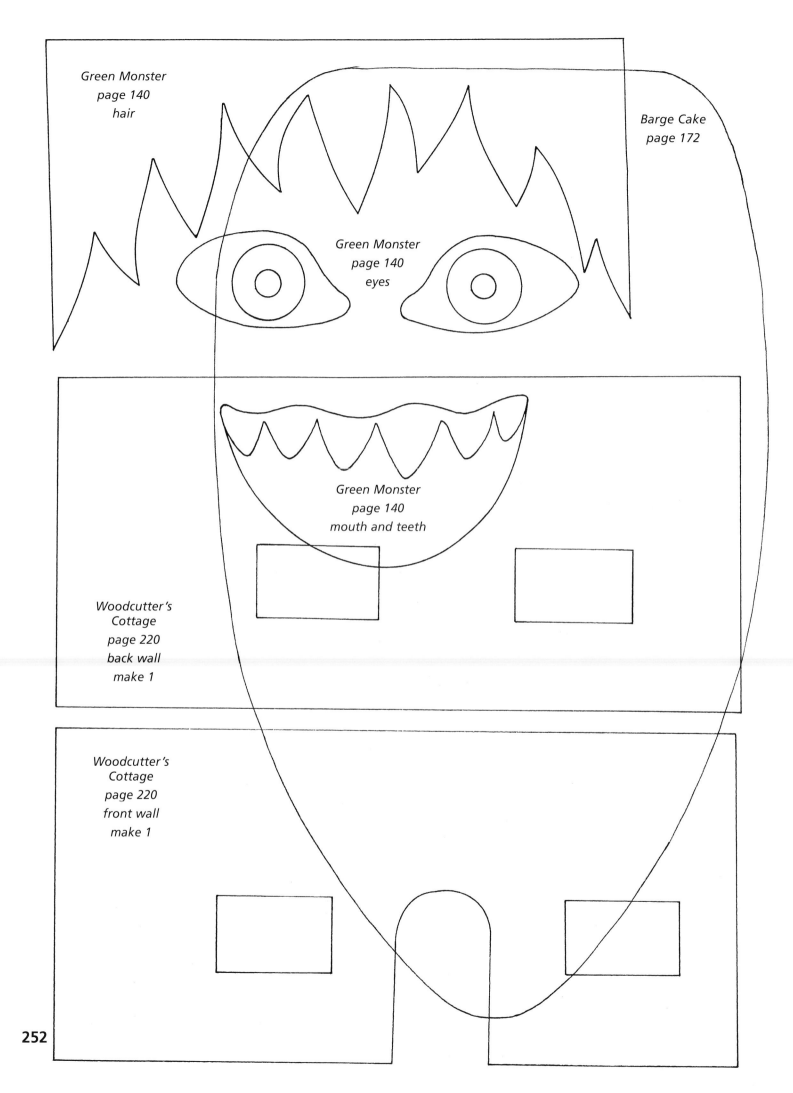

Green Monster
page 140
hair

Barge Cake
page 172

Green Monster
page 140
eyes

Green Monster
page 140
mouth and teeth

Woodcutter's
Cottage
page 220
back wall
make 1

Woodcutter's
Cottage
page 220
front wall
make 1

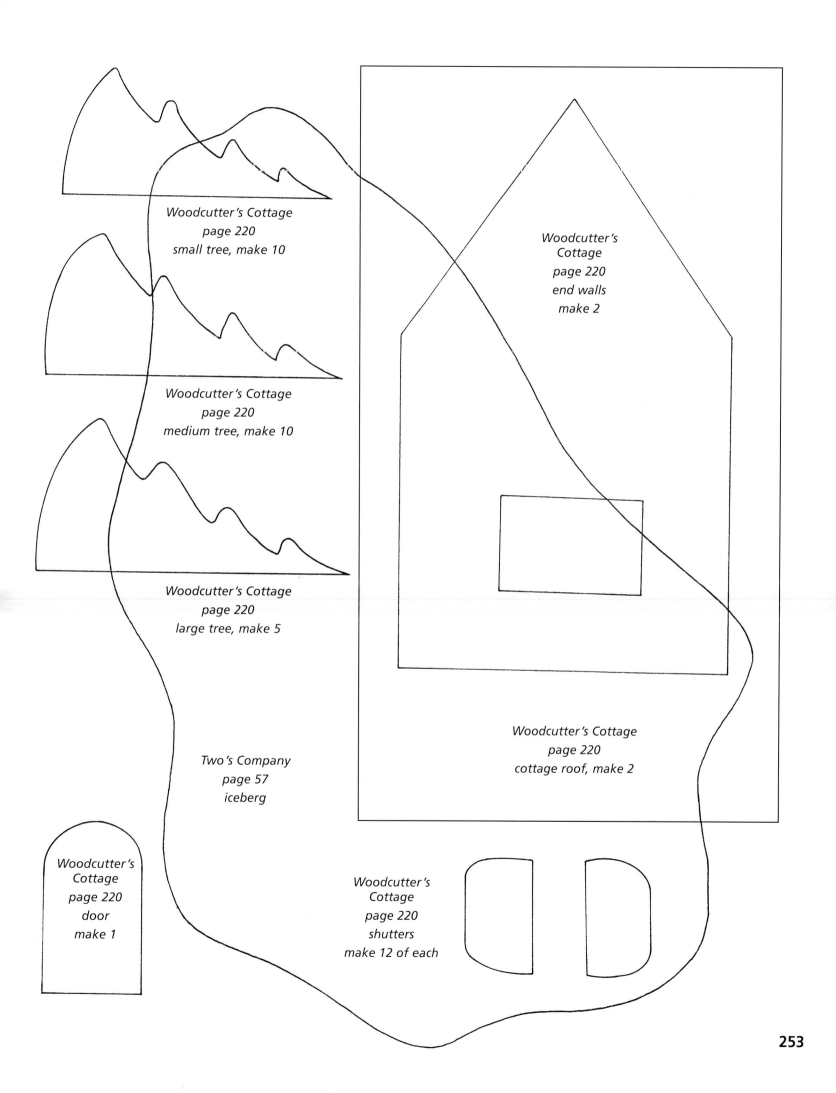

Woodcutter's Cottage
page 220
small tree, make 10

Woodcutter's Cottage
page 220
medium tree, make 10

Woodcutter's Cottage
page 220
large tree, make 5

Woodcutter's
Cottage
page 220
end walls
make 2

Woodcutter's Cottage
page 220
cottage roof, make 2

Two's Company
page 57
iceberg

Woodcutter's
Cottage
page 220
door
make 1

Woodcutter's
Cottage
page 220
shutters
make 12 of each

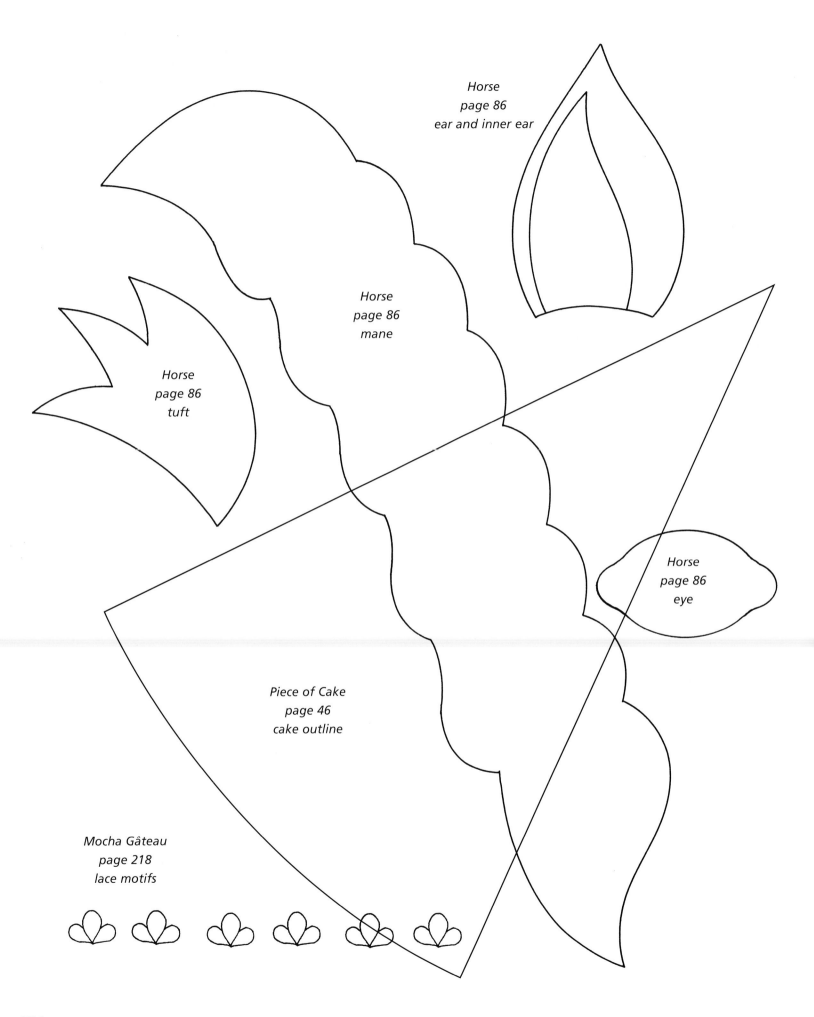

Horse
page 86
ear and inner ear

Horse
page 86
mane

Horse
page 86
tuft

Horse
page 86
eye

Piece of Cake
page 46
cake outline

Mocha Gâteau
page 218
lace motifs

1234567890

1234567890

NOTES ON USING THE RECIPES

☆ For all recipes, quantities are given in metric, Imperial and cup measurements.
☆ Follow one set of measures only as they are not interchangeable.
☆ Standard 5ml teaspoons (tsp) and 15ml tablespoons (tbsp) are used. Australian readers, whose tablespoons measure 20ml, should adjust quantities accordingly.
☆ All spoon measures are assumed to be level unless otherwise stated.
☆ Ovens should be preheated to specified temperatures.
☆ Where chocolate squares are listed in ingredients lists, this applies to American readers.

Acknowledgements

The authors and publishers would like to thank the following suppliers:

Cake Art Ltd.
Venture Way,
Crown Estate,
Priorswood, Taunton
TA2 8DE

Guy, Paul and Co. Ltd.
Unit B4, Foundry Way,
Little End Road,
Eaton Socon,
Cambs. PE19 3JH

Renshaw Scott Ltd.
Crown Street,
Liverpool L8 7RF

Other distributors and retailers

Squires Kitchen
Squires House,
3 Waverley Lane,
Farnham,
Surrey GU9 8BB
Tel: 01252 711749

Confectionery Supplies
31 Lower Cathedral Road
Riverside
Cardiff
S. Glamorgan
CF1 8LU
Tel: 01222 372161

Cakes & Co.
25 Rock Hill
Blackrock Village
Co. Dublin
Ireland
Tel: (01) 283 6544

Culpitt Ltd.
Jubilee Industrial Estate,
Ashington NE63 8UQ
Tel: 01670 814545

Beryl's Cake Decorating & Pastry Supplies
P.O. Box 1584, N.
Springfield, VA22151-0584
USA
Tel: 1-800-488-2749
Fax: 703-750-3779

Cake Decorators' Supplies
Shop 1,
770 George Street,
Sydney 2001
Australia
Tel: 92124050

Index